CHASING THE HARVEST

CHASING THE HARVEST

MIGRANT WORKERS IN CALIFORNIA AGRICULTURE

EDITED BY

GABRIEL THOMPSON

VOICE OF WITNESS

VERSO
London • New York

Assistant Editor
ALBERTO REYES MORGAN

Translators
PABLO BAEZA, HALEY CONGER,
PAUL DOMÍNGUEZ HERNÁNDEZ, SANDRA GARDUNO,
ARTEMIO GUERRA, MIRIAM HWANG-CARLOS,
MARIA MENDEZ, ALBERTO REYES MORGAN,
LAURA SCHROEDER, BARBARA SHEFFELS,
FEDERICO VARELA

Transcribers
CHARLOTTE EDELSTEIN,
KATIE FIEGENBAUM, ANNIE STINE

Research Editor
ANNIE STINE

Research Assistants
CHARLOTTE EDELSTEIN, MARY BETH MELSO

Copy Editor
MARK WILSON

VOICE OF WITNESS
First published by Verso 2017
© Verso and Voice of Witness 2017
Excerpt of "Cultivating Fear" © Human Rights Watch 2012

1 3 5 7 9 10 8 6 4 2

Verso
UK: 6 Meard Street, London W1F 0EG
US: 20 Jay Street, Suite 1010, Brooklyn, NY 11201
versobooks.com

Verso is the imprint of New Left Books

ISBN-13: 978-1-78663-221-0
ISBN-13: 978-1-78663-378-1 (HBK)
ISBN-13: 978-1-78663-220-3 (US EBK)
ISBN-13: 978-1-78663-219-7 (UK EBK)

British Library Cataloguing in Publication Data
A catalogue record for this book is available from the British Library

Library of Congress Cataloging-in-Publication Data

Names: Thompson, Gabriel, editor.
Title: Chasing the harvest : migrant workers in
California agriculture /
  edited by Gabriel Thompson.
Description: London ; New York : Verso, 2017. |
Series: Voice of witness
Identifiers: LCCN 2016055800 | ISBN
9781786632210 (alk. paper)
Subjects: LCSH: Migrant agricultural laborers—
California—Case studies.
Classification: LCC HD1527.C2 C43 2017 | DDC
331.5/4409794—dc23
LC record available at
https://lccn.loc.gov/2016055800

Typeset in Garamond by MJ & N Gavan, Truro, Cornwall
Printed in the US by Maple Press

CONTENTS

INTRODUCTION
"LOOK AT MY HANDS"

by Gabriel Thompson

In August of 1936, an ambitious young novelist named John Steinbeck set out in an old bakery truck for a firsthand look at the lives of California's migrant farmworkers. Notebook in hand, he toured labor camps and fields, beginning in the Bay Area and heading south. He knew that thousands of Dust Bowl families had come west, fleeing drought and economic devastation. Yet he still wasn't prepared for what he found. In an article for the *San Francisco News*, he described one family who lived in a cardboard home; when it rained, the structure would "slop down into a brown, pulpy mush." Another was holed up inside a tent "the color of the ground," with tattered canvas flaps that were "held together with bits of rusty baling wire." A third family had constructed a shelter from willow branches and slept under a piece of carpet. Steinbeck heard that a four-year-old boy in the camp he visited had died two weeks earlier of malnutrition. "This is the squatters' camp," he concluded. "Some are a little better, some much worse."

Steinbeck made several more trips in the coming years, doing research for what would become his classic novel, *The Grapes of Wrath*. The book follows the Joad family, who leave their desiccated farm in

Oklahoma carrying little more than dreams of a stable future. They instead find themselves in California contending with one emergency after another. The work in the fields is exhausting. The wages they earn are pitiful. They shelter wherever they can—squalid camps provided by farmers, ditch-bank settlements—until chased out by law enforcement. Life is spent shuffling across the state, earning just enough to keep moving along.

On its publication in 1939, Steinbeck's novel revealed the struggles of migrant farmworkers in California. But for the people still caught up in the westward migration, the fiction changed very little. Among those migrants was an eleven-year-old boy named Cesar Chavez, whose father had lost the family home in Arizona during the Depression. Chavez's family chased crop harvests up and down California—picking carrots in Brawley, thinning lettuce in Salinas— at times making homes out of garages and barns. Chavez himself dropped out of school in the eighth grade to work in the fields.

It was the grinding poverty of farmworkers that caused an adult Chavez, in 1962, to walk away from a stable job and move his family to Delano, one of the many sleepy towns in the Central Valley. He had an impossible dream: to organize a union of farmworkers. He didn't have much of a plan, and even less money. But he was stubborn and willing to sacrifice everything for what he would call *la causa*—the cause. Chavez traveled from town to town to spread word about his group, which he originally called the Farmworker Association. Others helped, too. Dolores Huerta, a fiery and fearless activist from Stockton, was often by his side. So was Gilbert Padilla, a World War II veteran like Chavez, who had been born at a California labor camp.

Three years later, on September 8, 1965, militant Filipino farmworkers, led by Philip Vera Cruz and Larry Itliong, walked out of Delano's grape fields in demand of higher wages. A week later, Chavez and his supporters joined the strike. The two groups eventually merged into the United Farm Workers (UFW). Teams of farmworkers and volunteers spread across the country, calling for a boycott of grapes in a campaign that galvanized the country. Chavez was featured on the cover of *Time* magazine. Some 17 million Americans refused to eat grapes in what was the most successful consumer boycott in US history. In 1970, the largest grape growers finally caved in and signed contracts. The impossible had become possible.

I had the chance to study the history of California's agricultural labor movement, along with the inspiring story of the UFW, while working on a biography of Fred Ross, an organizer who serves as a link between Steinbeck and Chavez. As a young man in the 1930s, Ross managed the same migrant labor camp near Bakersfield that Steinbeck visited numerous times while doing his research. Two decades later, in East San Jose, Ross knocked on the door of Chavez and encouraged him to become an organizer. Ross would go on to mentor many other important Mexican American leaders, including Dolores Huerta, and help direct boycotts and strikes during the 1960s and '70s.

While researching the Ross biography, I had the privilege of interviewing scores of people—farmworkers, volunteers, religious leaders—who had turned the UFW into both a union and a social movement. A key to the UFW's success was bridging the gap between farmworker and consumer. Then, as now, most consumers knew next to nothing about the conditions under which their food had been produced. So the UFW sent striking farmworkers into the cities, where they told their stories. What they revealed was a hidden crisis of labor abuse, unfair wages, and unsafe working conditions.

As the narrators in this book reveal, many of those crises continue to this day.

Roberto Valdez, a father of three, nearly lost his sixteen-year-old son to heat stroke. They had been harvesting grapes in Bakersfield on a 104-degree day; the company refused to provide a canopy for shade. Jose Saldivar was hospitalized for five days after suffering acute pesticide poisoning. He never learned what chemical he had been applying. Maricruz Ladino was sexually harassed, and then raped, by her supervisor; when she gathered the courage to file a complaint, she was fired. Other narrators, too poor to afford rent, have slept in the fields and orchards at times. Some bathed in pesticide-laden irrigation canals. Most, at one point or another, had their wages stolen from them. And nearly all faced crises of domestic stability common to migrant labor—a lack of stable housing, fathers often separated from children in pursuit of work, children taken out of schools to work in fields or to move to follow the harvest cycles, and the ever-present threat of deportation. That last concern is not only a crisis for the family of the deported, but often the entire community. Oscar Ramos describes the moment growing up in a labor camp when *la migra*—Immigration enforcement officers—raided the camp and took away the woman who was babysitting him and his sister while his parents worked in the fields. "She's in the van, looking back with a sad face, waving goodbye. And my younger sister and I are in the middle of the yard, like, *Well, what about us? What's gonna happen to us?*"

This century might not yet have produced anything like a *Grapes of Wrath* or national boycott to capture the attention of American consumers, but that doesn't mean farmworkers haven't been trying to share their stories. Two years ago, Roberto Valdez began using his cellphone to take videos from the fields. He narrated the short clips, adding details about the lives of his coworkers, and uploaded them onto the Internet. "The world needs to know us better," he said when we met at his trailer in Thermal, located in one of the poorest corners of the country. "No one comes out here; no one knows what we go through."

That's the purpose of this book: to hear directly from farmworkers who have stories to tell; to get to know them better; to learn what they've gone through, and what they're still going through.

Statistics describe lives where even seemingly minor setbacks—a sprained ankle, a broken radiator—can quickly turn into full-blown emergencies. The median annual income for California farmworkers is $14,000. They face numerous workplace dangers, from musculoskeletal injuries caused by stoop labor to pesticide poisoning and heat exhaustion. Nearly two-thirds don't have health insurance. A study of seven agricultural communities in California found that 10 percent of farmworkers lived in what researchers called "informal dwellings" like garages, sheds, barns, and abandoned vehicles. Formal dwellings aren't always much better. Families double or triple up in apartments, stuff into sweltering trailers, make homes out of primitive labor camps.

When Steinbeck visited the fields, he found plenty of white faces. This no doubt made some of his readership more sympathetic to the plight of his characters, but what he encountered was only a brief demographic shift. Perhaps a million ethnic Mexicans were deported during the Depression, and Dust Bowl migrants replaced them. When World War II began, Mexicans returned en masse to the fields as *braceros*, or guest workers.[1] Other ethnic groups have played important roles in California's fields, including immigrants from China, Japan, Yemen, and the Philippines. But during most of the twentieth century, the backbone of the agricultural workforce has been from Mexico.

In California's fields today, approximately 70 percent of workers were born in Mexico. As many as 50 percent or more are undocumented. This adds another layer of vulnerability to an already vulnerable workforce. The U.S. Department of Labor identifies agriculture as a "priority industry" for enforcement due to the presence of "high labor violations and workers that are reluctant or unable to exercise their rights." From 2010 to 2013, the DOL inspected more than 6,100 agricultural employers across the country. Farmworker Justice, a DC-based advocacy group, recently analyzed the results of those inspections. They found that nearly 70 percent of employers

---

[1] For more on the Bracero Program, see the Glossary, page 283.

violated key federal labor laws and provisions. (They also highlighted another chronic problem: the lack of enforcement personnel. Those 6,100 inspections, conducted over four years, reached just 1 percent of farms.)

The newest group to arrive in California's fields is indigenous Mexicans, most of whom come from the southern state of Oaxaca. It is estimated that they now make up one-quarter of the state's farmworkers. Many don't speak Spanish, a linguistic isolation that leaves them especially prone to mistreatment. As one narrator, Fausto Sanchez—himself an indigenous Mexican—told me, indigenous Mexicans working in the U.S. fields are the "invisible of the invisible."

Fausto first came to California in the mid-1980s, when he was a young teenager. He now works as an advocate for California Rural Legal Assistance (CRLA). In 2010, CRLA published a groundbreaking report on the state's indigenous Mexican farmworkers. They found that indigenous migrants lived in conditions that were "consistently appalling" and faced a wide range of labor abuses, from foremen who randomly docked their pay to fields that had no drinking water or bathrooms. One-third reported earning less than the minimum wage.

Fausto lives in Arvin, a small city fifteen miles southeast of Bakersfield. It's near where Steinbeck did much of his research. We first met in 2014, when I was reporting a magazine article. During one conversation, he told me that he knew some labor contractors who paid indigenous workers he knew as little as $25 for an eight-hour shift. Adjusted for inflation, that's less than what farmworkers made in Steinbeck's day.

My first direct contact with farmworkers came in 2008, when I was hired to harvest iceberg lettuce in Yuma, a city in Arizona near the U.S.-Mexico border. I spent the first day stumbling along the rows and dripping sweat onto the produce. The other members of the crew, all from Mexico, were bundled up in hoodies, their faces bone dry. When I lay down that night, my back seized up. After a week, I could barely walk. The crew's fastest lettuce cutter was Julio, a twig of a man with rippling forearms. Each morning he told me the same thing: "Your body will get used to it." That didn't seem possible, but he was right, sort of. A month later, I was still sore, but I'd forgotten what it felt like to *not* be sore.

I had come to Yuma because I was writing a book about the work done by Latino immigrants. An hour in the fields had taught me the first important lesson: this work took a great deal of skill. To watch Julio cut, trim, and bag a head of lettuce was beautiful, almost magical. An initial stab with the lettuce knife to separate the head from the ground, a perfectly placed second cut to remove the outer leaves, a quick shake to send those leaves to the ground, and a flick of the wrist to wrap the lettuce in plastic. The movement took Julio three seconds. My first attempt lasted nearly a minute. But I slowly picked up some tricks, and after four weeks, I was usually able to harvest my two rows without falling too far behind.

As we worked, we shared stories. Many of the men and women were guest workers who traveled each morning from the Mexican border city of San Luis Río Colorado. The wait in the border checkpoint line could be three hours; once across, they boarded a repurposed school bus for an hour-long drive to the fields. They weren't paid for this time, yet few complained about the arrangement. Most of the guest workers, like Julio, had grown up in deep poverty in Mexico's interior and traveled to the border searching for economic opportunity. Now they were earning $8.27 an hour—more than many jobs in their hometowns paid for an entire day's work.

Other crewmembers had crossed into the United States without papers and eventually became legal residents. (As far as I could tell, there were no undocumented workers on the crew.) Some had spent years shuttling between Yuma and Salinas, California, following the lettuce harvest. During breaks, they talked about the hardships of being on the road: how they slept in cars, were cheated out of wages, spent months away from their families.

But there was also joy present in that crew. One morning, just after 5 a.m., I boarded the bus to the sounds of an accordion and guitar. Humberto and Tomás, two of the crew's elders, were belting out a tune from the backseats. They played during breaks, too, the men and women rising from their plastic white chairs, tacos in hand, to dance. Our half-hour lunches were filled with jokes and laughter and sometimes food fights. Lots of people shared what they had brought. Nobody ate alone.

Part of the joy came from the work. This might seem strange to readers who think of farmworkers only as exploited, vulnerable, and miserable. Statistics do a good job of painting that picture, and they are indeed real. But the statistics miss a lot, too. They miss the joys that farmworkers also have: the pride in their work, the camaraderie of a crew, the tightknit families, the feeling of deep satisfaction that comes, as Rosario Pelayo says, from being in "a beautiful struggle."

There are 800,000 farmworkers in California, one third of the nation's agricultural workforce. In 2015, the crops they harvested fetched $47 billion. The scale of California's agricultural bounty can be hard to fully appreciate. I didn't, until I got lost one evening while driving among vineyards, looking for a narrator's house. That was in Kern County, a rectangle-shaped swath of land that surrounds Bakersfield, whose fields—of grapes, almonds, pomegranates, you name it—cover more territory than San Francisco, New York City, and Los Angeles combined.

In California, it's hard to find a spot where something isn't being grown. In the town of Newell, ten miles from the Oregon border, farmworkers move through fields of strawberry seedlings, pruning and plucking unwanted flowers. Nearly 800 miles to the south, men and women stoop over lettuce fields within sight of the border wall with Mexico. Drive from one end of the state to the other and you'll find countless towns that have crowned themselves a food capital of the world: Holtville (carrots), Castroville (artichokes), Patterson (apricots), Gilroy (garlic), Selma (raisins), Greenfield (broccoli). Others are more ambitious. Corcoran calls itself the "farming capital of California"; Salinas, the "world's salad bowl."

California has four major agricultural regions. The southernmost is Imperial Valley, a scorching stretch of desert that straddles the U.S.-Mexico and California-Arizona borders. The Imperial Valley's major crops are winter vegetables, especially lettuce. Just north of Imperial is the Coachella Valley, also hot and arid. Here is where the grape harvest begins. Move northwest 200 miles and you reach the Central Valley, which starts at the foot of the Tehachapi Mountains and runs 450 miles north, angling with the state. This is California's powerhouse, the most productive land on the planet. The Salinas Valley, south of the Bay Area, is much smaller—just 90 miles long and 40 miles wide—and enjoys cooler coastal temperatures that are perfect for growing virtually all vegetables and many fruits.

Each valley is an agricultural marvel. The cities and towns within each valley, however, tend to be very poor. This shouldn't be surprising, given the farmworker data outlined above.

But it does raise a question: What happened to the dream of Cesar Chavez? In its heyday, the UFW had tens of thousands of members, many of whom earned middle class wages, enjoyed healthcare and pensions, and had a voice in their workplace. The union also rewrote labor law. In 1935, Congress had enacted the National Labor Relations Act, which protected the rights of workers to form unions. But Southern politicians lobbied hard to exclude farmworkers and domestic workers, the two industries that employed the majority of African-Americans at the time. So the UFW wrote a new law for California, the Agricultural Labor Relations Act, which granted farmworkers the right to organize. Governor Jerry Brown signed it into law in 1975. To date, no other state in the country protects the rights of farmworkers to organize.

Beginning in the late 1970s, however, the union began to unravel. Chavez, who became increasingly preoccupied with maintaining control, pushed out many dedicated farmworkers and volunteers. The union spent less time organizing in the fields and lost dozens of contracts. At the time of Chavez's death, in 1993, the UFW was a shell of its former self.

Still, in recent years, the union has achieved some notable organizing victories in the fields, though only a small fraction of California farmworkers belong to a union. Today, the UFW's most important role is as an advocacy organization, where they have helped achieve a number of major victories to protect farmworkers. These include the passage of the first state law in the country designed to protect fieldworkers from heat stroke, and stronger federal protections for farmworkers against pesticides. I write this introduction two days after Governor Brown signed a historic bill, supported by the UFW, that finally granted farmworkers overtime pay after eight hours of work, like employees in any other industry.

The following narratives were collected in the spring and summer of 2016, a busy time for California's farmworkers. Many have only one day off a week—Sunday—so we usually met then. But people sometimes worked on Sundays, too, so we connected whenever we could. I sat down with Ismael Moreno, a seventeen-year-old high school student, just after he had returned from picking nectarines in 105-degree heat. Maricruz Ladino, who drives a large produce truck, often puts in more than 100-hour workweeks. She recounted her story from behind the steering wheel, interrupted occasionally when pallets of lettuce were loaded and unloaded. Silvia Correra talked to me several times over the phone while she pruned vineyards in Napa County.

The people interviewed here have harvested, at one point or another, just about every fruit grown in California: table grapes and wine grapes, peaches and nectarines, strawberries, oranges, lemons, watermelons. And then vegetables: all varieties of lettuce, onions, avocados, broccoli, carrots. Heraclio Astete, a former guest worker from Peru, spent his time in California's fields as a sheepherder. This sounded idyllic, until he began to tell his story.

There were no hard and fast rules for selecting narrators, only that they reflected some of the diversity of California's farmworkers and were eager to talk. I reached out to several organizations: especially helpful were California Rural Legal Assistance and the UFW, who passed along many names and numbers. Sometimes I sought out individuals whose backgrounds I knew something about. It was important, for example, to include narrators who could talk about specific human rights abuses that face California farmworkers, such as sexual harassment or the vulnerabilities of indigenous Mexican immigrants. But other times I knew only a person's name and address. I arrived with the faith that everyone, if given the space, has an important story to tell. I think this book bears that faith out.

There are seventeen narrators in this book. Ten are men and seven women (men make up about 75 percent of California's farm labor, though the challenges of migrant farmwork affect whole families). They live in all four of the major agricultural regions described above, with the majority coming from the Central Valley and the Coachella Valley. Along with current and former farmworkers, I have also collected the stories of people within their orbit. These include two farmers (or growers, as they are often called in California); a grade school teacher; a Migrant Head Start director; and a farmworker advocate. Still, every narrator in this book has spent long hours working in California's fields, regardless of their current occupations.

As I traveled across the state, I was guided by two overarching questions. How do the many challenges outlined above—wage theft, undocumented legal status, the general uncertainty of a life spent on the road—specifically impact the lives of the narrators? The second question was related to the first. In what way did farmworkers, despite such challenges, sustain themselves? Put another way: what formal support systems or protections are missing, and what informal systems have farmworkers developed in response?

But those were just jumping off points. Having worked for more than a decade as a journalist, I'm accustomed to listening to people talk about their lives. Yet I also tend to focus on a certain aspect of that person's life: the aspect that fits into the article I am writing. It was a wonderful change of pace to sit back and let the story go in directions determined by the narrators, and to have some of my assumptions challenged. Many narrators informed me, for instance, that California's half-decade-long drought hasn't impacted their work or their lives much. If anything, the drought has led to an increase in demand for farm labor as growers convert large acreage crops harvested mechanically (like wheat) to smaller-acreage crops like stone fruits that require harvesting by hand. I also sought to stay true to what my narrators saw as important in their own stories. One common thread that seemed to pass through all my interviews was a yearning for better opportunity and more stability for the children of farmworkers. Many narrators preferred to talk about the challenges of keeping their own children on track at school and on to college than abuses they may have faced in the fields. And so the struggle for educational opportunity emerged as a major unplanned theme in this book.

More than once, upon my departure, people mentioned that they had never before talked about a particular experience. They surprised me with their openness. They surprised themselves, too. Some of these experiences had been excruciating to live through, and sharing them was an act of courage. Along with courage, what shines through in each of these narratives—without exception—is a dogged optimism and pride. "Look at my hands," Roberto Valdez told me, an hour into sharing his story. Two fingernails were busted, there was a cut on his thumb, and the calluses on his palms were hard as bricks. "These are the hands that feed this country." He had a wide smile on his face. His is an important occupation, and he knew it.

EXECUTIVE
EDITOR'S NOTE

The narratives in this book are the result of oral history interviews conducted over a six-month period between the spring and fall of 2016. With every Voice of Witness narrative, we aim for a novelistic level of detail and (whenever possible) a birth-to-now chronological scope in order to portray narrators as individuals in all their complexity, rather than as case studies. We do not set out to create comprehensive histories of human rights issues. Rather, our goal is to compile a collection of voices that offers accessible, thought-provoking, and ultimately humanizing perspectives on what can often seem like impenetrable topics.

The stories themselves remain faithful to the speakers' words (we seek final narrator approval before publishing their narratives), and have been edited for clarity, coherence, and length. In a few cases, some names and details have been changed to protect the identities of our narrators and the identities of family members and acquaintances. The narratives themselves have been carefully fact-checked, and are supported by various appendices and a glossary included in the back of the book that provide context and some explanation of the history of farmwork in California.

We thank all the men and women who generously and patiently shared their experiences with us, including those whom we were unable to include in this book. We also thank all the frontline human rights defenders working to promote and protect the rights and dignity of all migrant workers throughout California. Without the cooperation of these human rights advocates, this book would not be possible.

Finally, we thank our community of educators and students who inspire our education program. With each Voice of Witness book, we create a Common Core–aligned curriculum that connects high school students and educators with the stories and issues presented in the book. Our education program also provides curriculum support, training, and site visits to educators in schools and invested communities. Visit the Voice of Witness website for free lesson plans, additional interview material, and to find out how you can be part of our work: voiceofwitness.org.

Mimi Lok
Executive Director and Executive Editor
Voice of Witness

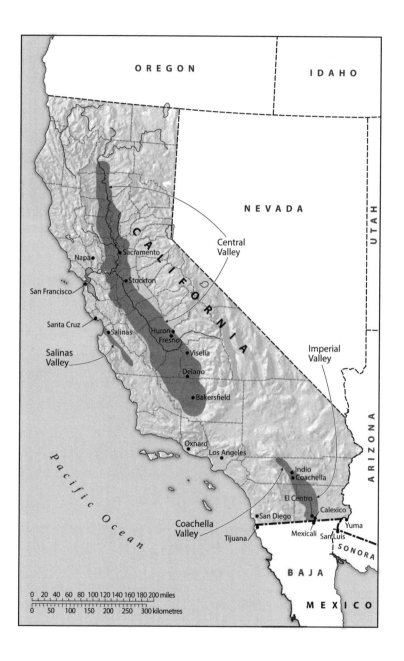

OREGON

IDAHO

NEVADA

Central
Valley

C A L I F O R N I A

U T A H

Napa

Sacramento

Stockton

San Francisco

Santa Cruz

Salinas

Huron

Fresno

Viselia

Salinas
Valley

Delano

Bakersfield

Imperial
Valley

A R I Z O N A

Pacific Ocean

Oxnard

Los Angeles

Indio
Coachella

El Centro

San Diego

Calexico

Yuma

Coachella
Valley

Tijuana

Mexicali

San Luis

SONORA

BAJA

MEXICO

0 20 40 60 80 100 120 140 160 180 200 miles
0   50   100   150   200   250   300 kilometres

MARICRUZ LADINO

AGE: *44*
OCCUPATION: *Produce truck driver*
BORN IN: *Sonora, Mexico*
INTERVIEWED IN: *Salinas, Monterey County*
AGRICULTURAL REGION: *Salinas Valley*

Sexual harassment and violence in agriculture is both widespread and underreported. For years, the everyday threats and assaults faced by female farmworkers was a story that mostly stayed in the fields. In the past decade, however, a number of investigations—made possible by the bravery of women who have come forward—have uncovered a human rights crisis. In 2010, UC Santa Cruz published a study based on interviews with 150 female farmworkers in California. Nearly 40 percent reported that they had experienced sexual harassment or assault, often from their supervisors, ranging from unwanted verbal advances to rape. Two years later, Human Rights Watch published a report, "Cultivating Fear," based on interviews with more than fifty farmworkers across the country, which concluded that the persistent harassment and violence faced by women in the fields was "fostered by a severe imbalance of power" between undocumented farmworkers and their supervisors.[1]

---

[1] To read an excerpt of the Human Rights Watch report, see Appendix V, page 310–18.

Maricruz Ladino knows all about that imbalance of power. "A supervisor can get you fired with the snap of his fingers," she says. And so she stayed quiet, putting up with her supervisor's daily harassment—and later, violent sexual assault—in order to hang on to her job at a lettuce-packing plant in Salinas. Then came the day she gathered the courage to walk into the company's office and file a complaint. She feared the worst: she could lose her job, or be deported. Both came to pass. But she has never regretted her decision.

We meet at a vegetable-cooling plant in early October, where Maricruz welcomes me aboard her truck, which is carrying pallets of iceberg lettuce eventually destined for Honolulu. While she waits for more produce to be loaded, she talks about growing up on the border, her intense drive to always keep moving forward, and why she eventually broke the silence about the abuse she suffered.

I'M THE GIRL THEY FOUND
IN THE GARBAGE CAN

I was born in 1972 in San Luis Río Colorado, Sonora.[2] I've been told that when my mom was pregnant, some friends of hers were going to bring her over to the United States so that I'd be born here. On the day they were going to pick her up, she was cleaning the patio. She wanted to leave a clean house when she left for Yuma.[3] But I was impatient.

My aunt lived next door and my mom began to yell out for her. There was a small pile of trash and my mom lay herself down on it so that I wouldn't hurt myself when I arrived. It was very romantic. My aunt arrived and helped her cut the umbilical cord. That's why they say I'm the girl they found in the garbage can.

---

[2] San Luis Río Colorado is a city of 150,000 on the Arizona-Sonora border. Across the border is the city of San Luis, Arizona, with a population of 30,000.

[3] Yuma, Arizona, is a city of 90,000 near the U.S.-Mexico border. In the winter, it is the major lettuce-growing region of the country.

My father was born in Tonalá, Jalisco, near Guadalajara.[4] My mom is from Ixtlán del Río in Nayarit.[5] They met in Ixtlán, got married, and then went to San Luis Río Colorado so my dad could work in the Bracero Program.[6] I'm not sure if he had to be on the border to sign papers or something. I never really asked. What I do know is that he had to be near the border so that he could work. He worked picking cotton on the U.S. side near Yuma and San Luis, Arizona.

My parents had six children—five girls and one boy. Each of us is separated by three years in age. I'm number four.

When I was a few months old, my parents made the decision to come to the United States to live in Yuma. It used to be much easier to get a passport or a tourist visa that allowed you to cross the border. We lived in a small adobe house; I close my eyes and I can still remember that poor house. There was only one room, and at the entrance there were a few steps where I would wait for my dad to come back from work. He was picking cotton and carried a sack the color of dirt. I'd run to him and he'd put the sack down and hug me. It was a beautiful thing. Now, I'm aware of the consequences of all the pesticides he was exposed to, but back then I didn't know any of that.

When I was three or four, my father made the decision for us to return to San Luis Río Colorado. From then on, he'd cross the border back and forth each day for work. You could walk from the house to the border crossing in only ten or fifteen minutes. Every weekend when he received his check, without fail, we'd cross to San Luis,

---

[4] Tonaláa, Jalisco is a city of 500,000 close to Guadalajara, the capital of the central Pacific state of Jalisco.

[5] Ixtláan del Rio is a municipality of 30,000 in the state of Nayarit, which is north of Jalisco.

[6] The Bracero Program was an agreement between the United States and Mexico beginning in 1942 to grant guest-worker visas to Mexican agricultural workers. For more information on the Bracero Program, see the Glossary, page 283.

Arizona to buy food. My parents would have us pick something we wanted to eat but could share with the other siblings. If I wanted a sandwich, I'd pick the bread, my other sister would pick the ham, and then the other sister the mayonnaise. It was something we'd all eat.

When I got older, around fourteen or fifteen, we had a neighbor that grew green onions. She needed people to help her clean and package them. My sisters and I asked my dad for permission to help this lady and make some money for the house. He got mad and told us no. He said he worked to provide for us, and if we needed anything we should ask him. But I was at the age where I wanted to help out, and I was curious about the work. I wanted to understand more about the world around me.

My father's sister, our aunt, lived across from that lady with the green onions. So we'd get back from school, quickly do our homework, eat, and then ask my mom if we could go visit my aunt. But we'd go over to the neighbor's house instead. We'd make up competitions with the younger children to see who could clean more onions and make bigger bunches, make more money. For us it was a game. For the lady it helped her keep up with her work. She'd only pay us two or three pesos per dozen of onion bunches, but we were happy.

Then came the day when my dad got home from work early. He asked my mom, "Where are they?" My mom told him, "Well, with your sister." He showed up and we weren't there.

As soon as we saw him, with only a look, we knew the scolding we'd receive. We got up, and with our heads hanging low, walked back home. When we got home, our father yelled at us for making him feel like we were lacking something, that he wasn't providing enough for us. But for us, working wasn't about anything we lacked. We wanted to help him so that we could all have more, but he never saw it that way. Now I see how we made him feel.

WE HAD TO STUDY TO BE SOMEBODY

I never found out exactly why my dad stopped working in the United States. He'd always say that he preferred to be with us. Sometimes he was away from us for a week or two—that wasn't a life. So he came back and got a job as a taxi driver in San Luis Río Colorado.

When he worked as a taxi driver, we never lacked anything. My mother also was not meant to work. He was the man of the house and she was supposed to take care of us and help him educate us. He never allowed her to work. She wanted to work. She would sell things to try and help.

My parents would always take us to school and pick us up. They didn't want us to be on our own. My dad wanted us to study and do better than he'd done. We had to study to be somebody. I liked school a lot, but I saw that keeping me in school was becoming more expensive for my parents. As I got older and high school came around, they had to buy me a uniform and books. My parents never said no—they would buy us everything—but I saw the difficulties they were having.

I graduated from high school when I was seventeen and entered the university, where I began to study to become a lab chemist and do analyses. But I didn't finish because I started dating a man from San Luis Río Colorado. We came to California when I was seventeen, in 1989, and got married the same year.

We moved to Five Points, a small ranch in the middle of the fields near Huron.[7] An aunt of mine rented us a small room. Within a short time of my arrival I became pregnant. My first daughter, Stephany, was born prematurely, in November 1990, when I was a week short of seven months. She weighed one and a half pounds and was in the hospital for a month and a half.

---

[7] Huron, California, is a municipality of 6,000 near Fresno. The population of the town more than doubles during harvest season.

Around the time my daughter was born, my husband and I began to have problems as a couple and we decided to separate. I think he went back to Mexico.

IT USED TO BE ONLY MEN THAT DID THIS JOB

After my husband and I separated, I cleaned houses to support my daughter and myself. When I was twenty-one, I began to work in the lettuce fields of Huron. I was beginning a new phase in my life. When I first started, I wasn't cutting or packing lettuce. I was up on the lettuce machine that goes slowly through the field, making sure it went straight along the rows, because Cal/OSHA required that.[8] I sat and watched the steering wheel, and sometimes made small turns, while behind me the rest of the people *worked*. I found my job boring. I wanted to learn what the others were doing. I was told to stay where I was, because working in the field was much harder. The supervisor said, "You won't know what to do and then you'll want to run away." But I was curious. And with the help of others, I began to learn how to pack.

With lettuce, there's a person that moves along cutting the heads. It used to be only men that did this job, but there are now women as well. The person moves down the row, cuts the lettuce, bags it, and puts it on a table that is located to one side. Then the packers twist that bagged lettuce until a ribbon forms at the top, then tape the ribbon so that the lettuce is wrapped nicely and box it so the package looks presentable.

Those first days were difficult. It was such a painful experience —my hands went through a lot of lettuce! A lady told me, "Don't worry, it'll last a week. When the swelling goes down and your bones stop aching, it'll almost be over." I was in such pain I couldn't

---

[8] Cal/OSHA is the agency that enforces workplace safety regulations in California. For more information, see the Glossary, page 283.

even hold onto the lettuce. Yet she was right, I only needed one week. They wrapped my hands up with bandanas to give them some support. Some co-workers offered some pills to help deal with the pain but I didn't take any. How else was I going to learn how to deal with the work than by just getting through it?

ON AUGUST 27, 1997, HE TRIED TO KILL ME

My two oldest sisters lived in Downey, California.[9] They wanted me to join them, so in 1992 I moved in with them. That's where I met my new husband, through the husband of a cousin. He was a truck driver and had been traveling through the Los Angeles area. That same year, in 1992, I moved to Coalinga to live with him.[10] But we weren't able to make a life together. We began to have serious problems. Serious in the sense that I have scars.

I had another two daughters with my second husband. Karla was born in 1992 and Sandra in 1994. In 1996 we moved to a remote ranch in Kerman, and the situation got worse.[11] Then we moved back to Coalinga, where supposedly everything was going to be different, but it never was.

On August 27, 1997, he tried to kill me.

It was the first day of school for my older daughters—the oldest was in first grade and the other two in Head Start. I sent them off and went to help my husband drop off cargo in Hanford, California.[12] I'd never eaten at a Denny's, and I saw one on our way and told him that I'd like to eat there on our way back. When we arrived in Hanford I

---

[9] Downey is a suburb 15 miles southeast of Los Angeles with a little more than 100,000 residents.

[10] Coalinga is a municipality of 13,000 located 60 miles southwest of Fresno.

[11] Kerman is a small city of 15,000, fifteen miles west of Fresno.

[12] Hanford is a city of over 50,000 in Kings County, approximately 30 miles south of Fresno.

began to unload big barrels of oil. An older man helped me unload—he'd take the barrels from me and hand them off to my husband. The man said to me that he'd help my husband so that I wouldn't get hurt. My husband took offense to this. He told me, "Go back to the truck! Can't you hear me?" I knew he was upset and that it would go badly for me. He was jealous.

After they finished unloading everything, he got back into the truck and began to hit me. Nobody could see. He began to ask where I knew that man from before. He said that he'd been so friendly to me because I was dating him. But I didn't know him; he was simply a kind man that didn't want me to get hurt.

On our way back we parked the truck and got into our car. He continued to hit me. We got to the Denny's and he stopped. My face was bleeding by that point. The people inside and outside of Denny's were staring at me. He told me, "Get out. You wanted to eat here, so I brought you here." I was embarrassed. He said, "You don't want to get out because you probably know somebody inside." He began again with his jealousy. He insisted that I wouldn't get out of the car because the men there knew me. We left.

To get to Coalinga you have to pass through a range of little mountains. I screamed that I couldn't stand it any longer and told him to let me out. That's where he stopped and told me to get out of the car. As he stopped, I opened the door to get out. He didn't allow it. He pulled me in and hit the gas hard. He started slowing down again and said, "All right, get out. I don't want you here if you want to get out." But he wouldn't stop.

I can't remember anything else. I saw black. Everything was dark. I could hear voices and I yelled out, "What happened to me! Tell me what happened!" That's all I remember.

I awoke in a hospital in Fresno, California. Everything looked blurry. I heard the noises of machines and the voices of my sisters and parents. My parents lived in Mexico at the time, so I don't know how or when they arrived at the hospital. I realized that days had gone by. My older sister massaged my head and said, "You're fine. We're with you."

I still didn't understand what had happened to me. There were no witnesses. There was a social worker in Coalinga who knew me, my daughters, and my husband. She knew about the domestic violence in my home. She could imagine what I was going through. When she found out what had happened to me, she came to see me. She told me, "You have to call somebody, or else nobody will be able to help you." She always said, "If you don't take action we can't do anything."

I was afraid of retribution. I was afraid of what my husband might do to my daughters or me. I was afraid; I kept silent. Back then I stupidly thought, *He's my daughters' father; I can't hurt him or my daughters will one day reproach me for that.* I wasn't well, so I wasn't thinking right. I can see this now.

I was in a coma for three weeks and in intensive care for weeks after that. It was a total of two and a half months that I was in the hospital. The one who never left my side was my dad. My husband was at the hospital for some time, too. I later learned that he'd told the hospital that I'd jumped out of the car. That was a complete lie. I asked the nurses to not let my husband in, but then they'd ask me why, so I had to keep quiet because I didn't want to say anything else. When you're young, you don't think things through. I never charged him with anything. I didn't want to tell my parents what was happening. A few months after I got out of the hospital, I went back to him. I had nowhere else to go.

He tried to beat me again, but this time I didn't allow it. I'd never resisted before, but then came the moment when I defended myself, to the point that I ended up in jail for three days for domestic violence. He started trying to hit me and I scratched his face, I ripped his clothes, I did what I could. Somebody called the police, I don't know who—maybe a neighbor. When the police showed up, I didn't have any marks on me, because I'd been like a cat when my husband tried to hit me.

When I had to go to court to face my charges, my neighbors and manager were there to support me. They explained that I was a good person who had defended herself. The judge saw the police reports from when neighbors had called because my husband was beating me. The judge let me go. I only had to go to anger management classes for six months.

I told myself, *This isn't a life.* I left my husband and rented an apartment in Coalinga with the help of friends who lent me money. One of those friends was a forewoman at a lettuce company in Huron. That's when I began to truly work in the fields.

I DIDN'T WANT PEOPLE TO SEE THAT I'D BEEN CRYING

Huron has a very short lettuce season. After that, though, there are peppers, peaches, many different fruits and vegetables to harvest. I worked all of them.

In 2000, the lettuce company I was working for asked me to go to Yuma with them and keep working. My parents had moved to Coalinga, and that day my dad noticed that I was sad and asked me what was going on. I told my dad about the job offer. "Tomorrow is the last day of work in Huron," I said. "My job is ending."

"So?" he asked.

I replied, "What do you mean, 'So?' Dad. You're trying to tell me to go to Yuma, but how am I going to do that? What about the girls?" I didn't even have a car back then.

"They'll stay with me," he said. "And you'll get on a Greyhound and go." He didn't have to tell me twice. I left. I wanted so badly to move forward, to help my daughters.

But it was very hard. In Yuma I covered my face with a bandana and wore sunglasses—I didn't want people to see that I was crying while I worked. I was far away from my daughters, far

MARICRUZ LADINO

from everything. I had to keep my strength up to keep working and sending them money.

I spent four months in Yuma, returned for one month in Huron, and then seven months in Salinas. While I was gone, my dad took care of my daughters in Coalinga. My mom frowned upon the idea of me traveling far for work. She didn't like the idea. I think my dad understood my situation better because he was reminded of his having to leave to feed us. I'm guessing that my parents fought between themselves. One wanted me to leave and the other didn't, but my dad has always supported me in everything.

DESIRE IS EXACTLY WHAT I HAVE

I worked only six or eight months as a lettuce packer. I always wanted to get ahead, to better myself, to earn more money. So one day I asked a supervisor, "What do I need to become a *mayordoma*?"[13] He smiled at me and said, "Desire."

I thought to myself, *Desire? Desire is exactly what I have.* They told me that I needed a class-B license to drive a bus, so I could transport a crew to the fields. A driving instructor said it sometimes took three or six months to get the license. I did it in fifteen days. That's how much ambition I had, how much hunger I had. When I got the license, I showed my supervisor and asked if there were any openings to be a mayordoma. In June of 2001, the company called me and said there was going to be a training session for mayordomos in Huron, to work in melons. I'd never worked with melons. I didn't know anything about a melon except how to eat it. But I thought, *Well, I've got to go.* When I was getting ready to leave for the meeting, the boss's son called and said it had

---

[13] A *mayordoma* is a supervisor of a work crew. For more about mayordomos, see the Glossary, page 287.

37

been canceled, and that he didn't know when the next training would be.

I said, "No problem, just let me know when there's going to be another training." And he said, "No. I'm not interested in giving you work. You're the person interested in working." At first I was offended. But eventually I realized he was right. The person who needs to work is me. So I kept asking when the next training would be: asking, asking, asking. The day of a new training came, and I showed up, really nervous but trying not to show it. I asked myself, *How am I going to do this? How can I direct people if I don't know the work?* But I was making $300 or $350 a week as a regular worker, and a mayordoma makes $600 a week. So I didn't want to miss that opportunity.

Little by little, I learned—from the workers themselves. I was sincere. I told them, "You know what, this is my first time. I'm going to need to learn from you." And they taught me a lot: how to cut the melon, how to move the equipment, how to use the tractors. They taught me what they knew, despite the fact that I was the mayordoma and that I was supposed to know more than they did.

A SUPERVISOR CAN GET YOU FIRED
WITH THE SNAP OF HIS FINGERS

Melon has a short season. When it ended, I became a mayordoma with a lettuce crew. I did that for two years, 2001 until 2003, going from Salinas to Yuma to Huron.

At first I felt very comfortable as a mayordoma. Then one day, a man walked over to me while I was watching how everyone in my crew was working. He got next to me, pointed to his crotch, and asked, "Who's giving it to you? Are you getting it from your boyfriend, your husband? Who's screwing you?"

I just looked at him and didn't say anything. He said, "Hey, I'm talking to you. Are you getting any?" And he repeated all the same lewd remarks. I looked at him and asked who he was. He said, "I'm your new supervisor."

This new supervisor bothered me for a long time. I cried. I felt very uncomfortable, but I couldn't complain to anybody, because I worried I would lose my job. A supervisor can get you fired with the snap of his fingers.

I felt impotent. It wasn't just him. Many other men made fun of me. They'd say, "Surely you are a mayordoma because you slept with someone, not because you did anything else to earn your position." I worked very hard to learn how to do my job, to learn how to take care of everything. And it was because of my hard work that I became a mayordoma, not because I'd slept with somebody.

THE STRONG ONE, DEVASTATED

I worked as a mayordoma until May 9, 2003. On that day I was in Salinas, and wanted to surprise my mother for Mother's Day. My parents had moved from Coalinga to San Luis, Arizona. While I was driving down to visit them, I was the one who got the surprise: my father had died. That was a very long drive.

I stayed with my daughters and mother in Yuma, trying to help out. It was very sad to come home to my parent's house in San Luis and not see my father. I couldn't let others know how I was feeling, because I was the strong one, the one that could withstand everything. The one that wasn't devastated, so that my mother wouldn't be devastated.

One day, I saw that my mom was sleeping. I didn't want to wake her, so I went to the backyard patio to sit outside. I turned the radio on. I don't really drink, but it was so hot that day, and there was a beer that had been forgotten in the fridge. I sat down and opened my beer. A song came on that my father used to like and I started to cry.

My daughters were inside and my mother was asleep. They were not going to know. No one could see me, the strong one, devastated. I was ready to give up. But when I felt my mother's hand on my shoulder, I stopped crying. I wiped away my tears and pretended as if nothing was happening. My mother said, "Cry, because if you don't cry it will hurt more. You have to let it out." I told my mom that I wasn't crying, that I just got something in my eye. It was very hard not to be able to let out all that sadness.

Thank god, when the lettuce season began in Yuma, I got a new job, this time as a supervisor. This was in the fall of 2003. By this time I knew how to do the work, how to direct crews, how to help more mayordomos. And so I began—not as a mayordoma, but as a supervisor. I was helping out the mayordomos, telling them how many boxes of lettuce we needed, checking the quality of the lettuce.

When I left, my daughters stayed with my mother in Yuma. During the summer vacation, I brought them with me to Salinas. And then when it was time to go back to Yuma, I brought them back. I did that for two years, until a co-worker told me about a position at another company.

In 2005, Maricruz began a new job, at a lettuce-packing plant in Salinas. Though the job helped her support her three daughters, she experienced constant sexual harassment from her boss, who pressured her to sleep with him. Then after a few months on the job, Maricruz's boss asked her to help him transport some boxes, and when they were alone he raped her. Maricruz, fearing retaliation, didn't report the rape immediately. However, after seven months and continued harassment, she filed a complaint against her boss with management.

An incident happened. It was … very unpleasant. I will try to explain what happened a little bit. It's something very delicate, very painful. It's not easy to talk about. All this time, the supervisor was telling me, "It's because of me that you have your position. If I want, I can fire you. Remember that you have three daughters, that you're the head of the family. If you don't do what I want, you're going to lose everything."

We could say that it was sexual harassment, but in reality, it was more than that. It was rape.

Before, like when I had that problem with the supervisor when I was a mayordoma, although I felt alone, there were people around. When this incident occurred, I was alone with this one person. At the moment, I didn't know what to do, how to act. I was in shock. I couldn't even talk. I simply didn't know how to react. It's like I was paralyzed.

I fell into a depression. I didn't know what to do. I kept working at the company for seven more months. I had two families that were depending on me: my three daughters in Salinas and my mother in Yuma. I was seeing someone at the time, but I never told my partner about what had happened to me, because I was afraid of his reaction, and because I was ashamed. As time passed, I kept thinking about what had been done to me. If I didn't speak up, the same sort of thing could happen to my daughters.

At the end of September 2006, I asked to speak to the owner's right-hand man. I didn't know English, so the company had someone translate. In the meeting, they told me, "Don't worry, everything will be kept confidential." I made the complaint at ten or eleven in the morning. By noon, all of the other employees were asking me, "Is it true that you complained? You really filed a complaint against this person?"

Imagine how I felt. It was supposed to be *confidential*. Everyone was watching me, whispering about me. At work the next day, they called me into a conference room, with lawyers and a translator. They asked me many questions, in different ways, waiting for me to say something that wasn't true, waiting for me to contradict myself. I couldn't tell them all of the details—exactly what happened at what time, how he did this or that—because I was ashamed. But it was easy to understand what had happened to me.

In October, some of the employees move to Huron for a month. I was going to stay in Salinas, but then the company told me to go to Huron. I worked there for one day, and then the bosses in Huron told me, "You know what, you need to return, because we forgot your check." They told me I needed to work Friday in Salinas, and I could collect my check when I was there.

I showed up for work at 8 a.m., as always. By then, they'd changed the position of the person who I'd complained about. The new supervisor said, "Give us a second, you don't need to start working. We're going to talk to you first." Then he told me, "You need to turn your work equipment in. You're fired. We don't have work for you anymore." Can you imagine? I supposedly had come back to work, but instead they wanted to fire me. I waited a week for my check. They never gave it to me.

In agricultural circles, everyone knows each other. All the mayordomos and supervisors and bosses know each other. I tried to look for work at other companies. And people would say, "Ah, I heard all these things about you. Are they true?" Sometimes they shut the door on my face. One company hired me, but at the moment that I went to show them proof of my license, someone mentioned the name of the person with whom I had a problem. I felt like they were saying, "We know who you are. We know what happened."

I felt humiliated. I left that office and didn't work there. People made stupid comments. Others wanted to know more. Yes, it's uncomfortable. Yes, you lose a lot of your self-esteem. I felt like trash. As a woman, I felt like I'd lost my dignity and worth. Sometimes I didn't want to leave the house so that I wouldn't see anybody that I knew.

The company I'd worked for still wouldn't hand over my last check. Someone gave me the phone number of a lawyer that I could call. I called this lawyer, and he gave me the number of an office that

I didn't know existed. It was for California Rural Legal Assistance (CRLA).[14] I called and made an appointment in late 2006 to see if they could help me collect the money that was owed to me.

I was ashamed to talk about what had happened. I hadn't gone there to talk about sexual harassment or anything like that. But one of the questions the man I talked to asked me was, "Why and how did they fire you?" And I told him, because I had filed a complaint. He said, "Complaint about what?" Little by little, it all came out—that there was a problem more serious than my unjust firing. But I had to talk a little bit more about the case, and it wasn't easy to do so. It was something very difficult, very shameful.

That was when CRLA filed a lawsuit. They also filed another lawsuit, with the EEOC, against the company.[15] It was all part of a strategy to make the case stronger. They asked me if I was ready to take this case all the way, and I said yes.

I had so much fear. Not fear about losing work—I had already lost it. I was afraid of what people were going to say about me. What action was the company going to take?

BY 2 P.M. I KNEW THEY WERE GOING TO DEPORT ME

Agents from ICE arrived at my apartment at six in the morning.[16] It was April 27, 2007—a date I'll never forget. They asked to speak to the owner of my partner's vehicle. I told them that he wasn't home.

---

[14] California Rural Legal Assistance is a fifty-year-old nonprofit that provides free legal services to rural poor throughout the state. Its advocacy work focuses on housing, labor, education, health, and leadership development. For more information, see Appendix IV, page 304–305.

[15] The US Equal Employment Opportunity Commission enforces federal employment discrimination laws.

[16] ICE stands for Immigration and Customs Enforcement. For more on ICE, see the Glossary, page 286.

It was true: he was at work. At the time, I thought it was just the police. They asked me to open the door. When I did, they told me again that they needed to talk to the owner of the truck. I asked, "Why do you have to talk to him?"

They searched through the house and asked for my identification. I still didn't really understand what was happening, but I showed it to them. They said, "OK, you're not the person we're looking for, but you have to come along with us." They wanted to verify with my fingerprints that I wasn't the person they were looking for. I told them that I needed to call someone to stay with my daughters. They hoped that the person I called would be my partner. But the person I called was a co-worker at the same company where I had made a complaint. This co-worker had always supported me in everything. He arrived at the house immediately. That's when ICE told me that they had a complaint that my partner was undocumented.

The company had reported my partner to Immigration. I don't want to say how I found this out, but I did. My partner had worked at the same company and they knew he was undocumented. They weren't sure of my immigration status, but if I didn't have papers and I got sent back to Mexico, it would take care of their problems with the lawsuit.

I went with ICE in their car. The only thing that they were going to do was bring me to San Jose to verify that I was who I said I was, and that I didn't have a deportation order. From the back seat, I called my partner, and told him that for absolutely no reason should he go to the house. He asked why, and I told him. I told him who was watching the girls. I called Jesus Lopez at CRLA and told him what had happened. Since I was in the back seat, I don't think they could hear me, and in case they had hidden microphones in the car, I tried to talk in a low voice.

While I was making these quick calls, ICE was doing raids. I'll never forget one of them. There was a man with his kids; I think he was bringing them to school. They parked one car in front of his car and two on the side. They parked the car that I was in behind his car, to surround him. The kids started to cry. It took a while before the person he called to take the kids arrived. I watched them round up more and more men and women. It was awful to see.

From Salinas they took us all to San Jose. By 2 p.m. I knew that they were going to deport me. They found out that I had had problems with domestic violence against my ex-husband. I'd broken the laws of the United States, so I wasn't a good person: I wasn't a person that would help the country. They supposedly wanted to get rid of bad people, people who could do harm. And I didn't have my papers, so there was absolutely nothing I could do to stop them.

They didn't put handcuffs on me until we got in the van that left San Jose for the airport in Oakland. Before we got out of the van in Oakland, they put restraints around my legs, too. On the plane, they read us the legal rights that we supposedly had. From Oakland we flew to Bakersfield, and from Bakersfield to Los Angeles, and from Los Angeles to San Diego. At each stop more people were brought on board for deportation. By the end, more than 100 people were on the plane.

They let me go in Tijuana at four in the morning. The first thing I did was to call my partner and tell him that I was in Tijuana and not to worry. He still thought I was in San Jose. It was a sad time, but at the same time I felt calm, because they hadn't gotten him. I felt like I could deal with it, because I knew the border a little bit, since I'd grown up here. I have family here and I'm not going to end up on the streets. I caught a bus from Tijuana to San Luis Río Colorado. Looking out the window, I was thinking, *How am I going to get back?*

The first thing my mom said was, "Forget about returning." My brother said the same thing. But in my mind I was always thinking, *I'm going back. I have to figure out how to do it.* I stayed a month. For me, it felt like a long time. My family had bouncy houses in Salinas that we rented out for birthday parties to make money, and we sold them so that I had enough to pay a coyote to get back. It took four or five days. I went through the desert in California. It was a bit difficult, but as you can see, it wasn't impossible. I got back to Los Angeles on a Friday night, and my partner and one of my daughters came to get me. When I returned to Salinas, I got in touch with Jesus Lopez at CRLA, and that's when they started a new case, along with my complaint. And thanks to them, I got a U visa.[17]

YOU COULD SAY THAT WHAT THE EXPERIENCE HAS DONE IS MAKE ME BRAVER

In 2010, Maricruz settled her lawsuit against the company under confidential terms, agreeing not to disclose the amount of the settlement or the name of the company. Since then, she has been interviewed by newspaper and radio journalists, and in 2013 was featured in the Frontline *documentary "Rape in the Fields," which aired on PBS.*

The dark side, the horrible side of working in the fields, is the abuse. To be afraid of the person who has power, the person who insults us, who threatens us, who can fire us whenever they want.

I want to share what happened to me to help find a solution, to prevent this from happening again. The pain that was done to me can't be erased, but it can be used to help more people.

You could say that what the experience has done is make me braver.

I can't say that I'm happy. I try to be happy. I try to have a normal life as a woman, as a human being. But all of this has caused problems, with my partner and with my daughters. But it doesn't matter. These things happened—they're in the past. I have to live now.

Today, I work as a truck driver. It's something I like, something

---

[17] The U visa, which allows undocumented immigrants to legalize their status, is available to victims of certain crimes who have suffered mental or physical abuse and are helpful to law enforcement in the investigation or prosecution of criminal activity.

that I dreamed of doing as a little kid, because my dad was a taxi driver. I wanted to be like him. It's still agriculture work, but it's a different stage. We bring the products from the field to cool them, and then we bring them to the stores, or to other trucks that will take them to planes, where they will be flown even further away. Some of the lettuce goes to Tokyo, Canada, New York, San Diego.

I work Monday to Saturday. I start at 7 a.m. On a short day, I work thirteen hours. On the longest days, I work twenty hours, sometimes up to twenty-three hours, when I take lettuce deliveries to San Francisco. On Sunday, I can't say I rest, because my daughters are waiting to hang out with me. They complain because of how little I see them.

Today, my oldest daughter, Stephany, lives in Yuma, where she owns a second-hand children's clothing store. She's married with three kids. Her youngest son just turned three. Karla and Sandra live here in Salinas. Karla is pregnant and will have her second child in a week or two. She graduated in May from Hartnell College with a major in sociology and will transfer to a four-year school next fall.[18] Sandra works as an administrator at a lettuce cooler and is at Hartnell, too, studying business and technology. I feel very proud of my daughters, and what they've achieved. And I think they are proud of me, for what I've achieved.

My partner is now my husband. He didn't know about the rape until the moment it appeared in the news. That was when I had to find the bravery to explain everything to him. It was very difficult, because at the beginning he was very angry and disappointed, but I think that in the end he understood. He has helped and supported me in every way.

I got my green card three weeks ago. The U visa gives you permission to live and work in the United States, but you have to stay

---

[18] Hartnell Community College in Salinas serves more than 16,000 students each year.

here—you can't leave. With a green card I can leave. The first thing I did with my green card was to buy a plane ticket. Being Mexican to the core, I promised that when I got a green card I would immediately go see the Basilica of Our Lady of Zapopan in Guadalajara.[19] I gave my work a week's notice before I left. The truth is that I didn't care if they gave me permission or not: I was going to go. Thank god I didn't lose my job! I flew with my mom from Mexicali to Guadalajara. From there we went to the Basilica to see the Virgin. I cried until I couldn't cry anymore, giving thanks that I was finally free.

---

[19] The Basilica of Our Lady of Zapopan is a seventeenth-century Franciscan sanctuary in downtown Zapopan, a city adjacent to Guadalajara, in the state of Jalisco. It is one of the most visited sanctuaries in western Mexico, and includes a wooden Virgin of Zapopan, which was made in the sixteenth century.

OSCAR RAMOS

AGE: *42*

OCCUPATION: *Elementary school teacher*
BORN IN: *Jalisco, Mexico*
INTERVIEWED IN: *Salinas, Monterey County*
AGRICULTURAL REGION: *Salinas Valley*

In 1970, when the United Farm Workers set up an office in Salinas, they chose a shuttered post office in East Salinas, the heart of the city's farmworker community. Next door to the union office was Sherwood Elementary School, where the children of those farmworkers were offered the kinds of educational opportunities that had been unavailable to their parents. The UFW office has since relocated, but Sherwood still stands, and continues to serve the children of migrant farmworkers. Of the school's nearly 900 students, 99 percent are Latino and 98 percent qualify for free or reduced-cost lunch. The vast majority are English language learners.

Oscar Ramos is intimately familiar with the challenges facing kids in East Salinas. He's taught at Sherwood for the past twenty years, and grew up in a labor camp on the outskirts of Hollister, a small city thirty miles northeast of Salinas. Ramos arrived in this country as an undocumented immigrant and worked in the fields until the eighth grade. Students are often amazed when they hear his story: a kid from the fields who graduated from college? "Yes," Ramos tells them. "And you can do the same."

We meet at Oscar's house in June, two weeks after school has let out. He wears a hooded Cal Bears sweatshirt—Oscar is class of '96—and we sit around his dining room table, where he shares stories about his upbringing, his teaching career, and why he isn't surprised when students fall asleep in class.

"DON'T TALK, DON'T SNEEZE, DON'T COUGH"

I was born in 1973 in Jalisco, Mexico.[1] My parents were already in the United States, but they used to travel to Mexico every year, especially during Christmas time, when work was slow. One of those times back in Mexico, I was born. After I was born they brought me to the United States. Obviously I wasn't legal, but I believe by that time my parents were in the process of becoming legal residents.

My dad had come here to the U.S. first. I'm gonna say it was in the 1960s. He came over because he had brothers who were here already, in San Jose. After a few years he saved up enough to bring my mom. She's from a little village called Lázaro Cárdenas.[2] We call them *ranchos*—there are ranchos all over Jalisco; my dad's from a bigger one called Cocula. In between there's a town, San Martín Hidalgo, and that's where they met.

When my parents were first crossing into the U.S., they didn't cross legally, but it was easier then. With all these advances in technology, helicopters, and infrared cameras, it's much more difficult now. I've heard stories where people could just cross in the car to the U.S. They wouldn't check every vehicle; they wouldn't ask you to open the trunk. They would maybe ask a few questions and kinda look around and say, "All right, you seem legit, go on." Now, no way.

---

[1] Jalisco is a state of 8 million on Mexico's west coast.

[2] Lázaro Cárdenas, a town of several hundred people, is named for a general in the Mexican Revolution who was the country's president from 1934 to 1940.

When I was two, my parents went back to visit family again and they decided that I'd stay in Mexico with my younger sister, who was a baby. I have six other siblings, but they're older. It was hard for my parents to have two young kids while they were working long hours, seven days a week, so my sister and I stayed with my grandparents for a few years in Lázaro Cárdenas.

In Mexico, I remember going out to the cornfields with my grandfather on horseback. I remember helping my grandma chase chickens for dinner. My grandma's job was to kill the thing, and I'd help pluck the feathers. They had chickens, cows, pigs—they had everything. So whatever we wanted, we wouldn't go buy it at the store—we'd go and kill it.

There was no running water and no electricity. I helped my grandma pull the rope to get water from the well. Old school stuff. You know, no technology. There was one phone in a little grocery store, and if anyone got a call, the store owner would get on a loudspeaker to make the announcement: "There's a telephone call from California." And my parents or whoever called had to wait 'til we got to the store to answer.

In California, my parents and siblings moved around a lot: San Jose to Morgan Hill to Gilroy to further east, to Visalia, Delano. I mean everywhere. Onion fields, garlic fields, apricot orchards, walnut orchards, and grapes, lettuce. Eventually, they settled in a labor camp at Hollister, where they worked for the camp owner.[3] He gave them first priority for jobs, so they had guaranteed work year round. That's when they decided to stop moving and went back to Mexico to bring the other two kids. This was in 1978. So when I was five years old, I made the trip back to the United States.

By that time my parents were legal residents. I think they were sponsored by the labor camp,[4] so they could cross the border without

---

[3] Hollister is a city of 35,000 in San Benito County.

[4] For more on labor camps, see the Glossary, page 287.

a problem. And all my other siblings were born in the United States. But I didn't have my documents, because I'd been born in Mexico. So we came across the border at Tijuana in a pickup truck with a camper, and my parents threw a bunch of blankets on top of my little sister and me, and a couple of my older brothers and sisters lay on top of the covers. Even though my little sister was born in the United States, we were always together, so she went under the blankets with me. We were kinda inseparable, so she went through everything I went through. She didn't have to, but she did.

My parents told us, "You can't make any noise. Don't talk, don't sneeze, don't cough; nothing until we're across the border." And I'm like, *Oh, I don't wanna get taken away from my family*. I mean, who goes through that? And those who do, it's pretty scary, so the mind remembers.

The border guards didn't really search much: they kinda just opened the camper, looked around, and moved some things within their reach. Then they said, "OK, you're good to go." We came across and that was it.

THE ADULTS FOUND IT FUNNY
TO YELL OUT, "LA MIGRA!"

We lived in the labor camp on the outskirts of Hollister, surrounded by fields. Eight kids and my mom and dad in a little two-bedroom— I don't even know what to call it—definitely not a house. A *casita*. I was young and I remember the rooms as being big. But I went back thirty years later, and people have bigger walk-in closets than where we were living. My first thought was, *How did ten people live here?* Lots of bunk beds. My two older brothers had a bunk bed in the kitchen. That was their bedroom.

Growing up, I was very aware of Immigration, the raids, and the danger of possibly being deported. I remember adults found it funny to yell out, *"La migra!"* You know, the INS, and it would terrify me.[5] I would run home and hide under the bed. I look back and I'm like, *That's horrible! Why would you do that to a child?*

Immigration agents would raid the camp regularly. In the summer, everyone would go to work except me and my younger sister. We'd stay with the babysitter, someone's grandma. That poor lady. I remember one day when I must have been five, she was watching us in the middle of the day, and Immigration showed up at the camp and took a few people. She got put in their van. She's in the van, looking back with a sad face, waving goodbye. And my younger sister and I are in the middle of the yard, like, *Well, what about us? What's gonna happen to us?*

There were no cell phones, but they had a system that worked fairly quickly. The labor camp had scouts that would go from field to field to make sure everything was OK, because Immigration would also raid the fields where people were working. The scout driving around would take off to the next field and tell people, "Run, hide, you might be next." When they took our babysitter, someone knew exactly where my parents were, so they went and told them, and they came home.

I started working when I was eight. We worked Saturdays and had some Sundays off, but not every Sunday. Here's the thing. People have asked, "Wow, you lived in the labor camp, and you had to go out and work in the fields. Ooh, what was that like?" And I think they're expecting a sob story. Yeah, it was very difficult. It was hard working those long hours out in the sun. You know, we wanted to go to summer school and my mom would say, "No summer school for you."

But we had each other. We had our siblings and there were other families in the labor camp that had kids our age. So we made

---

[5] *La migra* refers to immigration enforcement agents. Enforcement of immigration law was previously carried out on the federal level by the Immigration and Naturalization Service (INS), but since 2003 has been carried out by Immigration and Customs Enforcement (ICE) under the Department of Homeland Security. For more information, see the Glossary, page 287.

everything fun. If we were out in the onion fields, we'd throw onions at each other just to keep us on our toes. We'd have a transistor radio. We'd be out there and there'd be a song that everyone liked, and everyone would be singing. And the food, always the food. The sharing of the food was just wonderful. It wasn't like: *I packed my own lunch, everyone get away from me.* We all had lunch together, and we'd share whatever we brought. Everyone! We didn't have much, and other families didn't have much, but we'd share everything.

At the labor camp, the kids would get together and play marbles, spin tops. We'd play soccer, baseball, red rover. We'd play something we called "chang guys." I don't know where it comes from, I just remember that we played it. What you do is, you use a big stick to hit a smaller stick. Instead of home runs you'd get points—you would measure the lengths of the stick after you broke it in two, and those were your points. Our parents hated that game because we'd break the broomsticks. Two sticks and we'd have hours of fun.

We had a tiny black and white TV with those little rabbit-ear antennas. I remember my parents watching shows in English. They didn't know what the shows were about, but they liked them. The cop show *Chips* with Erik Estrada; they used to love that show! They didn't understand what the characters were saying, but they loved it.

BACK THEN THERE WERE ENTIRE FAMILIES WHO LIVED IN CAMPS

The guy that ran the labor camp had been illegal too. He crossed over and started working for a guy who owned some land. He built this relationship with that owner, and the owner was very grateful that he was loyal. So he allowed the man to rent a piece of his land where he could grow whatever he wanted and keep the profit. He did that year after year, and eventually he started buying land and became his own grower. He built the labor camp so people could live there and work for him.

Back then there were entire families who lived in the camps. Now there are no families. It's mainly single men, or married men who left their families in Mexico and just send money back. Back then it was full, and I'd venture to say there were people on the waiting list. Today, there's a lot of empty rooms.

Same thing with the work: you'd have entire families out there. As children we weren't supposed to be out there, but who was watching us? Eight years old and you're working with those sharp onion shears that are bigger than your hand. You're out there helping the family out. You don't see that anymore because inspectors are watching. Everyone's more vigilant about child labor.

Most of the land we farmed was in Hollister, but the labor camp owner also had fields nearby in Morgan Hill and Gilroy. The crop we hated the most was garlic. Other workers pulled the garlic out and faced the plants all the same way on the ground. Then we came in to clean. The roots were covered with hard mud and hard rocks. You needed a lot of strength to cut the roots. We used the shears you use to prune a rose bush, but these shears were thicker and heavier. You had to wedge the shear handle on your thigh to really get that grip and leverage. The first couple of weeks, when your body was still getting used to that harvest, your hands would be swollen, your thighs would be swollen. And whenever you got a cut, it was a really deep, deep cut because you're using so much strength.

You had to fill up these big baskets with garlic. But if you filled it up to the top and took it to get your little card punched, the foreman would send you back. The garlic had to be *over* the top. You pick up the basket and put it on your shoulder and walk to the big bins and lean in and dump it out carefully. If you dumped it without leaning over, the garlic could bruise and the foreman hated that. Sometimes if you didn't lean over, they'd say, "Nope," and they wouldn't punch your card.[6]

---

[6] When workers are paid by how much they harvest (piece rate), their output is

We were at the camp for five years. Then we moved across the street, to a house—an actual house with three bedrooms. That's where I turned ten. We weren't there very long, because by that time my father started working in construction and he applied for low-income housing. CHISPA, that's what he called it.[7] They pretty much pick names out of a hat, like a lottery, and if you got picked, you were gonna get a home.

You had to build your home. So the entire neighborhood where I grew up, people were given the territory and had to build their own houses. My father and my brothers built it. CHISPA provided the materials and everything; it was our job to put it together. Good thing my dad was in construction. Everyone on that block would help each other. You know, if walls needed to go up, everyone would go and help build those walls.

I think I became a legal resident by the time we moved into the house that my dad and brothers built. I can't give you specifics as to how I became a legal resident, I just remember going to wherever I needed to go. I had my picture taken. I remember having to sign documents. And I remember receiving my green card in the mail. I was very happy, like, *All right, there's no way they can kick me out now.*

HE WOULD MAKE THINGS HAPPEN

I was in fourth grade when I thought, *I want to be a teacher.* It wasn't like I had the greatest, most inspirational teacher. I just remember seeing what the teacher was doing and thinking, *Hey that was a great lesson, but it could be better.* I would do this instead of that. I think kids

---

often tracked by receiving hole punches in their individual work card for each basket or bucket they fill.

[7] CHISPA, or the Community Housing Improvement Systems and Planning Association, is a nonprofit housing developer based in Monterey County that has built and renovated 2,268 single-family homes and apartments for low and moderate-income people since 1980.

would enjoy it more. I wouldn't have that bookshelf there, it's kind of in the way. I would put it over here. So I thought, *I can do this job; I can be a good teacher*.

In eighth grade, I applied for a summer youth program. That's when I was finally able to stop working in the fields. In the morning, I'd come in and help a summer school teacher till noon. These were fifth and sixth grade students. A lot of them were in there because they needed extra help with English. When summer school ended, they sent me to be a teacher's assistant at a different labor camp in Hollister than the one I had grown up at. There were no classrooms, just a lot of benches outside. We had a big chalkboard, some school supplies, and I helped the teacher with the migrant kids. So that only solidified my decision to be a teacher.

I always liked math. In fifth grade, I would help my friends with their homework. I continued to do that in middle school. In high school, me and two other friends started a math tutoring center, which we got paid for. We were going to do it voluntarily, but the school said they would pay us. Like, excellent! I remember wanting to help people, and it felt great.

But I was always bad at paperwork, so I was going to miss the deadlines to apply for college and financial aid. I was like, *Oh well, I'll apply next year.* My friends said no, that's not gonna happen. I grew up with them, we worked the same fields, went through school together from the first grade. So they reported me to one of the counselors, Mr. C, who everybody loved. I mean, he would make things happen for students.

We knew each other, but he wasn't my counselor. He called me in and he said, "You're gonna sit here and you're not gonna leave this office until you fill out all your college applications and your financial aid forms." And I said, "Ah, I don't wanna do that." He called my mom, and my mom told him to keep me there all night if he had to. I didn't want to be locked up in that little office. So I filled out applications to UC Berkeley, UCLA, and UC Davis.

I wanted to leave but he said, "No, you still have the financial aid forms." So I filled those out and I said, "OK, *now* I can leave, right?" And he said, "No, now you're going to get in my car. I'm going to drive you to the post office. I want to see you mail those things out." And we went and mailed them. Then he said, "Now we go get ice cream and you're free to go."

I got accepted to all three schools. I thought I was gonna go to UCLA. But little did I know that my six friends had already had the discussion that we were all going to Berkeley. Seven of us got accepted to Berkeley that same year. So when I told them that I was going to UCLA, they told me, "No you're not—you're going to UC Berkeley with us." And I didn't question that.

WHO ARE YOU?

I graduated UC Berkeley in 1996 with a degree in history and inter-viewed for a part-time position as a parent liaison at a continuation school in Hollister, near the labor camp where I grew up. Just for the summer, because I was going to go back and get my master's and teaching credential. The continuation school called me the next day and said I had more experience than the candidates who had applied for one of their teaching positions. I told them, "You're offering me a full-time position that I didn't apply for, and I don't even have my credential." But they felt I was the right person and said I could take courses for the credential at night. So I agreed—in part because it was a history position.

It was very difficult. I knew half of the kids; I grew up with their siblings. I mean, I was twenty-two and they were sixteen, seventeen. And it wasn't what I had in mind. The school was for kids who'd been kicked out of regular high school. I was teaching history to kids who didn't want to be there, who didn't want to be challenged. So I did one year and that was it. It was a disservice to them and to myself, because I didn't have the experience to motivate and inspire them.

That summer of 1997 I was going to CSU Monterey Bay to get my teaching credential. Principals would come to the university and say, "We need teachers; come and see." I was resistant at the beginning —I didn't want to work and get my credential at the same time. But someone recommended Sherwood Elementary here in Salinas.

They gave me a tour, took me to meet some of the teachers. I met the librarian, I met the vice principal, I was out during recess. I felt welcomed. And not just by the teachers, but the students, too. Remember, I had just come from a year of students who didn't want to be at school and who couldn't wait to get out. At Sherwood, during recess, kids are out there playing, and they'd come up to me and say, "Who are you? What's your name? What are you doing?" They'd smile and I felt like, *Wow. The kids are coming up to me and they want to know who I am.* They were interested; they cared. I thought, *Yeah, this is a perfect fit.* I signed the contract the same day they gave me the tour. That was in September 1997.

I TELL MY STORY

Sherwood School is 99 percent Hispanic, low-income. Most of their parents work in the fields. In my mind, that's the kind of school I always wanted to teach at.

I tell my story to my kids every year. I didn't used to, but one year I thought I'd tell it just to see how they reacted. They went home and told their parents that I grew up in the labor camp and from the time I was eight I would work in the fields. During parent conferences it would come up. Parents would ask me, "Teacher, is that true? You know, my daughter told me that you used to do this."

Over the years, more and more parents know my story, and more students know my story, and it's helped me with them because they know that what I'm saying is genuine. Because I lived through it. I experienced it. I didn't learn about their experience through a book.

Like, "Oh I read that this is what it's like to be a farmworker." Everything is genuine. So I think that helped, telling them my story.

I've been at Sherwood for twenty years, and eighteen of them have been teaching third grade. This is why I like third grade: it's the age where you can have a mature conversation. Eight years old, nine years old—you know, they get it, they understand. You tell a joke and they'll get it and they'll laugh.

It used to be that we would lose half our students in the fall and winter, because most of those students had parents that were traveling for farmwork. They'd start leaving for Arizona in November and wouldn't be back 'til April.[8] The class you started with wasn't the class you ended up with. We had a fourth grade teacher who started one year with twenty-eight students. Only three of her original students ended that school year.

That constant movement is the entire *East of Salinas* story.[9] This particular student, Jose, he's always moving. Every year he would go to a different school. Sometimes during that same school year he'd move twice, and I think in one school year he moved to three different schools. And when he got to my class, in third grade, he wasn't going to finish the school year. He told me that he was going to move.

I'd read his file. I saw that he'd been to five different schools already. He'd never finished a grade in one of the schools, and I didn't want that for him. I talked to the principal. I talked to his mom. His stepfather was working in Arizona. And they agreed. I'd pick him up in the morning and drive him to school, and his mom would pick

---

[8] From about March to October, most of the nation's lettuce is grown in the Salinas Valley. Each winter, when temperatures drop, the lettuce harvest shifts to Yuma, Arizona. Many workers shuttle between the two regions, though increased immigration enforcement has caused these numbers to drop in recent years.

[9] In December 2015, PBS aired *East of Salinas*, an hour-long documentary by the filmmakers Laura Pacheco and Jackie Mow, which focuses on the relationship between Oscar and his student.

him up after work. I did that for a few months so he could finally finish one grade in one school.

Jose would come in and fall asleep, but I wouldn't wake him up. I knew why he was falling asleep, because that's the same thing that used to happen to me. His mom would wake him up at three or four o'clock in the morning when she took him to the babysitter's so she could go to work, and then he'd take a nap and they'd go to school. But once your night is broken up, it's not the same—you're gonna be tired the entire day.

We'd have snacks in the classroom, and he'd ask for two snacks. I knew why Jose was asking for two snacks—he wasn't eating; there was no food at home. So yeah, there are all these challenges that come with kids that move around and those are just some of them. I'm sure there's more that I'm not aware of.

Kids like that, they're usually very shy; they're very quiet. Because they figure, *Why speak, why make friends, if I'm gonna end up leaving? And why try hard because when I move to another school they're gonna be doing something different?* And they feel defeated.

Or they act up. *I get in trouble, so what? I won't be here much longer.* The principal suspends them and, *It's fine, I'm gonna be in another school.* So it's difficult for them and it's difficult for the teacher, too. Because how do you help a child like that? And if you start something that's working and then they end up leaving, what's gonna happen in the other school?

Jose finished third grade with me at Sherwood. After he left my classroom, I think he moved three or four times during the fourth grade. His family had a rent increase so they had to move. Wherever they move, it's a lower rent, but it's also less safe. The family witnessed a shooting and got a little scared, so they moved again. Eventually Jose settled down in one location, in an apartment. How long he'll be there, we don't know, but he's been there several years now. He's an eighth grader right now and doing great.

Over the years, what I've done is establish relationships with not just the students but with the entire family in case some of this stuff happens. Jose's family became one of our adopted families. There's a group of us former UC Berkeley students: most of us grew up in Hollister, but others we met from San Diego, LA, everywhere. We put money into a pool and we go and buy gifts for our adopted families. For parents it's mostly gift cards to grocery or department stores. For the kids, we get them the things we never got as children. Like a big remote control car, a skateboard, a bicycle. We really go all out.

I send out a description of the children and their situation. My friends come and we deliver these gifts to the kids. We don't just go in there and say, "Merry Christmas, here are some gifts." I explain to them who these strangers are that are with me, where they came from, how they had some of the same obstacles to overcome. And I tell them that the reason we're here is because we believe in them.

I see some of these kids and think, *They are amazing*. These are students like Jose, who despite everything they're going through still have a smile on their face every day and they're succeeding in school. They want to learn, they want to be there.

WE DON'T LOSE THAT MANY KIDS ANYMORE

Starting around 2002, 2003, at the school we started talking to parents during the parent conferences about how the moves back and forth to Arizona were affecting their kids, academically and socially, 'cause they were falling further behind and they were always having to make new friends. They would miss so much. We needed to find a way for them to have an uninterrupted school year. I would suggest to my parents, "Well, does the entire family have to go? You know, maybe you guys can go and they can stay with the sibling who didn't go to Arizona. Or, maybe just have dad go and you stay with the child."

And that's what's happening now. We don't lose that many kids anymore—sometimes just two or three a year. The children stay behind, the moms stay behind. But there are problems that come with that decision: now there are two bills to pay. They have to pay rent over there in Yuma, they have to buy food over there, and they have to send money back here. So the kids are getting what we wanted, that uninterrupted school year, but it's a strain on the families financially.

The families have made a conscious decision that education is important, that it's a top priority. And if they have to be tight with the money, then so be it. They're looking at the long term now. They want their child to graduate high school and go to college and get a degree and a career.

I have what is called a college wall in my classroom. It's a dedicated space to my university. You know, UC Berkeley posters, and pictures, a banner. Football and basketball and soccer. And I'm always referring back to UC Berkeley and my experiences at Berkeley, and we have this discussion about college. And other teachers have their own college walls. So every year students would get a teacher and they'd hear about their teacher's university and their experience. We wanted to plant the seed that college is possible; to let them know what it is and what it's like.

Recently we started taking sixth graders to UC Berkeley on field trips. They get to see the dorms, they get to eat at the dining commons, they get to sit at one of the big lecture halls with 600 seats. They get to see the kids with their backpacks, and the constant traffic. They get to meet some of the professors. The kids love that experience, and after that field trip of course they all want to go to UC Berkeley. We hope to show them it's a great experience. It's fun, it's going be difficult, it's hard, but at the end of the day, man, it's gonna be a great experience and life is just gonna be so much easier.

IT'S A LIFELONG RELATIONSHIP

Salinas has a gang problem. Now of course Salinas is like any other city, the violence is mostly in a certain area. Unfortunately, that's where the kids who I work with live.[10]

After school, teachers stay and do more work, plan for the next day, run copies. We end up leaving at four or five. When I first started teaching, as I was leaving I'd see kids playing outside. Playing soccer, playing football. Now you don't see as many kids out there. They're afraid. I shouldn't say the kids are afraid—the parents are afraid. They're afraid that their kids are going to get coerced into a gang or be an innocent victim if a fight breaks out or there's a drive-by or something.

Everyone is taking more precautions. I could see that with Jose. His brother and younger sister just stayed in the living room; that's what they did. They're just there. They watch TV, play, do their homework, ride their little scooter in circles around the living room.

There's a lot of violence in the neighborhood, and the kids witness it, they've been affected by it. We used to have a counselor on campus. He went to Sherwood as a child, had his doctorate and was retired, but decided to come back just to work at Sherwood. He knew all about East Salinas, 'cause his family still lived there. We would rely on him a lot. Especially those who had witnessed first-hand violence or whose family had been victims of violence. Now that counselor is not here anymore because of budget cuts. He wasn't getting paid nearly what he was worth, but with budget cuts, they're one of the first to go. He went from full-time to part-time to no time at all.

When I taught sixth grade one year, I'd talk a lot about making the right decisions, making the right choices. I told them, "Don't

---

[10] Salinas, a city of 155,000, has an estimated 3,500 gang members. In 2015, there were 40 homicides in the city—up from the previous high of 29 in 2009. More than half of the city's 40 homicides were likely gang-related.

make friends that don't have the same goals you do." Because we were talking about what they wanted to be in the future, where they would like to be. And everyone, of course, is very optimistic: I wanna be a doctor, and I wanna go to the military.

OK, well, find friends who have the same goals as you do. And if you have friends that aren't steering you in the right direction, they're really not your friends and you should probably stay away. And please don't think, *Oh you know, that's not gonna happen to me.* Because I've had students at Sherwood who thought the same way, and guess where they are? They're in prison, or they're dead. Not too many, but it happened.

Unfortunately, some chose the wrong path and ended up paying a high price. But the great majority are success stories, where they graduated and they got accepted to a university. Teachers from Sherwood —and we're elementary teachers—get invited to their high school graduation, and it's great to see so many of our kids graduating.

I have students in Hawaii, I have students in Oregon, I have students in Nebraska. They're my students in third grade, and they go to another classroom, but they're still my students. I keep in touch with them. I have students right now who are at UC Berkeley. I see them 'cause I have season tickets to the football games and I go to basketball games, too. We go have a coffee. I've become godfather to some of my students. It's a lifelong relationship.

FAMILY DINNERS

I used to do a lot of after-school programs for the children. Then I decided I should do programs for parents. From that I said I should do programs for entire families. I work with parents to help them become leaders of the school. Because our parents accept things without really questioning things. And that's not what we want. We want parents to get involved, and ask questions, and speak up, and demand.

There was no parent-teacher organization at our school, but now it's big, it's huge. So it went from just the students, to students and parents, to entire families, and then to helping them become leaders. A lot of them say, "Well, I can't help my kid, 'cause I don't know English, or I only had a third-grade education." So I have workshops where I teach them how they can help their children: basic things they can do to help their kid succeed in school. As easy as, you know, show me what your homework is today and show me when it's completed. Just little things like that can be crucial.

In the peak season, it's normal for parents to work ten hours a day. But then you have an open house and parents are there. I do family science night, and they are there for two and a half hours working with their kids, building projects. You see their faces and, yeah, they're tired. But they're there, they're helping them. I always end my programs with a dinner. We all go to the cafeteria and we all have dinner together. They get to sit with their kids, and they eat, and they get to talk about what they did. Because that's not part of our culture; that's not the way it happens. It's, you know, kids come, sit, eat, and the parents are over there doing the laundry, doing something else. We don't really have family dinners with everyone sitting together talking about their day and how it went. So it's great that they participate and they actually get to sit together, have dinner. We'll order pizza, they have their project there, and they're talking about it. You know, I love seeing that.

ROBERTO VALDEZ

AGE: *48*

OCCUPATION: *Farmworker—various crops*
BORN IN: *Guanajuato, Mexico*
INTERVIEWED IN: *Thermal, Riverside County*
AGRICULTURAL REGION: *Coachella Valley*

Thermal, California, is, as the name suggests, hot. A few weeks after I first visit Roberto Valdez, he posts on Facebook that the temperature has just hit 120 degrees. "I humbly ask you, my God, to protect my fellow farmworkers who don't know how to defend themselves," he writes. "Please guide their bosses to show them mercy and give them the chance to rest in the shade."

An unincorporated community in Riverside County, Thermal has fewer than 3,000 residents, and is located in the eastern part of the Coachella Valley. This is one of the poorest regions in the country: nearly half of Thermal's residents live below the poverty line, and the median home value is just $22,000. Valdez lives in one of the many trailer parks that dot the land within the reservation of the Torres Martinez Desert Cahuilla Indians, a tribe of 800 members.

I arrive on a cloudless and relatively cool Sunday morning in May and find Roberto behind his trailer, cleaning out a wooden shed. Inside the shed are scattered tools, boxes of laundry detergent, and cases of bottled water. A dusty Pearl drum set is in the far corner. Roberto plans to convert the shed into a studio, where he and his son, Angel, can play music. Roberto first introduced his son to music more than a decade ago, when Angel was sixteen and recuperating in the hospital after nearly dying from heat stroke and meningitis. To cheer up his son, Roberto brought an accordion into his room. They've been playing together ever since.

After Roberto shows me around his backyard, which opens into a vast desert, we head into the trailer and sit at a kitchen table. As he talks, he occasionally excuses himself to bring documents from his bedroom: his daughter's recent eighth-grade report card (straight As); a photo of Angel with then–California governor Arnold Schwarzenegger; and an award given to Roberto by the United Farm Workers, which recognizes Roberto's "leadership, effort, and dedication to improving the lives of farmworkers."

IT'S IN MY BLOOD

I'm from a *rancho* called Los Angeles, in Guanajuato, Mexico.[1] This ranch is the kind of place where everybody gets up early in the morning and says hi to one another, how are you feeling this morning, that sort of thing.

I was born in 1968. My wife Leticia and I have known each other since we were eleven years old. My parents sent me to grind corn at the mill on her ranch, and that's where we got to know each other. We used to chitchat, and I used to hide her shawl to tease her. I was thirteen when Leticia's brother got married, and Leticia and I danced together at the wedding. There was a connection, a chemistry that started then and that's never left.

The first time I came to the U.S. was in October 1985. I was seventeen years old and not yet married. There wasn't really a way to move forward in life in Guanajuato, and I thought I could make a

---

[1] Guanajuato is a state in central Mexico, northwest of Mexico City. *Rancho* in Mexico often describes small agricultural villages.

living in the United States working in the fields. I didn't know any English, but I knew many others like me from Guanajuato who came to the U.S. to work without knowing English.

I crossed from Mexicali into Calexico.[2] I worked for eight months in El Centro, near the border, in the broccoli and lettuce fields.[3] When I returned to Mexico, the U.S. had just passed immigration reform, but I didn't know how to ask for a letter to prove that I'd worked here already. So I couldn't fix my papers, even though I'd worked for eight months.[4]

After I returned from El Centro, I came back to Guanajuato. That's when Leticia and I really got together. We got married in July of 1987, and in 1988 we moved to Mexicali. I'd already seen that life was different in Mexicali, that there were more opportunities so close to the States. I had the idea that I could cross to the States to work in the fields from May to October, and then return to Mexico. But I wasn't able to make it across. The first time I tried, I swam. I'm really good at swimming—I'm not afraid of water. The group I was with crossed the American Canal and then walked for three hours, until Immigration caught us.[5] The Immigration officers said not to try to cross that way again, because it was really dangerous.

---

[2] Mexicali is a city of over 800,000 in the Mexican state of Baja, California. The Calexico-Mexicali metropolitan area is a major border crossing between the state of Baja in Mexico and eastern California in the United States.

[3] El Centro, California, is a border town of over 40,000 and a major hub of the Imperial Valley.

[4] The Immigration Reform and Control Act (IRCA), passed in 1986, provided permanent legal residence status to undocumented immigrants who had lived in the United States since December 31, 1981. A special provision of IRCA also allowed undocumented immigrants who had performed at least ninety days of farmwork between May 1985 and May 1986 to legalize their status. For more information, see the Glossary, page 286–7.

[5] The All-American Canal stretches 80 miles along California's southern border from the Colorado River to the Imperial Valley. The canal is a dangerous obstacle for migrants crossing into the United States—many hundreds of drowning deaths have occurred in the canal in the past few decades.

The next time I tried to cross was around the area of the Laguna Salada.[6] I went with a group of eleven people led by a *coyote*, and we didn't bring nearly enough water.[7] I also remember there's a kind of snake you find in that area that I was really afraid of. But we made it to the border and there wasn't a wall, not even a fence back then— just a little barbed wire. The water we brought in our small bottles lasted only a day and a half, and on the other side of the border the person who was going to pick us up didn't show. I was very hungry and I thought, *I'm not staying here.* I said to the coyote who'd brought us, "You know what, I'm going to go to the freeway and I'm not coming back." The others in the group didn't want to let me go, but I went. I walked to the freeway, Interstate 8. Immigration didn't stop me. I hitchhiked, and an old man and woman stopped for me. I told them I was going back to Mexico. They asked me, "If you're already here, why would you go *back*?" But I didn't want to take any more risks. I was done trying. The couple dropped me off in downtown Calexico, and I took a bus to Mexicali. When I got to our house, Leticia was surprised. She said, "What are you doing here! You're supposed to be over there!"

I decided to stay and work in Mexico. In 1991, I got a job in Mexicali at a company called Bimbo, which is a national bread company.[8] I was one of 116 applicants. We all had to take an exam and only fourteen people passed. It was my job to set the production schedules for the amount of bread that we were toasting. It was a nice job, an honest job, one of the best I've had. I worked there for six and a half years.

---

[6] The Laguna Salada is a basin that is part of the delta of the Colorado River, located southwest of Mexicali and near the U.S.-Mexico border.

[7] *Coyote* refers to a guide who helps migrants illegally cross into the United States. For more information, see the Glossary, page 284.

[8] Bimbo, headquartered in Mexico City, is the world's largest baking company, with 165 manufacturing plants in Mexico, the United States, Canada, and Spain.

At first there was one shift. Then they started a second shift. The person who had my position for the afternoon shift had gotten the job through a friend of the supervisor. This guy was very irresponsible. He burned a lot of bread and he threw away a lot of toast. He didn't know how to synchronize the temperatures. So when I'd get to work the next morning, the area was a complete mess. And what did I do? I filed a report about what the conditions of the area had been like when I began to work. The supervisor didn't like that, since I was getting his friend in trouble. He started harassing me, filing reports saying that it was me who was burning the product and leaving the area dirty. So that caused a whole lot of problems.

During my time in Mexicali, my wife and I had two kids—our son Angel and our daughter Rosa. Around the time I started having problems with the supervisor, I was also getting ready to baptize Rosa. I set a date and asked for permission to take the day off and the company denied it. So I went to my supervisor and said, "Hey, why are you denying this? I need a day off to baptize my daughter." He said, "Look, you don't have permission; we have to deliver these orders."

I decided not to go into work—I went to Rosa's baptism instead. When I returned to the factory, the supervisor was there waiting for me. He told me that he was suspending me for fifteen days. "No sir," I told him. "I've never missed work. You can see it right here in my file. It's not fair." He said I had to sign the paper agreeing to my suspension. I said, "No, I'm not signing anything. Give me my letter of resignation instead if you want. I'll sign *that*." And, yes, he was happy to do so. He gave me the letter of resignation, and I was so pissed off that I signed the paper and left.

I'm the kind of person who can't stand someone disrespecting me or anybody else. I don't allow it to happen: it's in my blood. It doesn't have to be about me. If I see someone else being disrespected, I leave everything I'm doing in order to defend that other person, even if I don't know them.

IF THERE'S NO WATER, YOU NEED
TO GET USED TO TEA

When I left Bimbo my family already had our tourist visas to visit the United States. It was 1997 when we first came to the U.S. as a family. Angel was eight at the time, and Rosa was two. Our plan was just to visit my wife's brother, who lived in a small town near El Centro. After we'd visited a while, Leticia's brother took me out to the fields around El Centro. I looked at all these green fields and said, "This is divine, this is beautiful." I asked him how much a worker earned here. He said $350 a week. I thought, *Wow, if my wife and I worked together, we'd earn $700 every week!* It seemed like a lot, but I didn't take into account the fact that we were going to have to pay really high rent, car insurance, and everything else.

When we returned to Mexicali, every day my daughter Rosa would tell me, "I want to learn English. I want to study." She'd heard her cousins speaking English. We didn't have our papers, but I said to my wife, "Let's go to the other side." I was ready for a move. People like me, wherever we go, we make a home.

We still had valid tourist visas, and we made the move that same year, in 1997. We worked our first season in the grape fields in Bakersfield for Sal Giumarra.[9] In order to get the job, we had to work three days without getting paid. According to the bosses, we wouldn't get paid because they were "teaching us how to work." I started on Wednesday around 10 or 11 in the morning and worked on Wednesday, Thursday, Friday, and Saturday. Three and a half days without pay. I never got that money. But I stayed on at the vineyard.

---

[9] Salvadore Giumarra was the longtime President of Giumarra Vineyards, one of the largest table-grape companies in California. Today Giumarra has grown into one of the largest farming and distribution corporations in California, with additional farms in Washington and Mexico. Bakersfield is a large city in the San Joaquin Valley and a major agricultural corporate hub.

My family and I settled in nearby—we paid $120 a week for a room in a labor camp near Lamont.[10] There wasn't much in our trailer—just a small bed and space for our backpacks, where we kept our clothes. Leticia and I lay down on the floor on top of a blanket, and the children took the bed. We didn't have air conditioning in the trailers. Instead, they had these coolers on top of the apartments that blew damp air to all the rooms.[11] The coolers didn't work—we'd be soaking in sweat. And our labor camp was surrounded by fields and vineyards. When they fumigated the vineyards with pesticides, we slept nearby with our coolers blowing the chemicals into our trailer. We didn't have any protection.[12]

We didn't know what we'd gotten ourselves into. If they send you to Mars or Japan or any other place, you might not know what to do with yourself, the right way to act. You don't know about how life is lived where you are. If you're used to drinking water and there's no water but only tea, you need to get used to tea. So we just lived in the present and did what we could to get by—trying to get used to the way things were. Now I know we could have gone somewhere else and rented an apartment on our own—away from the heat, away from the pesticides. Now I know more about the business, but back then we just did what we saw other people doing.

ONE QUESTIONABLE GRAPE

After that first trip as a family to California, we ended up living in Mexicali in the winters, where I worked as a bricklayer, and we'd come back to California every season in June to work in the vineyards.

---

[10] Lamont is an unincorporated town of 15,000 located about ten miles south of Bakersfield. For more on labor camps, see the Glossary, page 287.

[11] This type of system, called an evaporative cooler or swamp cooler, adds water vapor to the air and is a cheaper alternative to air conditioning.

[12] For more on agricultural workers exposure to pesticides, see Appendix III, page 296–300.

In the United States we'd be making about $7 an hour. So starting in June, first we went to Coachella, then to Bakersfield, and then we'd go back to Mexicali in November.[13] We lived eight years like that, from 1997 to 2003. We could do it because we had a tourist visa. It was only a tourist visa—not a work visa—but we still worked, even if we weren't supposed to.[14]

People who've worked in the field can do any work without difficulty, because we're working people. The work itself isn't the problem. But I remember once, my co-worker and I were working for a company in Coachella, and if you accidentally picked a grape that was unripe or rotten or stained they stopped you and they gave you three days off without pay. The bosses there were really strict. It wasn't fair to be suspended for just one questionable grape. I used to tell the supervisor, "Hey man, come on, why are you going to send me out for three days? It's just a little grape." He said those were the company rules. The saddest thing is that the foremen we worked for were people who come from the place where I'm from. Do you know what I mean? They have the same experiences and backgrounds as the other workers. They know where we're from, and they know our needs. But to keep their jobs, they do things they shouldn't to their workers.[15] And that is actually bad for the companies they work for, because, let me tell you, any company must be both humane and productive. Any company depends on the customer to survive, but they also depend on the worker.

A company is the support for thousands of families. I'm not against companies, because they're what allow us to eat, to pay our taxes. But it's wrong when a company or a supervisor they

[13] The route Roberto describes is about 700 miles round trip.

[14] A B-2 visa, or travel visa, permits carriers to legally travel throughout the United States but not to earn money for work.

[15] Many farms throughout California rely on labor provided through independent labor contractors. This structure allows farmers to hire the right size labor force for a given day's work.

hire demeans the worker who harvests the product. That's how I see it.

I TOOK ANGEL TO WORK WHEN
HE WAS TOO YOUNG

In 2003, there was a person who worked at my daughter Rosa's school in Coachella who told me, "Roberto, you must settle your family in one place—either here or in Bakersfield. Your kids need more stability." I took the advice. After that, we stayed here in the States to work year-round. I rented a trailer at this park, and we've lived here since, full time. Leticia and I both worked. We'd weed fields for green beans, lettuce, broccoli, cauliflower. We'd plant chili, cucumber. Harvest whatever we were asked to harvest.

I made a mistake with Angel—I took him to work when he was too young. He started working with me when he was thirteen. That was around the time Leticia had another baby, our second daughter, Dolores. So I'd take Angel to the fields. When our youngest daughter was old enough, we'd leave her with Rosa back at the camp while Leticia, Angel, and I went to work. But he was still young. And in August 2005, when he was sixteen years old, he had an incident. It was when we were working for Giumarra in Bakersfield.

Giumarra wanted us to fill up forty boxes of grapes a day, each person. We had a forewoman who was very strict. She wanted to get as much work out of us as possible. One day in August, my boy came to me and said, "I'm feeling pretty bad. I'm shaky and tired." So I told him to take a rest and drink some water. The forewoman saw him and said, "What are you doing? No, no! You're getting paid for your time. Get back to work."

We kept working, but then Angel just couldn't do it anymore, so he sat down. He was shaking and sweating and had a headache. I got something for Angel to drink, and a supervisor came by to see what was going on. I thought Angel might need an ambulance, and

I talked to the supervisor about it. The supervisor said that he'd take Angel to the doctor himself, and that I should keep working.

By the time it was five o'clock in the afternoon, Angel and the supervisor still hadn't gotten back. Then it was seven o'clock, and still nothing. I went to the forewoman at the labor camp and asked her why he hadn't come back. She said somebody was taking care of him, that he'd been taken to a doctor, and that I shouldn't worry. But I was worried. I said I wanted to go and see him or I'd call the police. I shouted, "What's going on, I want to know about my son!" And she just looked at me and said, "No. You can't go." I couldn't believe it. I said that I had the right to see him—he's my son. I wanted to know where he was.

They brought Angel back home around 11 p.m. He couldn't even talk to me. He could walk a little bit, but he'd get exhausted right away. After a little while he was able to talk a little and I found out it was a lie that they'd taken him to a doctor. The supervisor had taken Angel to a truck with air conditioning, put ice under his armpits, and driven around with the AC on. He was never taken to a doctor.

Angel spent the whole night sweating and vomiting. The following day, Leticia and I went to work and Angel stayed home to rest. We would have rather stayed with Angel, but we had no choice if we wanted to keep our jobs—if we stopped working for a day, we'd be fired. We made him comfortable and had arrangements with the bosses for someone to pick him up at 9 a.m. and take him to the hospital.

We were worried, but we went to work. It just so happened that Cesar Chavez's organization was in the fields that day.[16] Some members of the union showed up around the time of our morning break. They walked up and said, "Hello comrades, we come from the

---

[16] Roberto is referring to the United Farm Workers, the farmworker union founded by Cesar Chavez and others. For more on the UFW, see Appendix IV, page 305–6.

farmworkers union. We've come to see if you have any problems, if there's anything you need." Many of the people I worked with had told me, "Those bastards just want to get some money out of the company. They won't ever do anything to help us." And as soon as the forewoman saw them show up, she told us workers, "No, no, no! I don't want anybody to talk to them. If one of you talks to them, you'll be fired." The organizers just said, "Anybody who'd like to, come outside and we'll answer your questions."

The organizers were walking around among the workers, and when the supervisor wasn't looking, I stood up from where I was having breakfast under the vines in the field and said to one of the organizers, "My son had heatstroke yesterday, and I'm not sure if the company is getting him to the doctor or not." The organizer I spoke to said he'd find someone to help me and then left.[17]

At around 12:30 I visited the Giumarra offices again to check on where they'd taken my son. They didn't really have clear answers for me about how he was doing or where he was. Eventually I found out he was at Memorial Hospital in Bakersfield and I went to see him. He was still very sick, and the doctors hadn't learned anything about his condition, so I took him home again and made him comfortable.

The next day we went to work again with Angel at home resting. And in the afternoon we had a knock on our door. It was a man from Chavez's organization who introduced himself as Roman Pinal. He came in to see Angel and told us that he could take him back to the hospital for us. So we got Angel into Roman's vehicle and they went off to Memorial Hospital.

We couldn't be with Angel the whole time he was at the hospital, since we had to work. But Roman Pinal was like an angel sent by

---

[17] Giumarra may have been under special scrutiny by labor organizations such as UFW following the heatstroke death of Giumarra worker Agustin Gudino the previous month. Aside from Gudino, three other Giumarra field workers had collapsed due to heatstroke that summer.

god. He didn't ask us for money, he lived and slept there in hospital, he would drink coffee to stay awake and argue with the doctors and keep me up to date.

A couple of days after Angel was admitted to the hospital, Roman told me, "I'm sorry. We don't know if they're going to be able to bring him back." Apparently my son had slipped into a coma. I couldn't believe it. My son was dying. I went to visit him right away, without telling Leticia what was happening. I didn't know how to tell her. And when I got to the hospital, it was true. Angel couldn't talk or move or anything. I'm a faithful man. I haven't shaken hands with God, but God exists. On the way home from the hospital, I pulled over to the side of the road. I couldn't even raise my head. I talked to God and said, "What do we owe you? *What* do I owe you? What is it? Let him live—he's young, let him live."

I couldn't stand hearing what the doctors told me about Angel's condition. He had heatstroke and an infection.[18] I got home, but I didn't want to tell my wife everything that was happening. Instead I just told her, "Things are very difficult. I want you to know that we're going to go through a very bitter time, but if God gives us a hand, Angel will get better." We didn't pray. Just in our hearts we wished for God to let him be here with us.

We went to the hospital the next day, where we spent the entire day and night. I remember pacing outside, just waiting to find out what was going to happen. We went home, and then the next afternoon around 4 or 5 p.m., Roman visited us in the camp. He'd been at the hospital. "Roberto!" he said. I was prepared for anything. He hugged me and told me, "Guess what? I have good news—Angel woke up!"

---

[18] Aside from heatstroke, Angel was diagnosed with meningitis caused by the West Nile virus. Doctors believed the heatstroke weakened his immune system and led to the onset of meningitis.

We went to the hospital right away. My son was so skinny. He held my hand. I asked, "How do you feel?" He told me, "I feel weird." I told him, "It's over; everything is over. There's nothing to worry about. I'm here; we're in good hands." I tried to keep him calm, then kissed him goodbye and left. When I left, the pain of happiness hit me. I kneeled in the hallway and told God, "Thank you. Who do I repay for such a favor?"

Angel was in the hospital twelve or thirteen days. The doctors said it was the heat, and also because of a disease he got from a mosquito bite. But the big trigger was the heat. I never got any help from Giumarra. Not a single supervisor came to tell me, "We're really sorry." They didn't want me to be at the hospital because a few journalists had found out about Angel and were coming to interview me. A cameraman from *Al Rojo Vivo* came and taped me.[19] This TV broadcaster was coming; this other journalist was coming. Angel's story became known throughout the state. Not only had Angel been denied a break, there wasn't even shade in the fields provided for workers that needed a rest to escape the sun.

I ASKED THE SENATORS TO HAVE COMPASSION FOR US

In 2005, the death of twelve agricultural workers in California from heat stress led to the creation of heat regulations enacted by the California Division of Occupational Safety and Health (Cal/OSHA). The new standard required those hiring farmworkers to provide water and shade, to allow breaks to workers complaining of heat exhaustion, and to have a plan in place for workers who experience heat stroke. Roberto was invited by the UFW to testify about his experiences in the California Statehouse as the regulation was being considered.

---

[19] *Al Rojo Vivo* ("Red Hot") is a current events news program on Telemundo.

After Angel's story became better known, my family was invited to the state legislature in Sacramento. I remember standing in a large assembly room, like a courtroom, in front of twelve senators. They had chairs for us to sit on, but I stayed on my feet the whole time. I told them about what had happened to Angel. I said, "The hands that you see are the hands that harvest the lemons you use to make the lemonade you're now drinking. The strawberries that your children eat, we cut them. The grapes that you see in the markets, we cut them. We're dying out there in the fields."

And we cried. A lady that was there, a congresswoman, she cried. I asked the senators to have compassion for us, to make changes to the law to protect farmworkers. From that year, farms throughout California had to make sure to provide shade in the field.[20] This is something that Angel and I were able to help achieve.

The United States is a big country; we must keep on fighting so that it's not only a big country, but the best, the most humane. We must fight for that. If we have the means for planting and harvesting, why not have the means to treat people better?

THE WORLD NEEDS TO KNOW US BETTER

Before Angel got sick, I had never paid attention to the disrespect we workers received from the supervisors and bosses. I took the scolding for granted. But I talk to supervisors now and say, "You think you're worth more than this worker. You're not. You're worth the same, but you are poorer, because in your head the worker is worth less." That's what I tell them because that's the way it is.

I don't regret telling anybody my story—not Salvadore Giumarra, not the governor of California, not the President of the United States. Because this is the reality we live in. I'm a person

---

[20] For more on legislation to protect farmworker safety passed in California, see Appendix III, page 289–303.

who didn't study. I never learned how to write numbers, or use punctuation. I don't know anything about that stuff. But I do know that everyone is hurt by insults, and everyone is hurt when they're mistreated, and everyone is hurt when they are ignored.

Getting respect in the fields is still a problem. Supervisors don't treat me nicely. When somebody wants water, I always call for it to be brought over. The drinking water is kept on the machine, and if you leave your spot to get water, the supervisor might tell you off. They want you to keep working fast, so you don't fall behind. They say I complain too much. They say, "Let them work for a while before taking a break."

I recorded my first video last year. I've recorded about eight or nine so far. In one video, a supervisor was scolding a woman in the grape field. The supervisor was saying, "Why have you done so few boxes? I'm not going to pay if you're doing thirty boxes while the rest of the crew is doing eighty or ninety." I was recording it. I placed my phone on my chest and I didn't talk. The supervisor yelled at the woman. "You choose—you do your best or you don't come anymore!"

I told the supervisor, "Hey! You need to be more thoughtful. Look at the woman and look at me." I can work and I'm stronger. She was overweight, but I didn't say it that way, not in front of her. Of course we're not going to harvest the same amount of grapes. But she has the right to receive her daily bread. It's better for her to do this than to be shoplifting.

I make the videos so that people can see the way we work. The world needs to know us better. [Roberto plays a video on his phone of him narrating from the field.]

This is some of the work that we do in the United States. You might work as bricklayers, welders, nursing assistants, professors, doctors, and here we work humbly as farmworkers who have always worked in the fields. In these fields the temperature can reach 116 degrees. We are from El Salvador, Mexico,

Honduras, Guatemala. We do our best. Our children are waiting for us at home ...

This is the labor force of the United States. These are the people that nobody wants, earning their bread every day. These are the people that the politicians don't want, but while they sleep at this hour, all these people are working in the fields across California. And a greeting to Donald Trump, who doesn't want us—I invite him to come here and find out about our work. This here is celery, which gives flavor to his soup. We're not criminals, we're working people. This is the United States, amigos.[21]

When the company realized I recorded the video, they came to work and talked to me in private. I told the man who was sent to scold me, "Look, this is the last time you talk to me in private. If you don't want me to carry my phone, if you don't want me to record videos, it can't just be to me—you must tell us altogether." The supervisor said, "Hey, I just want to know why you recorded a video and uploaded it." I said, "Everybody wants to kick Latino people around and insult us. And some people let this happen." I told him, "You're Latino!" He comes from Mexico. It offends me how Trump thinks of us. I said hi to him and invited him to come to see our work. I also called Jorge Ramos to come and see what the criminals—as Trump calls us—are doing.[22] Why are journalists constantly talking about how long Salma Hayek's dress is? Why do they follow stories like that? The real stories are here.

The supervisors don't allow us to bring phones to the field anymore.

---

[21] This video, which was shared by the United Farm Workers, has been viewed more than 300,000 times on Facebook. Another of Valdez's videos, also shared by the UFW, has more than 150,000 views.

[22] Jorge Ramos is a journalist and anchor for Univion who has been called the "Walter Cronkite of Latino America."

THERE ARE MANY THINGS
THAT I CAN'T CONTROL

My children are growing up. Rosa studied here in the United States —elementary school, middle school, high school, and then moved on to college. She's studying journalism at Cal-Poly Pomona; she has DACA.[23] We pay her rent; I pay for everything. And now little Dolores is in the eighth grade. She doesn't have any kind of documents yet. Neither does my wife.

Angel lives here in the trailer with his family. He's twenty-seven years old and fixed his papers thanks to his wife. He's a citizen now. I always felt proud of him. I still do. As a boy he always wanted to be close to his dad. I taught him how to sell clothes—we took shirts from the United States and sold them in Mexicali. He was a very good student in Mexico, and here as well. He graduated from Rancho Mirage High School in Thermal. Now he works digging ditches. His mood changed after he nearly died. He can't control his behavior; sometimes he gets angry and insults me or shouts at me. He wasn't like this before. He used to be very loving with me, very sweet.

As for my family back in Mexico, my father died in Mexico on May 16, 2014. I never got to say goodbye to him. My mom is sick now; she's also going to die. She has diabetes and I'm here. I can't go visit her—I don't have the luxury of being able to go and come back. There are many things that I can't control. But I do my best in one way or another.

Yesterday we worked in the field, picking banana peppers. We started at 6 a.m., a group of sixty or seventy people. We filled six big rigs with peppers. Sometimes you can earn $160 a day, but it's very tough. They should give us all gloves, but they don't. We should

---

[23] The Deferred Action for Childhood Arrivals, or DACA, was created in 2012 through an executive order by President Barack Obama. The policy allows certain undocumented youth to receive renewable two-year permits and be protected from deportation. For more information, see the Glossary, page 284.

all wear sunglasses but they don't give us sunglasses. There are flies around, the kind that bite. This is our work, look. [Roberto shows another video.] These are the boxes we use. This is how we work, behind a machine tossing peppers onto it. These are the puddles we walk through to get to the peppers.

Not so long ago some people died while pruning palm trees. There's a lot of material for journalists here. Look, in this video the boy harvesting raisins is not wearing a mask or gloves. He can't even see through the dust. That's not right. We should all be ashamed of this. Look!

HERACLIO ASTETE

AGE: *62*

OCCUPATION: *Former sheepherder*
BORN IN: *Junín, Peru*
INTERVIEWED IN: *Bakersfield, Kern County*
AGRICULTURAL REGION: *Central Valley*

Along with fruit and vegetable crops, California's agriculture also includes livestock, from dairy cows and egg-laying hens to hogs and even ostriches. Then there are sheep and lambs—and the unique challenges faced by the workers who care for them. These sheepherders are predominantly temporary guest workers, often called "H-2A workers" after the type of visa they hold.[1]

Theirs is a lonely occupation. Living out of primitive trailers that are dozens of miles from the nearest town, sheepherders can go weeks without seeing another face. It is also the poorest paid job in the country, with some sheepherders still earning around $750 a month; with their long hours of work, that amounts to about a dollar an hour. In a 2000 report by Central California Legal Services, ninety percent of sheepherders reported that they weren't given

---

[1] Traditionally, H-2A workers have not had much of a presence in California, but that is beginning to change. In 2012, the state had just 2,600 H-2A workers. In 2016, it had 9,300, representing a nearly four-fold increase. Labor shortages and an aging farmworker population are reported to be the main factors driving this increase.

a day off over the entire year. When asked about their best experience as a sheepherder in the United States, many responded: "None."

Like many sheepherders, Heraclio Astete came from Peru, where he grew up caring for flocks of sheep in his hometown. And like many of the workers who responded "None" to the survey, he had a lot of complaints about workplace exploitation. When he suffered a potentially life-threatening work-related illness, he decided to do something about it.

GOING TO SCHOOL IN LIMA
WAS A DREAM FOR ME

My name is Heraclio Astete, and I was born in Peru, in Junín.[2] It's a city in Peru's central mountains. My parents were farmers, and they worked raising animals. We had sheep, horses, cows—we lived in the city but spent most of our time in the country.

I have great memories of my childhood, because I was able to spend so much time with my parents and my five sisters. The thing I remember best about Junín were the festivals. We'd always go. Every year there was a big festival on August 6, which is the anniversary of the Battle of Junín.[3] It's the town's biggest party, and everyone has a great time. As a child I'd be in parades with my classmates, and there'd be all sorts of sports competitions—track and field, cycling races, soccer—that we'd watch or participate in.

I have strong memories of Junín, but for much of my childhood, I was in the country. My parents' farm was outside town near the village where my mother grew up. It's called San Pedro.

My sisters and I started helping with herding the animals at six or seven years old. We'd stay with them out in the fields, then we'd

---

[2] Junín is the capital of the Junín region in the central highlands of Peru.

[3] The Battle of Junín (1824) was a major military victory for the United Liberating Army of Peru, led by General Simón Bolívar, against the Royalist Army of the Kingdom of Spain.

bring them back to the barn at night. I was working at the same time that I was going to school. So on school days, we'd be up at 5:30 to take the animals out to the fields to graze. Then my sisters and I would travel into the city for breakfast, before heading off to school. Sometimes we took our homework back to the country to work on while we watched the animals in the fields. Then every weekend was spent entirely on the farm. Financially we weren't too comfortable, but we were sort of middle class.

In Peru I had the chance to go to primary school, high school, and university. I went to the Universidad Guzmán y Valle in Lima.[4] I'd been to Lima before, but going to school there was a dream for me—all of us in the provinces aspire to make it to the capital.

At university I studied education, because I always liked spending time with kids. I graduated in 1983. And after I graduated, I went home. My mom made a special request of me—she wanted me to start a little school in San Pedro. At the time, children from the community could go to nearby villages for primary school, but there was no secondary school in the area. So I promised my mom I'd start one.

In San Pedro there were more or less 500 people, but no real centralized village. Everyone lived spread out on their ranches because they were all farmers, but there was one old house that marked the center of the village that was called the communal house. That's where I started the school. To start, I had about twenty-seven students. The second year it had grown to thirty-four. I was the first director of the school and one of the first teachers. We ran it as a community-managed education center, and then after two years, the state took over and it became a government-funded public school.

After the state took over the school, I went back to my hometown of Junín to teach. But the school I'd started kept growing. It's still there today, and now it even has electricity.

---

[4] Universidad Guzmán y Valle was founded in 1822 and is known primarily as a training university for educators and administrators .

EVERY TIME I VISITED THE SCHOOL I FELT LIKE I WAS TAKING MY LIFE IN MY HANDS

I taught in Junín for eight years. They were difficult times, though. I was teaching when Shining Path was on the rise.[5] It was a real tragedy for my country. Between the insurgents and reprisals from the government, you didn't know when you went out on the street if you'd come back home.

Shining Path targeted teachers. I believe Shining Path's thinking was that teachers were the ones responsible for their students' ideology, and if students were to have the right ideology, teachers would have to be replaced. Although it was more complicated than that—when teachers went missing, it was never clear whether it was Shining Path or the army of Peru that was responsible.[6] I had colleagues from other districts and villages disappear, and we'd never find out what happened to them. Every time I went back to San Pedro to visit the school I founded, I always felt like I was taking my life in my hands.

During the eighties, I got married to a woman named Aída and had a son and a daughter. In 1991, my wife was pregnant with our third child, and there simply wasn't any money. The government had fallen apart completely, and government employees such as teachers were barely getting paid. So I tried to make the best decision I could for my family, and I looked into leaving the country to make money. I decided to go to the United States.

---

[5] Shining Path was a notoriously violent Maoist guerrilla group that took up arms against the Peruvian government in 1980.

[6] Right-wing paramilitaries operated by the Peruvian government sprang up in the 1980s in response to the rise of Shining Path. Some paramilitaries such as Grupo Centro also targeted teachers who they believed might be aligned with Shining Path ideology. In 1992, Grupo Centro kidnapped and murdered a professor and nine students from Universidad Guzmán y Valle, Heraclio's alma mater, in what is known as La Cantuta Massacre.

I had a brother-in-law who had already been in the north for many years with the H-2A program.[7] He'd made the decision to work in the U.S. for the same reason—because social problems were worsening in Peru and the economy was a complete disaster.

To participate in the H-2A program I had to apply for a U.S. work visa. To do that, I went to Lima. There's an agency there that represents a U.S. farming company—Western Range Association.[8] My brother-in-law worked for the company, and he'd already talked with the boss here in the United States, so the boss asked the American government for my visa. I arranged my paperwork with the company in Lima, and then they sent me the visa and I was able to travel. I was told I would work as a sheepherder. It was something I'd done all through my childhood, so I felt I was prepared.

I signed a contract that stated that I had to stay in the United States for three years. If things worked out, I could renew the contract for another three years. But I just wanted to make money to support my family and then come home.

---

[7] The H-2A Visa is a work visa specially designated for agricultural workers. For more information on the H-2A Visa, see the Glossary, page 285. Though most H-2A visas are designed to be short-term, the program carves out special exceptions for sheepherders, allowing for three-year contracts. The original law also excluded sheepherders from minimum-wage protections.

[8] The Western Range Association was formed as the California Range Association during World War II in response to a labor shortage on sheep ranches throughout the state. It was originally a lobbying group that successfully introduced legislation to allow sponsorship of Spanish Basque sheepherder guest workers who were fleeing oppression under General Francisco Franco. Today, the Western Range Association is an organization of independent sheepherders and a lobbying group established to hire workers through the H-2A program. In recent years the organization has consisted of over 200 independent sheep farmers hiring nearly 1,000 farmworkers, with many from Peru.

THAT NIGHT WE CRIED TOGETHER, AND THEN THE NEXT DAY WE GOT TO WORK

I left for the States in October 1991. I flew from Lima to Los Angeles to Idaho, where I first worked. I remember landing in Idaho, and everything was covered in a blanket of snow. Everything I saw was white. I'd never seen anything like it. We had snow in Peru, but not much. A Mexican worker from the company came to the airport to pick me up, and then we drove hours away from the city to get to the ranch. We drove through a little town called Castleford, and then the ranch was about 20 miles further out from there. We arrived at the ranch in the afternoon and there I met other Peruvians who were also working at the ranch. We spent some time together and talked and told our stories. That night we cried together, and the next day we got to work.

We started really early, at about 5 a.m. There were six of us with the animals, and a supervisor. I was hired as a sheepherder, but my first job was actually to work in a cow feeding lot. Every day we had to carry bales of hay around and distribute them to all of the cows for food. That work lasted more or less until 11 a.m. and we barely had time to cook and eat lunch, and then we had to go back out with the animals.

One of the things I remember most from Idaho was the cold. I started working in October and it had already snowed. In November or December, it would sometimes get to 10 degrees, 15 degrees below zero. It's very hard during winter because of the cold. Even though we had thermal coveralls, we almost couldn't stand it. We had gloves too, thick leather gloves. But despite that, we were always terribly cold because we were outside for as much as twelve hours a day. All of us from time to time would think, *What am I doing here?* But we all had families back home that we needed to send money to.

Finally we'd head inside at 6 or 7 p.m., depending on the time of the year. We didn't rest until the end of the day, and then we were still responsible for the well-being of the animals. There were no Saturdays or Sundays. There was no punching in or punching out. We were at the will of our bosses, and we worked almost 365 days of the year.

In Idaho we earned $750 a month, and it didn't matter how many hours a day we put in. To get it to our families we'd plead with the boss to have him wire funds to the Bank of Peru. Back then there was no Western Union or any agencies that wire money between banks. Every year we had one week of paid vacation. But none of us had any place to go, so we'd stay put.

I was in Idaho for two years, but then the boss sold off some of his animals, so there were two of us left redundant. One day I was told I was being sent to California. I think the other extra guy was sent to Montana. I was a Western Range employee, and I was in the United States legally only because they'd hired me. So I could be moved by the boss to wherever they needed me. I didn't know anything about California. The word California meant nothing to me, other than I knew it was a state.

So for the last year of my first contract I was flown to California and driven to Delano.[9] It wasn't as cold, but work in California was harder than work in Idaho in some ways. For one, instead of staying in a bunkhouse with other workers, I stayed by myself in a trailer in the pastures that didn't have heat, air conditioning, or a bathroom. I felt like a nomad.

My job was a twenty-four-hour-a-day job. On a typical day, I'd get up at 4 or 5 a.m. and check on the animals. Then I'd go around and work on the fencing—we worked with fencing that could be moved depending on where the sheep were grazing. Then in the evening I'd be back with the flock again. Even at night, I'd have to stay alert.

---

[9] Delano is a city of over 60,000 located 30 miles north of Bakersfield in Kern County. It was the site of the UFW's first strike, and the site of much of the UFW's organization work throughout the '60s and early '70s.

Most days it was just me and the animals out there together. There were a lot of restrictions, and the bosses didn't want workers socializing much. In those days, we weren't even allowed to have a television, radio, or newspapers and magazines. If the bosses found any of these things they'd say we were distracted and wasting time. There were many times that a boss told me I wasn't allowed to have this or that. The bosses were also very suspicious of visitors, and if my boss saw tire tracks on the road near my trailer, he'd grill me about who had passed by. We weren't supposed to have visitors.

So I was entirely by myself, with nothing to do. The entire day was spent simply taking care of the sheep. My only companion was a little dog named Lagún. The boss, a Basque Spaniard, had named him. Apparently in Basque the name Lagún means "friend." And indeed he was my loyal friend. But I wasn't around other people much, and I'd talk to myself like a crazy person when I was alone. And then maybe once a day the boss would come by to check on me, but I was often in the pasture when he stopped by, so I didn't see him.

Sheep are peaceful animals: they don't make any trouble at all. They do require a high degree of care, though. I was in charge of grazing anywhere from 1,200 to 2,000 sheep. Near Delano we had to be wary of foxes, coyotes, and rattlesnakes. Coyotes can do a lot of damage, especially during the fall lambing season. That's when you can't really sleep the entire night, because you have to stay alert for predators. The sheep would sleep near the trailers and Lagún would bark whenever there was a wild animal near. Then I'd hop up and go scare off the coyote or whatever it was.

It was terrible in months like July and August trying to sleep inside the trailer. Sometimes I couldn't sleep at all because it was so hot. Many times I would go sleep outside because of the heat and also to keep an eye on the sheep, but mainly because of the heat.

During this whole time, my wife and children were living in Junín. We didn't have phone lines or access to phones, so the only way I could communicate with her was by letter, and those often arrived late or got lost. It was by letter that I'd found out my second daughter was born. I didn't hear until two months after it happened. It was very hard to be away from my family for those three years. I was used to a different kind of life, and adjusting to life in the United States was difficult. I struggled with a lot of things I wasn't used to, and one of the main things was loneliness. But I wanted to improve my family's financial situation, so that's why I stayed.

I WAS BACK WITH MY FAMILY
FOR ONLY TEN MONTHS

Finally, in 1994, my contract ended and I went back to Peru. I got to meet my new daughter for the first time, and she was already old enough that she was walking. I wasn't able to get a teaching job again, but I had a plan to invest some of the money I'd made while in the States. I bought a new vehicle and I was set to be a driver. Unfortunately, transportation laws changed just after I bought the vehicle, and the one I'd bought didn't qualify anymore for a commercial driver registration.

I couldn't use it to make money, and I had no other job, so I started thinking of what else to do. I talked to my old boss about having another chance to come back to Delano, and he said the job was still available. I talked to my wife about it, and she didn't like the idea of me leaving again, but she understood that I didn't have any other good choices. So I applied for another H-2A visa, and got accepted again.

I was back with my family for only ten months. In October 1994 I went back to Delano under a new three-year contract. I had the same job, the same tasks, the same hours as before. Everything was the same.

"IF YOU WANT TO DIE, STAY AT THE RANCH"

I completed a three-year contract, then I started another contract. My plan was to finish the second contract and then finally head back to Peru for good. That would have taken me from 1994 to 1999. But things didn't go as I'd planned them.

In July 1998, I was out setting fences with some of the other workers. We went out at dawn. After the sun came up it was a very hot day in the desert, and I was feeling very uncomfortable. We'd brought ice water with us, and I drank some to cool off, but it didn't seem to help. I was sure I was just fatigued. We continued with the work, and after the fences were repaired we fed the animals. There was always work to be done.

Late that night, I began to feel a fever coming on. I felt chills, and my body ached. I thought maybe I'd been dehydrated and overheated. But I started coughing and felt worse and worse. The coughing got worse, and by early the next morning, I was spitting up blood when I coughed.

That next morning, my first task was to go feed the rams, which were separated from the rest of the herd. But I couldn't do it. My body wasn't even responding to my brain's commands. Around 8 a.m. my boss came by my trailer to find out what was going on. He came into my trailer, and I couldn't even get up. But he began to scold me. "Why aren't you out feeding the rams?"

I told him, "I'm very sick. I need you to take me to the doctor." Well, once he saw that I was spitting up blood, he agreed to make an appointment to take me to Delano to see the doctor. Then he left and didn't return again until the afternoon.

When he came to my trailer at 1 p.m., I was very feverish. I felt like my head was going to explode. He got me to the doctor, and they ran some tests and gave me some medication for the fever. We went back to the ranch, and after three days we went back for another doctor's appointment and they diagnosed me with valley fever. Valley fever is a disease caused by a fungus that infects some of the soil in California's deserts. It's possible to breathe in the fungus through dust. It was something I'd caught while working in the pastures.

After the doctor explained what was wrong, I was sent to Bakersfield for more tests and to see a specialist.

I had to pay for everything myself. Western Range didn't want to take responsibility for my treatment, so all the money that I'd saved up to that point had to be spent on paying for my medicine and doctors.

I was able to call my wife using a phone card and I told her I was sick. It was a terrible blow to my family to hear what was going on. Not only were they worried for me, but being sick, I couldn't send them any money or save any, and that was the whole reason I was in California in the first place.

My case of valley fever was bad. I went back to live in the trailer, but I wasn't getting healthy. The doctors recommended I have complete rest to heal, but the bosses wouldn't give me time off. My boss would say, "*You* have to feed the animals. These animals don't have somebody else here to feed them." Sick as I was, I couldn't stop working.

On a trip to see the doctor in Bakersfield, I met with an ex-employee of Western Range, a fellow Peruvian named Victor. I told him my story, and he said, "If you want to die, stay at the ranch. If not, you'll need to get out." He told me I should talk to a lawyer and try to get worker's comp to help pay for my treatment.[10]

In early 1999, after six months trying to keep up with my job while sick, I left work and moved to Bakersfield. Because my sickness was clearly work-related, I started receiving workers' comp and established myself in Bakersfield. Workers' comp paid me 75 percent of my salary from Western Range. And I received treatment at Mercy Hospital for my valley fever.

---

[10] For more on workers' compensation insurance, see the Glossary, page 288.

I wasn't getting a lot better, though, and by the end of 1999 something strange happened. The fungi had eaten away at my right lung so much that it caused a perforation. I needed more expensive treatments, and that's when Western Range began talking to me about flying me back to Peru. They mailed me a plane ticket and told me that they'd found a clinic in Peru to take care of me. They said it would be better if I was with my family. And on top of that, they promised me an extra $2,000.

It sounded like a lot, but I had compatriots from Peru around me in Bakersfield that I could talk to. I found out from some of them that a few other Peruvians had caught valley fever and Western Range had flown them home, but that the company had then immediately cut off contact. I heard about Peruvians who had died because nobody in Peru knew how to treat the disease. None of the doctors there are familiar with valley fever, because the fungus and disease are pretty limited to parts of the United States.

So I told Western Range that I wouldn't leave until I was dead or cured. I'd arrived in the States in good health, and the work itself was what caused my illness. I returned the ticket for Peru that had been sent to me.

I focused on my treatments, which consisted of taking two Diflucan pills a day.[11] I also had surgery performed on my right lung, because I couldn't get rid of the encapsulated fungus that was eating it from the inside.

My wife came to the United States in 2000 with a humanitarian visa because of my poor state of health. The Peruvian Embassy processed the visa. She came here by herself and left our three kids. My wife was here for only one month. She had to go back because my children couldn't stay by themselves.

So by around 2001, I was in the United States by myself again

---

[11] Diflucan is commonly used to treat fungal infections, especially in those with weak or compromised immune systems.

and I was finally starting to get better. I had no papers to stay in the U.S., but I was able to find a job working on a farm that grew produce.

IT FELT LIKE A BIG ACHIEVEMENT

After I left sheepherding, I began to organize a sheepherders' union in Bakersfield with Victor Flores.[12] He's the fellow Peruvian who had helped me in the first place after I'd come to Bakersfield for treatment.

Victor and I would go out at night to meet with the sheepherders in all the different pastures and fields. We collected signatures to see if they were for or against joining a union. We also gathered their stories—we had to show that there was abuse of the sheepherders going on.

The largest meetings we ever had for the union was of maybe three or four sheepherders. There weren't ever any larger meetings because individual sheepherders were so isolated by their work. Between individual sheepherders there are sometimes 40 or 50 miles. We'd go individually from one to the other to talk to them. It was difficult to organize, because they don't have permission from their employers to leave the area. It was a big problem for us, but we struggled and made it work, and we eventually filed the paperwork to form a union.

Then later in 2001, there was a hearing in Sacramento about the conditions faced by herders with guest-worker visas. It was a huge experience for me. After having fought for the benefits and dignity of the least protected workers here in the United States, it felt like a big achievement.

---

[12] Victor Flores started the Sheepherders Union after being pushed out of his H-2A herder contract and ending up working as a dishwasher in Bakersfield. According to Flores, he was pushed out of his contract and transported away from the ranch where he worked after he began asking for more food rations.

I testified about my own experience to state senators and a special commission. Victor also spoke. He explained how after a dispute with his boss he'd been dropped off at a hotel in Bakersfield with nothing.

We wanted better living conditions for H-2A herders. Better housing, food, and working hours. One of the problems was that we weren't paid for all the hours we worked, and we were made to do work other than sheepherding without any additional pay. For example, some workers might have come over as sheepherders but then were put to work in the fields harvesting crops, driving tractors, even though we weren't getting paid near what other fieldworkers were getting paid per hour.[13] And we wanted to make it so ranchers couldn't just move you around wherever they wanted or abandon you whenever they wanted.

During the testimony, the statehouse was filled with ranchers.[14] Western Range had been informed about my union work, and they were there as well. I ran into the Western Range agent who had signed me up for the program in Lima back in 1991. He said to me, "Why are you doing this? I did you all a favor by letting you enter this country." I said, "That may have been a favor, but what we experienced here was exploitation. A real favor would have been advocating for better conditions for us."

That year, the California legislature passed a law protecting us. It required a graduated increase in pay over the next few years, as well as better living conditions such as electricity, toilets, and access to better food and fresh water.[15] It also allowed for breaks every day,

---

[13] The H-2A exceptions for herders exempt them from the minimum-wage standards that apply to other agricultural workers.

[14] During the hearing, representatives for the ranchers argued that workers were not mistreated, and that a steady decline in profits made adding additional amenities and benefit protections for workers impossible for most ranchers.

[15] In October 2015, the federal Department of Labor announced that they were

and vacation. It was a big achievement for all the workers. Unfortunately, in the years that followed, the law wasn't enforced much. The Department of Labor didn't do much to make sure ranchers were following the guidelines.

Things have got a little better over the years. The treatment of the workers on the part of the bosses has improved some. Now, a sheepherder is allowed to have a cell phone, radio or television in his trailer. They can also go out more and participate in the community, like go to sporting events.

What hasn't fully improved is the living situation—that's only improved on a case to case basis. Now there are some trailers with solar panels that have power, so they have air conditioning, for instance. But some trailers are still like they were decades ago.

THANK GOD MY CHILDREN UNDERSTAND
THE SACRIFICES I HAVE MADE

Today, I still live in Bakersfield with my wife. I work for the same farm that I worked for after I left the ranch. It's a good company—they respect the laws protecting their workers. My wife was able to get a tourist visa to come live with me. Eventually I got my papers fixed so I could stay here, and she's working on it right now. Still, I can't leave the U.S. and come back.

We also have two of our kids here with us. My first daughter Gisela is here—she's twenty-seven. I also have a twelve-year-old son named Jiomar. My oldest son and my second daughter are still in Peru. I saw my oldest son two years ago when he came to visit on a tourist visa. My second daughter I haven't seen in over twenty years. The only time I've spent with her was during the ten months I was

---

raising the wages of H-2A sheepherders to about $1,500 a month, which will be phased in over three years.

back in Peru in 1994. I only know her through speaking to her on the phone. I'd love to visit her, but I can't go to Peru and come back here. But my children in Peru are doing well. My oldest boy is a doctor. My daughter is a nurse, and she's working on a post-graduate degree. Thank God my children have been able to understand and value the sacrifices that I've made.

ROSARIO PELAYO

AGE: 77

BORN IN: *Jalisco, Mexico*
OCCUPATION: *Retired farmworker and labor leader*
INTERVIEWED IN: *Calexico, Imperial County*
AGRICULTURAL REGION: *Imperial Valley*

In a black and white image in a forty-year-old newspaper, Rosario Pelayo stands in front of a cement wall with four other women, their right fists in the air. Above their outstretched arms, block letters read: "Imperial County Sheriff's Office And Jail." A few of the woman are smiling, but Rosario, whose mouth is turned slightly upward, looks utterly defiant. "She was arrested so many times she had her own jail cell," her daughter, Leonor, says with a laugh.

The photo appeared in the March 29, 1974 issue of El Malcriado *(The Brat), the newspaper of the United Farm Workers. Three years earlier, Rosario had moved to the United States with her husband and five children. She began working in the grape fields in the spring of 1973, just weeks before a major battle erupted between the UFW and the Teamsters, then a corrupt union with close ties to the growers, over who would represent California farmworkers.*

Rosario, known to friends as "Chayo," had already met Cesar Chavez, the founder of the UFW, and was impressed by his quiet determination. She soon dedicated her life to what Chavez called "la causa"—the cause. She woke early to walk the picket lines, where she exhorted her coworkers to strike for higher wages and respect. She stared down foremen twice her size. She stood in front of grocery stores, asking customers to boycott grapes. She was handcuffed and jailed and pushed to the ground. She was hit by armed police officers—and she hit back.

Today, Rosario lives in a tidy townhouse in Calexico, just miles from the border wall that divides the United States and Mexico. Inside, paintings of the Virgin of Guadalupe and Pope John Paul II hang from the walls. On the living room table is a Spanish-language Bible open to the Book of Matthew. Between sips of bottled water, Rosario recounts her history as a UFW activist matter-of-factly. Anyone in her situation would have done the same, she tells me. Her sturdy faith—in the Pope, in Jesus, in the cause of the farmworkers —seems to have driven out the spaces most of us reserve for worry and fear. Like many UFW veterans of the 1960s and '70s, she looks back at her time with the union as the highlight of her life. But as her story moves into the '80s, a decade in which she and many other farmworkers were pushed out of the union, it also becomes clear that she can't shake a lingering sadness at what could have been.

I FOUGHT A GOOD FIGHT

I have really nice memories of my life. I had six children, seventeen grandchildren, and soon I'll have twenty-one great-grandchildren. They've all heard my stories. They can't believe my stories sometimes, and they say, "Really, that happened?" I tell them it did. My life was a beautiful experience. I fought a good fight. There were days when the only thing we had out on the picket lines was a bottle of water and one taco. And I still haven't lost the spirit. Sometimes you feel sad. But at the same time you don't have any regrets because you get to say, "We fought for something."

I was the oldest of fifteen kids, and I was born in 1938. About 100 people lived in our town, which was called Santa Rosalía, in

Jalisco.[1] In Mexico, my father worked in the fields all his life. And so did my siblings and I, since we were very young. Before I helped in the fields, I helped in the house. When I was three or four years old, I started cooking. My parents would put a drawer on the floor so that I could reach the stove. I made beans, corn tortillas, chilaquiles, eggs, molcajete salsa. I think those early experiences are why I love cooking today.

I started to work in the fields at seven. I rode horses and milked cows, and my siblings and I would help plant and harvest. In Santa Rosalía, there was no school after third grade in the town, and my father wouldn't let me leave to go to school elsewhere. I remember a doctor lived on the ranch—he'd been a doctor in the army, but had retired to the ranch after being wounded. He begged my father to let me continue with my schooling, and he said he'd take care of the expenses. But no, my dad wouldn't listen.

Still, we were happy. Yes, we were poor, but we always had food on the table. We had very responsible parents, very affectionate. My mother didn't go to school but her parents raised her well. She loved reading novels about saints. Saints, oh my! She would get very excited about the saints. She could read well, write—not so much. She had fourteen siblings, too.

I got married when I was fifteen years old. I lived in Jalisco for five years after my marriage. My first daughter, Leonor, was born in Atengo, Jalisco.[2] And like everywhere else, you know, things happened in our family. My father-in-law was killed over a piece of land. It was envy. His cattle went inside a neighbor's land to graze, and the neighbor got angry, so he and his family killed my father-in-law. It wasn't a fight that my father-in-law had picked. The neighbors thought my husband's family might seek revenge, so they threatened us. That's why my husband decided we needed

---

[1] Jalisco is a state of 8 million on Mexico's Pacific coast.
[2] Atengo is a municipality of about 5,000 in central Jalisco.

to move, and how we ended up going to Mexicali, along with his brother.[3]

I ENJOYED BEING NOSY

We moved to Mexicali in 1960, when my daughter was three, and stayed there until 1970. In Mexicali I didn't work or anything. I was a housewife—I had six children to raise during this time, and I stayed home and took care of the kids. Antonia was born in '62, Jorge in '63, Modesto in '65, and Ramon in '68. Then Estela in 1970. During that time my husband worked in the melon fields, the carrot fields, lettuce. First he was a loader and then he worked as an irrigator for many years.

We got our documents in 1971 through my husband's employer and moved to Calexico, California.[4] My husband was already a member of the union at that time, of the United Farm Workers. The union had an office here; they were starting to organize in Calexico. Since my husband was a member, I could go to the office, and I enjoyed going over there, being nosy. So we started participating in the union and from there, little by little, we began to organize people.

I saw Cesar Chavez for the first time in Calexico, in a meeting he had with us. I thought, *Yeah, this guy really wants to fight for the workers; we have to help him.* I remember he was short! But also very patient, calm. I had a lot of faith in him and I knew that he was really going to do something. I remember how good he was at communicating with workers. He stayed at our place many times. We lived in a big house and he had his own room when he visited. Once we had a party in Mexicali. It was a family gathering in the seventies. We invited him to come; we didn't think he would. But he arrived with

---

[3] Mexicali is a border city in Mexico of nearly 700,000 people, and the capital of the state of Baja California. It is across the border from the smaller California city of Calexico.

[4] For more on work visas in the United States, see the Glossary, page 285.

his dogs, Huelga and Boycott.[5] I have a picture of the party. We made *birria* and my daughter Leonor danced with him.[6]

THAT'S WHEN THE PRESSURE STARTED

In 1970, after waging a five-year campaign that included a national boycott of grapes, the United Farm Workers signed contracts with California's largest table-grape growers. When the contracts expired, in 1973, the companies signed new contracts with the International Brotherhood of Teamsters, a union with a long history of corruption and collusion with California growers. Thus began a new round of strikes and boycotts, which began in Coachella and spread to the San Joaquin Valley.

I first started working in 1971. I started in the grape fields in Coachella, for a company called Karahadian. It was rough, you know? Because we worked all day and it was very different than back in Mexico. You had to work for eight or nine hours under the sun without a break. There were farmers who didn't provide any water for the workers. There were no bathrooms, and you had to go find a secluded spot for privacy. Later that year I also went to work in lettuce in Calexico. We traveled like that and worked for two years. When I started there was a lot of pressure building in the area, and the UFW began to organize and explain the ways we could have better working conditions. But first we had to ask the farmers to give us those rights, right?

I remember the first time that a representative of the union showed up in the grape fields in 1973. When all of us workers saw that the union people were on the road near the grape fields, carrying

---

[5] *Huelga* means "strike" in Spanish; Chavez named his dogs after the UFW's two most effective strategies.

[6] *Birria* is a spicy stew, traditionally made from goat meat or mutton, native to Jalisco.

flags and signs, we went out. Not all of us came out, but most of us did. I grabbed a flag and started to yell at the other workers to leave the fields, because we were going on strike. From that day on, I'd wake up at 5 a.m. and go to the fields to picket and ask the workers not to break the strike.

The Teamsters really came after us in Coachella. We often talked with them about why they broke the strikes. They told us that they were working for the farmers and were getting paid to do that. The Teamsters treated the farmworkers as if they were slaves. The gorillas beat up a lot of people.[7] They beat a priest up; they broke his nose.

One of my sisters had moved to California as well, and her family was part of the movement. While we were striking, my family, along with my sister's family, lived close to the picket lines with my brother-in-law. At the time, my brother-in-law worked as an irrigator at the farm where we were striking, and the company he worked for gave houses to their employees. So my husband and I stayed there in that house with them, along with our six kids, who ranged from very young up to my sixteen-year-old daughter. And my sister's family was there, too, so it was a full house.

One afternoon, after being at the picket lines, we came home to eat lunch. There was a knock at the door, and my brother-in-law went to answer. We all went out to see who it was. The kids, too—you know what kids are like. It was six men, and they immediately started cursing at us and yelling, saying the farmer wanted us out of the house. They were Teamsters. The men were armed—some had the shears used to cut asparagus, some had tire irons or chains, some carried bats.

The Teamsters threatened us, but they didn't have time to beat us up because we called the union's office, and the UFW sent people

[7] Members of the UFW called the Teamsters *gorillas*, a Spanish word that can refer to the animal or hired thugs.

out right away to check on us. In fact, a lot of people who were on strike came out to the house, and the Teamsters left.

Later, the farmer even disconnected the water supply. A lawyer went to talk to them and they connected the water supply again and we stayed a bit longer.

I was angry. Not afraid. We didn't show them that we were scared. But after pressure from the farmer, my family left to live in a house in Calexico. I stayed to continue with the strike, and then I went up to Delano to continue the grape strike there.[8] And we were also working on a boycott. We would go around to the grocery stores and ask customers not to buy grapes. Some of the customers would ask us what we were up to, and we'd tell them that we were fighting for better wages, to be treated better at our jobs in the fields.

In Delano, only my oldest son Jorge stayed with me. He was eleven years old at the time. We kept each other company and he liked being there. Sometimes we had nowhere to go, so we stayed in the park—it's the only park there is in Delano. We slept on benches, in our cars. A lot of strikers were sleeping in cars around the park. The union ordered food for us when they had money. And when they didn't, we ate whatever we could.

Very early in the morning we'd continue with the strike. The police followed us every day: they knew which cars were ours. We talked to workers, told them to leave the fields, to stop working, that they were breaking the strike and we weren't going to be able to get the benefits that the union was offering to give us. And that's what we did all day long. We stayed there until workers left the fields. We were close to the highway and we weren't obstructing the fields, because the police would come to get us if they saw we were directly interfering with the work or on the farmer's property. But I did cross

---

[8] Delano is a city of over 60,000 located 30 miles north of Bakersfield in Kern County. It was the site of the UFW's first strike, and the site of much of the UFW's organization work throughout the '60s and early '70s.

into the fields, many times. And that's when the police would come and take me to jail.

"YOU'RE AFRAID OF ME, AREN'T YOU?"

The foremen couldn't come out of the fields to where we workers were striking, because the police could arrest them as well for confronting us. And like I said, I wasn't supposed to go into the fields, since that would be trespassing. But sometimes I'd take the risk. The foremen would run after me with knives in their hands, try to chase me out. But I'd keep coming back to talk to people.

Of course when the police found me, they'd take me straight to jail. So yeah, they'd arrest me, handcuff me, they'd push me. I'd tell them, "You're afraid of me, aren't you?" And then they'd tell me to shut up.

I remember once I was arrested during Lent. When we got to jail, the police tried to get my fingerprints. But instead of just putting my fingers in the ink, I let my whole hand "slip" and get covered in ink. It was just an act of rebellion. And when I did that, the police hit me.

When I was taken to the jail cell, all the people who'd already been arrested were already inside kneeling on the floor, forming a prayer circle. The police had taken the priests, the nuns, and everybody from the field. Since I was struggling with the police, they grabbed me by the hands and feet and tossed me right into the prayer circle. How was I not supposed to be angry? With everything they were doing? You would have been as well.

When I got out of jail, I was back on the picket line. There's this movie, a documentary called *Fighting for Our Lives*.[9] I'm in it, yelling, "Strike, strike, go on strike!" You can see me jumping all over the

---

[9] *Fighting for Our Lives*, which documented the UFW's 1973 campaign against the growers and Teamsters, was nominated for an Academy Award in 1976.

place. I said, "Coworkers, come out, come to the strike!" And they did. I didn't really care if I was sent to jail or whatever. How can I explain this? I didn't care about what happened to me. I had faith that we had to win, that we needed a union, and that we had to fight with all of our hearts.

I SLAPPED THE THREE OF THEM

The summer of 1973 was remarkably violent. Along with the Teamsters, who stalked the vineyards carrying chains, knives, and baseball bats, the UFW was confronted with law enforcement officials who openly sided with the growers. On the picket line, workers were harassed, tear-gassed, and sometimes beaten by local deputies. In August, two UFW members on strike were killed. Nagi Daifullah, an immigrant from Yemen, was struck by a police officer with a flashlight; he hit his head on the ground and died hours later. The next day, Juan de la Cruz was shot to death while walking a picket line. In response, Chavez called off the strike, citing the dangers faced by picketers, and restarted the grape boycott. Hundreds of UFW volunteers spread out across the country to encourage consumers to stop eating grapes, while most workers returned to the fields.

In 1973, when the grape season was over, I came back to Calexico to work in the lettuce. The next year there was a huge strike in El Centro. I was sent to jail again.

A cop was in the lettuce fields, hitting some of our female coworkers with his baton. I got really angry. I didn't even think about it: I just wanted the police to listen to me. I was carrying a flag with the union's logo on it, and I started hitting the police officer. Two other cops grabbed me to stop me, and I started hitting them with the flag as well.

The first policeman I hit was the sheriff. He was tall, more than six feet, well-built. I grabbed him by the hair and made him kneel to the ground. The other one tried to grab me and I slapped him.

I slapped the three of them. So they took me to jail and everybody made fun of them, because a woman had hit them. But they took me to a tiny cell that was too small to even sit. It was like a cage. They told me it was for people who misbehave, and they didn't give me food or water.

I couldn't move, and there was water dripping from the ceiling onto my head. I think it was a torture method. And they didn't let the union lawyers go inside. I'd been there for twenty-four hours by the time they let the lawyer in—that's when I got out. I think the bail they had to pay to get me out was $20,000.

After the one-day lettuce strike, Rosario continued to work in the fields, harvesting grapes in the spring and summer in the San Joaquin Valley, then returning to Calexico for lettuce work in the winter. On January 19, 1979, after their contracts with vegetable companies had expired, the UFW called another strike. Nearly 2,000 workers walked out of the fields in the Imperial Valley, shutting down a number of companies for several weeks.

We went on strike again in 1979. I worked at Cal Coastal, in the lettuce fields. It was a strike against all companies in general, because they didn't want to sign union contracts. It was the longest strike; it lasted three years. My husband had to take care of our children, and during the three years that we were on strike, the only money we got was $20 per week and some food from the union.[10] We got help to pay the rent because we went to welfare and they paid our rent and gave us food stamps.

I worked with Marshall Ganz and Jessica Govea. May she rest in peace. They were two very professional organizers.[11] Jessica especially was always sensitive to what was happening to us. We had to be at

---

[10] Roughly $70 in 2017 dollars.

[11] Marshall Ganz and Jessica Govea were leaders of the UFW and members on the executive board together in the late seventies. Jessica Govea passed away in 2005.

Calexico at two in the morning to talk to people on the buses, try to get them not to go to work. Then I went from one place to another, making sure people didn't have any problems, that they were getting their food packages, their $20 per week. We'd come back from being on strike and get to the union office between 7 and 8 p.m. and check in. The meetings sometimes lasted three hours. I slept one or two hours, if I was lucky.

Cesar Chavez believed that the lettuce strike was destined to fail. He pushed for a boycott instead. But many lettuce and vegetable workers wanted to expand the strike, and they did so—against Chavez's wishes. When the harvest moved to Salinas, thousands of workers walked out, leaving unpicked crops to rot in the fields. A number of major vegetable companies quickly signed contracts with the UFW, which raised the starting wage to a standardized $5 an hour (nearly $17 an hour in 2017 dollars). The contracts also created union representatives from each company, whose wages were paid for by the company. Farmworkers elected their own paid representative—fellow farmworkers—whose job it was to enforce the contracts.

But Rosario's employer, Cal Coastal, held out three years before finally signing a contract in April 1981. It was only then that she returned to the fields, where she packed broccoli. Six months later, the UFW held a national convention in Fresno, where the union would elect new members of the executive board. The board didn't have a farmworker on it, and the paid representatives decided to run a slate of two farmworkers—again against Chavez's wishes. One of the farmworkers they chose was Rosario.

I HAD ALL OF THEIR SUPPORT, RIGHT?

In 1981, I was nominated to be part of the executive board of the union by the other workers. I worked in the fields, and they wanted a worker to be part of the board. I accepted because the laborers nominated me, and I thought, *Well, I know I don't know anything about this but if they back me up* ... I had all of their support, right?

Unfortunately, there were a lot of politics involved and we were kicked out of the union. Frankly, what happened is that when we were in Salinas, Dolores Huerta passed out some fliers saying that we wanted to take Cesar's place. That *that* was the reason why some in the UFW wanted me to be a member of the executive board: in order to kick Cesar out. But that wasn't true. Workers wanted a person that still worked with them in the fields to be part of the board. That was all. Nobody was going to take his place. His place was his, period.

At the UFW convention the organizers disconnected our microphones. They wouldn't let us speak, and we left. People say that if you get angry, you lose, right? But it wasn't worth it because it seemed that the situation was really going to get bad and we decided it would be better to leave.

I was very discouraged. Everyone at the convention was discouraged, everyone was sad.

I was very resentful, because I had fought for so long; I mean, with all my heart. I didn't do it because I really wanted to be part of the executive board, but because my fellow workers had nominated me and I thought, *Yes, if they are OK with it, I will do it to continue with the fight.*

YOU HAVE TO FIGHT FOR WHAT YOU WANT

Right after the convention I had an accident at work. I was working for Cal Coastal, packing in the broccoli fields. I went to the bathroom, a porta potty, but they hadn't installed it properly and it wasn't on stable ground, so when I went in, the whole porta potty fell backwards. After some other workers got me out, I felt dizzy and sick. They took me to the doctor and I learned that my spine was fractured. I couldn't walk much for the next year. The doctors kept sending me to San Diego to get tests and everything, and finally I had surgery. I sued the company and got $20,000, but I was permanently disabled. I couldn't work in the fields anymore.

My doctor said that I had to take care of myself after the operation. I learned to walk again, little by little. But I could never be like I was before. Eventually I was able to cook my own meals, but I couldn't bend over at all for a while, so I needed people to dress me. My kids helped a lot, especially Leonor. After two years of therapy, they sent me to a program to see what other kind of work I could do. But I hadn't had much schooling and the only work I knew was in the field, so there wasn't anything else I could do.

I started drawing, sewing, and reading. I got really involved in the church. I go to Our Lady of Guadalupe in Calexico. I'm Catholic. We have many groups there that I joined. I go to church seven days a week! Right now, I'm in a class that reads the Bible and studies for two hours every day. We bring food to the park for the homeless. I am still involved in helping people.

There are people at the church who work in the fields. Right now, the conditions are very bad for farmworkers. There's a lot of discrimination and oppression. They force them to do too much work. Some of the farmworkers at the church know about my history. Not a lot, but a few. One of my sons worked in the fields, but he got hurt six years ago. A tractor ran over his arm and he didn't have insurance. He can't use his arm now; he doesn't have any strength.

I saw so many injustices in the field. They used to treat the farmworkers as if they were slaves. We didn't get breaks. There were no bathrooms in the field, no cold water with ice. I had faith that we had to win. We needed a union and to get it we had to fight with all our hearts. We worked together so nicely. We didn't care if we if didn't get any sleep or if we didn't eat.

When the union came in there were a lot of changes. We started to get ten-minute breaks. Growers started treating people with more dignity. We got bathrooms and fresh water with ice and a medical plan. So there were improvements. But you have to fight for what you want.

FAUSTO SANCHEZ

AGE: 47

OCCUPATION: *Indigenous program community worker,*
California Rural Legal Assistance
BORN IN: *Oaxaca, Mexico*
INTERVIEWED IN: *Arvin, Kern County*
AGRICULTURAL REGION: *Central Valley*

In John Steinbeck's classic novel The Grapes of Wrath, *the Joad family leaves Oklahoma and arrives, after an arduous journey, at a migrant labor camp near the town of Arvin, where they find work picking grapes. Located on the southern edge of the San Joaquin Valley, the region is still a center for grape production in the United States, and continues to rely on thousands of migrant farmworkers each summer for the harvest.*

Fausto Sanchez was one of those migrants. An indigenous Mixteco from the Mexican state of Oaxaca, he first came to the Valley as a teenager in the 1980s. After several years in the fields, he enrolled at a local adult school, and has used his language proficiency—he speaks two Mixteco dialects in addition to Spanish and English—to advocate for indigenous farmworkers.[1]

---

[1] It is estimated that almost half of the workers picking fruit and vegetables in the United States are working in California. Over 120,000 of those workers speak an indigenous Mexican language. Indigenous language speakers from states such as Fausto's Oaxaca make up as much as 40 percent of new arrivals in California's fields, a spike of migration that has sped up since the passage of NAFTA in 1994.

We meet at California Rural Legal Assistance's storefront office on Arvin's main street. A sign on the window reads SE HABLA MIXTECO—*we speak Mixteco. Inside, stacks of blue-and-white flyers outline the labor rights of farmworkers. Fausto sits behind a large desk, wearing jeans and a polo shirt, and for several hours he shares stories about his long and circuitous path from a remote Mexican hillside to Arizona and then California, and his lifelong fascination with language.*

A TOWN WITH YELLOW EARTH

My family says that I was born in the mountains, under a tree. While my mother was pregnant, she had to take care of the goats, lambs, and cows. She went out one day to the mountains with one of my brothers to tend to the animals, and she started going into labor. She wasn't able to get all the way to the house, so my brother went to let everyone at home know that I'd been born. The rest of the family got ready to go get her, but before they were able to leave, my mother had already gathered me in her *huipil*—the local dress that women wear in Oaxaca—and brought me to the house.[2] That was in 1969.

I'm the fifth of nine children—three boys and six girls. The village where I grew up was called Santo Domingo. It had about 200 people; we all spoke Mixteco, not Spanish. Our house was made of wood planks, and I remember that it measured six by seven meters. That's where the whole family lived, in one small space, with no electricity and no water. There was a school in town, but it only went up to second grade. I only went to two months of primary school, like kindergarten.

Santo Domingo was in the mountains, about 3,000 feet above sea level. But it's a town with yellow earth—not good land for farming.

---

[2] The state of Oaxaca is in southwest Mexico and best known for its large indigenous population, which includes at least sixteen different cultures. More than 1 million Oaxacans speak an indigenous language, and many indigenous speakers do not also speak Spanish.

My parents took care of animals, and my father also cut down trees for lumber. He tied them to a horse to take them to Juxtlahuaca—the largest town in the area—to sell them and earn a little money.[3] At the time there were no major roads for cars, so it took about two and a half hours, walking along a path that went over the mountain and down to the river.

The only way to survive was to own animals. If you needed money, you'd go and sell livestock. My father had two horses, three or four cows, and lambs. But as time passed, the animals began to die, and there were more children, and the crops he farmed on the land were no longer enough for all of us to eat. So that's why we had to leave, so that we could find a way to feed ourselves.

THE LETTERS TALK

I was seven years old the first time we left for Sinaloa.[4] Sinaloa is famous for its produce such as tomatoes, cucumbers, squash, and eggplant. It's good farmland and people from Oaxaca and Guerrero go to Sinaloa to find work.[5] There was even farmland in Sinaloa that the people called the "Oaxacan farmland," because there were so many Oaxacans working it.

We went by train the first time. The train trip took four days, night and day, and there was a lot of noise. *Pum, pum, pum, pum*—that was the sound it made. The journey was special, but also a little uncomfortable for us, because vendors on the train sell a lot of things—food, sweets, treats—and we didn't have any money. My father had brought a large

---

[3] Santiago Juxtlahuaca is both a town and the municipality head—akin to a county seat—and is one of the oldest towns in Oaxaca, dating back to the twelfth century.

[4] Sinaloa is a state of nearly 3 million people on Mexico's northwest coast. It is the most agriculturally productive state in the country, known as *"el granero de México,"* or Mexico's breadbasket.

[5] Guerrero is a neighboring state to the west of Oaxaca and has a population of 3.5 million people.

sack of dried tortillas—*totopos*, which are like what they call "chips" in the United States. And that's all we ate along the way.

We arrived in Sinaloa with our faces and clothes very dirty from the smoke on the train—we were all black. We ended up at a farm called Nogalitos.[6] At that time, my parents and older siblings were harvesting tomatoes, cucumbers, whatever they had been assigned. Each person had a different job, but all of them worked. The first time we were in Sinaloa and my family went to work, I didn't go with them—I stayed at home with my little brother. He was five at the time. I'd get up and if there was something to eat, we would eat, and then we'd go outside to play. We'd play with marbles, run around. There was no school, and there were a lot of other children at the labor camp.

My brother and I liked to go play in the canal. One time the police grabbed us because it's forbidden to bathe in the canals. I didn't know. They chased me, grabbed me, and put me in the back of their car. I was crying a lot. My brother escaped, but they took me to jail in Villa Juárez, the town where the police precinct is located.[7] My father came and paid the fine to get me out. He was mad and said, "I don't want you going in the canal anymore." I told him OK. But four or five days later, my brother and I went back to the canal. My brother would start as the lookout, making sure that no one came. Then he got in, too.

There were 300 or 400 people living in Nogalitos. The people were from Oaxaca, and most spoke Mixteco. The camps had rows of houses, like mobile homes right up against one another, sided with large sheets of black tar paper. Whatever we said, whatever we did, all of the other families could hear. There was no electricity and the floors were dirt. Whenever anyone cooked, all of the smoke would get

---

[6] Nogalitos means "little walnut trees."

[7] The town of Licenciado Benito Juárez, better known as Villa Juárez, has a population of 24,000 and is located 12 miles southwest of Culiacán, the capital of Sinaloa.

trapped in the house, since there wasn't really any ventilation. We'd wake up covered in black soot! But no one complained. Nobody talked about how the place was bad. I don't know why. I think it was nothing more than people would arrive, be offered work, be given somewhere to live, and they would just start working. There was no inspector, no one to come and see what the conditions were like.

Two years later we returned to our town to be part of our community again. My father was made a head of the village, something like a village representative, and he would go to represent the interests of the village in the municipality in Juxtlahuaca. Sometimes he'd take me. There were lots of signs in front of the main building, the municipal offices, and my dad would say to me, "Listen, take notice of the letters and talk with them, because the letters talk." Of course, I didn't know how the letters could be able to talk. My father didn't know how to read, but he knew the letters meant something. From then on I was curious to know: *How is it that the letters could talk? How could I speak with them?* And the idea stayed with me. I always thought about learning to read and write.

I was nine years old when my parents decided that we were going to go to Sinaloa again. We were at the bus terminal in Juxtlahuaca, ready to go. By chance, an uncle of my mother's arrived. He told my parents about a woman who was looking for a boy to live with her and help out around the house. The woman said that she'd take care of the boy. In exchange for doing chores she would feed him, and send him to school to learn to read and write. I told my father that I wanted to stay with the woman.

He said, "Really?"

"Yes," I told him, "I want to stay."

He told me it would be OK. I remember he went out and bought me a black T-shirt with a Cepillín design.[8] I was more excited than

---

[8] Cepillín is a clown who had a popular TV show in Mexico beginning in the 1970s. He was originally a dentist, and his name means "little brush."

sad about leaving my family, because I really wanted to go to school. I wanted to learn to read and write and to speak Spanish. I knew that way I could go where I wanted and have more opportunities. If you know how to read and write it's a lot better, because Mixteco is not going to help you get ahead.

And so I went to live with the woman.

I RAN AND RAN AND RAN

The woman I moved in with was from a family that had come from Spain, so she spoke Spanish. She had straight hair and her three children had light-colored eyes. They were people who lived comfortably —or as they say, people who had money. The house was big. There was a bathroom and kitchen, rooms and more rooms, and many trees and plants. When I arrived she gave me a place to sleep on the back patio, outside the house. She gave me blankets and a woven mat to sleep on. The house had many rooms. She never explained to me why she wouldn't give me a room to stay in.

Every morning at five the woman woke me up and I had pick up my blankets and mat and take them to the garage. I had to throw water all over the patio to clean it. And then I had to sweep, take out the garbage, clean up and gather the fallen leaves from the trees, and throw them out. When I returned I had to go run errands to the plaza to get milk, bread, tortillas—everything that they needed. Sometimes the woman would make enchiladas and empanadas and I'd sell them at the plaza. Then I'd return, give her the money, and go to school from one in the afternoon until six. When I was done with school, I'd go out again, because she would have made bread to sell. I'd go home, have my dinner, wash the plates, go and retrieve my mat and covers, and go out on the patio to sleep.

This was all when I was nine years old.

At first it didn't strike me as strange that I was sleeping outside, because in Santo Domingo sometimes I'd sleep outside with my brothers amongst the trees. But as time passed, I did begin to feel bad about it. The woman had godchildren from the church, and when they arrived she'd treat them very differently. She'd give them hugs, ask them how they were, say, "Hello my child." When the god-children stayed at the house, she always had a room for them with a bed and blankets. So while I slept out on the patio, I thought, *Wait, something here isn't right. Why have I been living with her for so long and she doesn't give me a room to sleep in?*

I wasn't friends with her children. I knew four of them. Like if you have a brother or a friend—you talk, play, do things. With them it was a dead end. They'd make me do things all the time. "Come here," "clean these shoes," "sweep the kitchen," "take out the trash." "You're a servant, a worker, and I'm the owner of the house. I'm the one who's in charge."

When I arrived I spoke very little Spanish. And the children at school made a lot of fun of me too, because I didn't speak Spanish. They'd grab me, we'd fight, many times for the same reason—because they would say that I was a *tata*, a *ñerro*, a *huarachudo*.[9] So I studied. First, second, third, fourth grade. I think it took me a year to learn Spanish—that's all anyone spoke.

I lived with the woman's family for four years while my family was in Sinaloa. One time my family sent me a backpack, through an uncle in Juxtlahuaca, but nothing else. I didn't regret having gone to live with this new family, but I became very angry at the way that they treated me. I was mad because they never said to me, "We care about you," or "Give me a hug," or "How are you?"

I wanted nothing more than to leave. When I was thirteen years old, my father returned. I saw him approaching the house, and I ran out to him. He said, "I've come to get you." After he said that, I just started running from the house. I ran and ran and ran, almost to the

---

[9] These are slang words meant to describe, roughly, an ignorant person from the mountains who doesn't speak Spanish.

edge of town. I didn't take anything from the house—my diploma, clothing, shoes—nothing at all. And when he caught up with me, my dad asked, "Fausto, why are you running?" I said, "I don't want to be there one minute longer!"

YOU HAD TO BE HIDING FROM IMMIGRATION

From there, we went to Santo Domingo, and I was with my parents for two or three months. Then one of my older sisters came from Sinaloa with a brother, and at thirteen or fourteen I went with them to Sinaloa while my parents stayed in Santo Domingo. I started to work for myself—my own wages. What I made was now mine! I felt free.

In the fields where we worked, each crew has a note taker, or checker, and that was my job. I signed in workers, noting how many boxes each person was filling each day, how many containers of tomatoes they filled. And I got water for the crew. I also worked in the store selling things to the people who lived in the labor camp. Working in Sinaloa was OK, but sometimes we Oaxacans did face discrimination. When there were young Sinaloans in our work crews they'd often look down on us. A lot of times they'd be tall and light skinned, or have green eyes, and they'd make fun of how short we were, or our dark skin, or the way we spoke. They'd call us "little Oaxacans." Things like that make you feel bad.

After the season was over in Sinaloa, I went to Baja, California.[10] Then I came to the United States for the first time, along with some other Mixteco farmworkers who wanted to make money working in fields. There were a few months a year when the work wasn't very good in Sinaloa or Baja, and that's when farmworkers would go to the United States.

---

[10] The state of Baja California has 3.3 million people, and is made up of the northern half of the Baja Peninsula (the southern half is Baja California Sur.) The state's agricultural center is the San Quintín Valley, about two hundred miles south of San Diego; the workforce is predominantly indigenous Oaxacans.

The first time, I crossed the border at Tijuana with a group of people from my home town led by some coyotes that we'd paid.[11] I was fourteen or fifteen; it was around 1985. We were above where the houses in Tijuana are and we looked down and saw Immigration waiting for us. The coyotes told us that we had to wait until midnight, because that's when the Immigration agents changed shifts. We'd have about a half hour to run. Midnight arrived and there was no light at all. It was pitch black. They said, "It's time to run." We ran and crossed a canal filled with water up to our chests.[12] When we came out there was an iron fence, but it had already been broken and pushed to the ground. Past the fence, we came to an alley and some small houses, and maybe 200 feet from the houses was a road where a taxi was already waiting. The drivers know that people who cross will need a ride. We took the taxi to San Diego, and from San Diego we took a bus to Kerman.[13] I don't remember the name of the person in our group, but there was a guy who already knew some people in Kerman.

A grower who lived near the canal in Kerman offered us a house and a job. It was a big green house, and all of us living there were Mixteco. We went straight to work in the onion and garlic fields. To work in the onion fields we used big scissors. You pull the onion out of the ground, cut the root and the point off, and then put the onion in a plastic container. You put the container in a sack. Then they paid

---

[11] Tijuana is a sprawling city of 1.7 million, across the border from San Ysidro, the southernmost district of San Diego. Once the most popular crossing spot for undocumented migrants, increased border security in the San Diego–Tijuana corridor—launched in 1994 by Bill Clinton and called "Operation Gatekeeper"—has caused the migrant stream to move east, to the more inhospitable deserts of Arizona. *Coyote* refers to a guide who helps migrants illegally cross into the United States. For more information, see the Glossary, page 284.

[12] The All-American Canal stretches 80 miles along California's southern border from the Colorado River to the Imperial Valley. The canal is a dangerous obstacle for migrants crossing into the United States—many hundreds of drowning deaths have occurred in the canal in the past few decades.

[13] Kerman is a small city of 15,000, fifteen miles west of Fresno.

us either 80 cents or one dollar per sack. In one day, sometimes you earned $15 or $20, depending on whether the onions were good and big or not.

What I noticed most in the United States were the cars. A lot of cars, big highways, and then the houses and the buildings too. Enormous. And that you had to hide from Immigration. You couldn't walk around during the day; you weren't free to go to the store. When you got up at five in the morning, you went directly to the field. Then you'd return to where you lived. At night, or on Saturdays or Sundays, you'd do your shopping, because on Saturdays and Sundays *la migra* wasn't out.[14] But Monday through Friday, a lot of Immigration officers were around, with their cars and everything. Many of my friends who risked leaving home during the week—well, they got caught and sent to Mexico.

After two or three months working in Kerman, the work was over. A number of guys from the house started leaving, with many going back to Mexico. Pretty soon there were only a few of us left in the house, and they were planning on leaving too. I didn't know anyone else in town, and I had no connections to help me get other work, so I decided that I wanted to return to Mexico, too. I brought my clothing, my shoes, and left with the last few housemates for Sinaloa.

Each time I'd come back to Sinaloa, I'd say, "I'm back!" And the man in charge of the store would say, "OK, then get to work." Then the jobs would end in Sinaloa and I'd go with the man to work in Baja California, and whenever I'd go back to Sinaloa, he'd give me work again. But the store wasn't open all year. It was only when there was work in the fields. There were a few months—two or three months—when the work wasn't very good, and I used those times to come back to the United States.[15]

---

[14] *Migra* is short for a Border Patrol or Immigration agent. For more on immigration enforcement agencies, see the Glossary, page 286–7.

[15] In the 1980s, it generally cost $50–$200 per person to pay a coyote for travel across the U.S.-Mexico border, making frequent trips somewhat affordable for

WE WENT LOOKING FOR A BIG
TREE TO LIVE UNDER

I think it was 1986, or maybe '87, I was sixteen or seventeen when the group I was with walked three days in the desert to get to Arizona. We had a guide, a man who led us through the hills. He knew all of the hills. And so we went with him to a place I believe was called Casa Grande. There we paid another man who took us to Chandler and led us to an orange orchard.[16]

Then we went looking for a big tree to live under. We went to the dump and got mattresses. We'd put one mattress on the bottom, another mattress in between, and another one on top. Three mattresses, so you're up high. Then you take a big piece of plastic, securing it in the middle, and it goes down the sides. So that's where you sleep. If it rains or leaves fall, nothing is going to happen because you'll be there under the plastic. To bathe, well, there's a big canal. And you get far away from there if you need to use the bathroom.

We slept under the orange trees, and that's also where we worked. In my crew there were about six people. Ten trees that way, there's another group, and so on. I think there were thirty, forty people living in that field of oranges. The supervisors give you a ladder of about eighteen feet, and a bag that's bigger than you to throw over your shoulder. You go up and fill it, and then go back down with it. I think I lasted an hour. I filled up only one bag. *No more, no more.* I told the foreman that I wasn't going to do the job, because it was too hard and I was afraid to fall. He said that was all right. So I didn't work, but all the men who came with me kept working. I'd go with them to the field and just eat the oranges. When I wouldn't work, I was the one who'd cook, so the other guys wouldn't get mad.

---

seasonal workers making annual crossings. In recent decades, the cost per person has risen to $5,000–$15,000 per person.

[16] Chandler is located about twenty miles southeast of Phoenix. Once a small agricultural town—its population was 30,000 in 1980—it is now one of the fastest-growing cities in the country, with a current population of more than 240,000.

After oranges, the group I was with went to work in pecans in the area. Starting with the nuts, I began to work. The farm had a machine that would shake the trees and pick the nuts up, but a lot of the nuts would fall on the ground. So the supervisors would give us a bucket, and we'd use the bucket to fill a sack. I think they were paying $3.50 a sack. And sometimes, for nine, ten sacks, they'd give me $30, $40 a day. It was a lot of money.

We were in Chandler for three months. Then, some of the men went back to Mexico and left me and two other young guys. We didn't know where to go, but we ran into a group of Guatemalans in Chandler. They told us they were going to Florida. So I asked my friends if they wanted to go, and they said, "OK." In their car, the Guatemalans told us that in Guatemala, there's a lot of war, and so they were asking for political asylum. They said that if we filled out and signed paperwork they had, and Immigration grabs us, maybe they'd let us stay. I asked my friends, "What do you think?"—talking to them in Mixteco, right, so that we're not overheard. And my friends said, "Well, no. Because what if they kick us out and send us to Guatemala? If *la migra* gets us, we're going to tell them the truth."

So we left, and in New Mexico, sure enough, *la migra* got us. They got us at the gas station and took us away in a Bronco. There were six or eight people lying down on the floor of the Bronco—the men on the bottom and the women on top. We were stacked in a cross formation, some this way and some that way. They took us all the way to Texas. It was really uncomfortable, because the women on top of me were heavy. We were knocking our heads against each other. They threw us out in El Paso, Texas, and sent us to Ciudad Juárez.[17] Then I went back to the fields in Sinaloa. I don't know what happened to the Guatemalans.

---

[17] The border city of El Paso is in the western corner of Texas. Opposite El Paso is Ciudad Juárez. Running between the cities is the Rio Grande River (or, as it is known in Mexico, *El Río Bravo*—the fierce river).

LET'S GO TO WHEREVER WE GET TO

I married my wife, Alberta, on March 8, 1988. She's also from Oaxaca, from a town further away—San Juan Mixtepec. But we speak the same Mixteco.[18]

We first met in 1983, when I was living at the labor camp in Baja, California. I was sharing a room with my younger brother, and she and her family got a room next to us. But it's not the way it is in the United States, where you see someone and you approach and just talk to her. Our ways in Oaxaca are different. I saw her and I liked her, but she was always with her sisters, her brothers, her mom and dad. So I'd just stare at her. I didn't say anything to her that first year, but I'd talk to her younger brothers, looking for a way to get close to the family. Then they went back to Sinaloa. After I returned from Kerman I came back to Sinaloa to work at the store. That's when someone told me she was living nearby. I rode my bicycle out to their place, but I only saw her brothers, so I took them to the store and bought them candy. And that was that.

Later, in Baja, she happened to live right next to my parents, and sometimes I'd see her, but I still didn't say a word. In 1987, I asked my dad to ask her father for her hand in marriage. Her father said OK—but that I'd have to wait a year. I told my dad that one year was a really long time and that I didn't want to wait. That's when I went to Arizona and told my dad not to talk to her parents again. Well, I don't know—I couldn't find anyone that I liked more than her, so when I returned to Baja I asked my dad to go again. I think her parents scolded him, but they said yes in the end. Right away we went to the registry office in Baja and got married, and then came to Sinaloa together.

Four months later, in July 1988, my wife and I came to the United States. Because we had heard about the amnesty, I decided I should bring my birth certificate and documents in case I wanted

---

[18] The Mixteco language has many regional dialects.

to apply.[19] We walked three days, and my wife was at the front of the group the whole time—she's a strong woman. We got to an old American town, Sasabe, and the coyotes gave us a lot of food, but it was out of a can.[20] Prison food. So we ate, and they put us in a house outside of town, surrounded by abandoned cars. We were there until night came, and then they took us to Chandler. From there, we found someone who took us to Madera.[21]

I didn't have a specific plan about a place to go, only that the plan was to come to the United States. It didn't matter where. Let's go to wherever we get to. In Madera, we were working in the grape fields. We left Madera to go to Corning, to work olives, and then after that we went back to Madera, to prune grapes.[22] We were living in a van, I think about ten of us. At night we would lie down on the ground, under the trees. Others slept in the car. And when it rained we all climbed in the car and slept sitting up, because it wasn't possible to lie down. There was no privacy. There was nothing.

At the time, my brother-in-law was living in Arvin, and he asked us to come live with him and his sisters. That was in November or December 1988. Since then we've been here. There are about fifteen people in Arvin from my hometown of Santo Domingo. And from San Juan Mixtepec, where my wife is from, there must be 250 or 300 people. I think that if we were to move to a different place, we'd lose that connection with the people. Where there are people from our hometown, that's where we will be.

---

[19] The Immigration Reform and Control Act, passed in 1986, provided permanent legal residence to eligible migrants, including those who could prove that they'd worked in agriculture in the United States during a certain time period. For more information, see the Glossary, page 286.

[20] Sasabe, Arizona, is a small community and border-crossing station.

[21] Madera has a population of about 60,000 and is twenty-five miles northwest of Fresno.

[22] Corning, a northern California town of 7,500 people, is about 250 miles north of Madera.

PREJUDICE AGAINST INDIGENOUS
PEOPLE CAN BE A PROBLEM

After moving to Arvin I went to Kerman to get information from the farmer, to show that I'd worked for ninety days.[23] Then I had an appointment at the Immigration office in Fresno—they asked me where I had worked, what kind of work I had done, other questions. That's how I got my green card.[24] My wife got her green card, too, because she was married to me.

In 1990, I started working at the Greenway packing plant, in Bakersfield, packing carrots. Then an opportunity came up to learn how to operate a forklift—that was something I really wanted to do. So for seven years, from 1992 to 1999, I was a forklift operator, while Alberta worked in the grape fields. She still works in the fields today.

We have three children, all born in the United States. The oldest is Daniel, then comes Alex, and then Cesar. They are in their twenties now and studying in Los Angeles. At one time they went to work with their mom in the grape fields, but they didn't like it. It's a hard job. Like I said, my wife is a strong woman.

When my kids started going to school, I decided to go to school, too. In 1997, I learned that California Rural Legal Assistance was looking for people who spoke Mixteco and Spanish, so that they could become interpreters.[25] I signed up, got the grant, and went to Salinas for interpreter training. Then I came back here to Arvin and went to look for work as an interpreter—in the courts, in the clinics,

---

[23] Proof of ninety days of previous farmwork was required for green card eligibility as part of the Immigration Reform and Control Act. For more on the IRCA, see the Glossary, page 286–7.

[24] Fausto is referring to an H2-A agricultural work visa. For more on the H2-A visa, see the Glossary, page 285.

[25] California Rural Legal Assistance is a fifty-year-old nonprofit that provides free legal services to rural poor throughout the state. Its advocacy work focuses on housing, labor, education, health, and leadership development. For more information, see Appendix IV, page 304.

in the hospitals. But the first thing they would ask me was if I spoke English, and I would say to them, no. They'd say, "OK, let's talk later." And they would never get back to me.

So in 1998 I enrolled at the adult school in Bakersfield to learn English and get credits for my GED. I went four times a week, from Monday to Thursday, 8:30 in the morning to noon. I still worked at Greenway in the afternoon. I'd come in at three and leave at midnight or one in the morning. Sometimes I'd leave at 5 or 6 a.m., but I wouldn't fail my classes. I got my GED in 2001. After that I went to Bakersfield College and graduated in 2011 with a certificate in Human Resources.

While I was attending classes, a friend told me that CRLA was again looking for a person who would want to work with them and who was bilingual—who could speak Mixteco and Spanish. That's how I came to work for them. I started working with CRLA on April 26, 1999. I work in the Indigenous Program. I give presentations in schools, or for community agencies, or the people at the consulate; or I talk to the clients, or go to the labor commission, or the radio, or the television. Where I work, I'm by myself. When the day is done, I close up the office. I do have a supervisor, but she's in Oakland—I'm always bugging her whenever anything comes up.

I remember a case I helped with a couple of years after I started with CRLA. Around 2002, there was a pesticide company spraying some carrot and potato fields here in Arvin. They didn't follow guidelines for the pesticide they were using, and a cloud of it drifted into the homes of fieldworkers nearby. The pesticide burned the eyes and throats of the people it reached, and some of them had migraines for months. Some had eyes that burned for a long time. It was a dire situation.

I helped CRLA prepare a case against the pesticide company and the farm. I helped interpret for the Mixteco families. We'd have meetings with lawyers, and I'd sit with them and explain the situation, explain what was being said. We helped get compensation for some twenty-five or thirty families. I think there were three or so Mixteco families. I helped them participate in the lawsuit, so they knew what was going on.[26]

Prejudice against indigenous people from other Mexicans can be a problem. People from other states like Michoacán, Guanajuato, and Sinaloa think that indigenous people who can't speak Spanish are dumb, that they are not intelligent. They make fun of them. They bully them. We are native people from Mexico who have our own language, our own culture, and our own way to celebrate the holidays. But I don't think that makes us less valuable than other people, or less intelligent, right? So another part of my job is supporting indigenous people that are working here in the United States.

There's a lot of indigenous people here, not only Mixtecos, who never had the opportunity to go to school, and many of them can't speak Spanish well, can't read and write. There are a lot of problems with communication. Employers sometimes take advantage of that. For instance, I know of many Mixtecos who are promised a certain salary by a grower or labor contractor and are then paid much less, and the Mixteco worker can't read or write or know who to speak with to complain. Or maybe the person hiring the indigenous worker doesn't explain fully what the pay will be, and the worker doesn't know how to ask questions.

The challenges aren't only with employers. There are language barriers and cultural barriers for other services as well. I think

---

[26] In 2002, at least eighty-four residents of Arvin were exposed to a cloud of the pesticide metam sodium that had drifted from a nearby farm into their homes. Because the pesticide had been improperly applied, leading to the pesticide drift, lawyers with CRLA were able to bring a case against the farm and the pesticide application company and win a settlement of $775,000 in 2005. The state of California also fined the applicator company $60,000. Immediate symptoms of exposure to the pesticide cloud included burning eyes and upper respiratory problems. Long-term effects included vision and respiratory problems, persistent headaches, and diarrhea. The eighty-three cases of exposure due to the pesticide drift were part of around 1,300 cases of pesticide poisoning identified by California in 2002. For more on pesticides and legal protections in California, see Appendix IV, page 304.

sometimes these can be harder for women. For instance, a lot of women from Oaxaca come from the countryside where they've never visited a doctor, and when they give birth they use midwives. So many women are reluctant to go to the doctor, especially because they're afraid they'll get a male doctor. Husbands can get jealous. And very few doctors or nurses speak Mixteco.

In Arvin we try to integrate Mixtecos through cultural events and make them feel proud, but we also try to introduce our culture to other people within the community who don't know much about us. We have community meetings, where we tell people they don't have to be afraid. We tell them that the law protects everyone, whether they have documents or not. If they haven't been paid, they have the right to that money. So that is something I work towards—making sure Mixteco people have the information they need about their rights. But my favorite part of the work is when we win a case with the workers. When we get involved in a lawsuit about wages, or some other issue they have had in the fields, and win the case for them. They are very happy, and so are we.

We are only asking to be treated with respect, right? Because we are here, our children were born here, they go to school here, and they are not going back to a country they don't know. We only want to be OK, like any other person from any other country who came here and grew up here. We are here as well, part of a country of immigrants.

In fact, our ancestors lived here in the Americas for a long, long time and the only thing that makes us look like foreigners is the political division of the border, but other than that indigenous people have always moved around—there were no borders until politics invented them.

JOSE SALDIVAR

AGE: 62

OCCUPATION: *Irrigator and pesticide applicator*
BORN IN: *Nayarit, Mexico*
INTERVIEWED IN: *Coachella, Riverside County*
AGRICULTURAL REGION: *Coachella Valley*

Farmworkers tend to change jobs frequently. Sometimes they move from one town to the next as the growing seasons change. Other times they may work for numerous companies while living in a single place, as labor demands for specific crops fluctuate. In an occupation that is often defined by instability, Jose Saldivar has lived an uncommonly grounded life. For the past forty years he has worked at a single company, HMS Agricultural Corporation.[1] He also has the advantage of having been a member of the United Farm Workers, which has brought benefits that are out of reach for the vast majority of farmworkers: a pension, job security, paid vacations.[2] "I'm very lucky," says Jose, a broad smile on his face.

But that doesn't mean everything has been easy. Even with the protection of a union, Jose has faced many workplace hazards over his long career.

---

[1] HMS Agricultural Corporation employs about seventy workers and is today a certified organic grower of citrus and other fruits.

[2] For more on United Farmworkers and California Rural Legal Assistance, see Appendix IV, page 304–6.

He regularly handled pesticides without proper safety equipment, leading to one acute case of pesticide poisoning. He has also seen how less fortunate farmworkers, many of whom migrate to Coachella each summer for the grape harvest, are forced to sleep in the fields and bathe and wash their clothes with pesticide-contaminated water from irrigation canals.

We meet at the office of California Rural Legal Assistance in downtown Coachella. Outside the streets are deserted—it's 1 p.m., and what had begun as a pleasant morning is turning uncomfortably hot. We gather inside a large conference room with walls lined with legal texts. Jose is trim and fit, with close-cropped gray hair parted neatly on the side and a wide mustache. He speaks deliberately, pausing to search at times for the right word, as he describes the changes he has seen in the field and how, with the help of CRLA, he was able to finally ensure that Coachella farmworkers without homes would have a safe place to bathe.

WE WERE LOOKING FOR A BETTER LIFE

I was born in a village called Acaponeta, in the state of Nayarit in 1954.[3] My family moved to Mexicali when I was six years old.[4] We moved for the same reason that I later came to the United States—we were looking for a better life.

I came to the United States when I was eighteen years old. It was May 1972, more or less. My aunt knew someone who helped people enter illegally. This guy came to Mexico, said that he could bring me with him, and I said yes. I imagined my life in the United States would be much better than the one I was living in Mexicali. I saw that people coming from the United States had nice cars and dressed well, and where I was from, we didn't have nice cars or clothes.

---

[3] Nayarit is a small state on Mexico's western coast with a population of about 1 million people.

[4] Mexicali is a border city in Mexico of nearly 700,000 people, and the capital of the state of Baja California. It is across the border from the smaller California city of Calexico.

The group I went with walked six hours in the desert from Algodones to Yuma, without seeing a single person. And then from Yuma we rode the train to Mecca.[5] It was a cargo train—we didn't need a ticket. You just jumped onto a ladder when it was slowing down. People would lose a foot if they didn't get on the right way.

In Mecca, I got a job for a company that gave me a little John Deere tractor that ran on propane. There was no training for how to drive the tractor—nothing. It had a tank behind and we sprayed an oil that killed weeds. The government banned the oil in 1980, I think. It was very toxic—very harmful to many living things.[6] That was my first job.

After that, I switched to working at a nursery. I changed jobs for the money, what can I say? The first job paid me $1.80 an hour, and the nursery paid $2.30. The nursery boss was a good boss. At break time at 9 o'clock in the morning, his wife would show up with a box of donuts and a thermos of coffee. At noon she came with tea and juice. They were the only bosses I've ever had that were good bosses.

When I was twenty-one I got married. My wife already lived here in the States. She worked in the fields, picking lemons and oranges and grapefruit. I knew her from the church. We were friends, and I asked her to be my girlfriend something like a hundred times in three months. She told me, "No, I already have a boyfriend." I kept

---

[5] Los Algodones, which means "cotton plants" in Spanish, is a Mexican border town in the state of Baja California with about 5,000 people. It is less than ten miles from Yuma, Arizona, a city of more than 90,000 that is a major lettuce and vegetable producing region. Mecca, California, is a community of less than 10,000 on the north shore of the Salton Sea in southern California's Coachella Valley.

[6] Jose might be talking about Lindane, a commonly used pesticide before 1980. The EPA proposed a ban of most uses of Lindane in 1980 under the Carter Administration, though that proposal was later relaxed to a ban on only certain uses. It was finally banned again for most uses by 2007. Lindane exposure is known to cause health effects such as nervous system disorders, and it is also believed to be a carcinogen. Lindane is also harmful to wildlife and categorized in the United States as a persistent organic pollutant.

insisting, insisting, insisting until she became my girlfriend. What attracted me to her was that she rejected me! That's the truth.

I DIDN'T KNOW WHAT CHEMICALS
I WAS SPRAYING

In 1978 I started working at a company called HMS. I've now worked there for thirty-nine years. At first I began by weeding. Then they had me work as an irrigator. Later, I started to add fertilizer, insecticides, and pesticides to the irrigation water.

I began working with a pesticide called Nemacur in 1986.[7] I injected it into the water and used it on the grapevines every year after the harvest was finished. The Nemacur would kill the worms that cause vines to get infected.[8] Apparently, the owner of the company didn't know that I was working with Nemacur. The supervisor I was working for told me to do it, and I assumed the owner agreed.[9]

When I handled Nemacur, the supervisors gave me overalls, plastic boots, gloves, and one of those masks with a filter. They gave me protection, but what they didn't tell me was that I was doing this illegally, since I wasn't trained or licensed to use the chemical. And

[7] The pesticide Nemacur belongs to the organophosphate family, a class of pesticides commonly used in agriculture. Organophosphates are neurotoxins, and when exposed to high doses, victims can die because they are unable to breathe. Each pesticide has a "Material Safety Data Sheet" that lists the dangers and precautions that must be taken when handling the chemical. Nemacur's data sheet describes it as "very dangerous—poisonous if absorbed by skin contact, inhaled, or swallowed."

[8] Various species of nematodes are common pests in California vineyards. Some species of nematodes are vectors for the fanleaf virus, an infection that lowers grape crop yields.

[9] A significant number of California farmworkers are not employed directly by a grower. Rather, they are hired, organized into work crews, and paid through farm labor contractors, who manage most labor transactions for the grower. This middleman management system has led to widespread abuse. For more information on farm labor contractors, see the Glossary, page 284.

they never told me that the chemical was dangerous. I assumed it was hazardous because of all the special gear, but I didn't know the risks, or that it could really hurt me.

One year, the owner came and started talking about how the labor contractor I worked for didn't use Nemacur. He said that they had another person that was trained to do it—he had a license to do it. And I stopped him and told him that I had been applying Nemacur for three years.

He told me, "No, that's not possible."

I told him, "Yes, every time that the grapes were harvested, I used it afterwards." After I talked to the owner, the supervisors never had me work with Nemacur again. It's been a few years now that Nemacur has been prohibited.[10] It's not used anymore. The year I stopped using it, a guy from another company was handling it and he got sick and they sent him to the hospital. I don't know what happened to him.

I never got sick from Nemacur, but in 1990 I did get sick from another chemical. HMS had planted a small orchard of grapefruit. One day my supervisor told me to move the tractor to the orchard and that we were going to spray the trees. They arrived with bags full of powder, and I emptied them by myself. The supervisor gave me a sprayer. I brought the sprayer to the tractor and began to spray the trees, steering the tractor with one hand and spraying with the other. But driving and spraying was awkward for me, and the pesticide that I was spraying leaked onto my hand, soaking it. At that time, they still didn't give us gloves or boots. They didn't give us any kind of protection. I told the supervisor and he said, "Don't worry, there's nothing wrong." So I continued. In the afternoon, when I got home, I began to feel dizzy. I told my wife, "You know what,

---

[10] The Environmental Protection Agency banned the production of Nemacur in 2007. In October 2011, the EPA ordered that any existing stock of Nemacur had to be used by 2014.

take me to the hospital. I don't know what's wrong with me. I feel really bad."

I arrived at the hospital very anxious, and I had a bad headache. The nurse told me maybe it was some kind of chemical that was affecting me. After I told her what had happened they put me in the emergency room. A doctor came and asked me what chemical I had sprayed. I didn't know. He said, "You have symptoms of poisoning."[11] After my illness was reported, safety inspectors called the farm and asked what I'd been exposed to. Nobody could answer, not even the supervisor. But you know what? When the inspector went to the company's shop the next morning, he didn't find anything. The bags that had been there weren't there anymore.

I was in the hospital for five days. I had an IV, and was feeling a little better after the second day. I never found out what chemical I'd been exposed to. But from then on, the company never had me spray pesticides from a tractor into the air. I'd only mix pesticides into the crops' water supply.

All of this happened when Cesar Chavez was working to prohibit the pesticides. But at the time it still wasn't law that workers had the right to protection from pesticides.[12] Later, little by little, when Chavez enforced it, a few growers began to give us gloves, boots, overalls, masks. Before that, they didn't give any of those things to us, even when they made us spray chemicals. From about '78 until '95, nothing, except for when I sprayed Nemacur. I didn't know what chemicals I was spraying, either.

---

[11] The Environmental Protection Agency estimates that as many as 20,000 farmworkers are poisoned by pesticides in the United States each year, though the actual number is likely much higher. For more on California farmworkers and pesticide exposure, see Appendix III, page 296–300.

[12] Cesar Chavez was a farmworker leader who, along with Dolores Huerta and Gilbert Padilla, founded what became the United Farm Workers in 1962. At its peak, the union represented tens of thousands of workers. During the 1980s, Chavez led campaigns to raise awareness about the dangers pesticides posed to both workers and consumers. For more information, see Appendix I, page 278–80.

I have protections because of the union. My company is the only company around that has a union. The other people who're working in the fields don't have the protections I have. And they are doing the same things that I was doing years ago. They are forced to do them. Why? They do what they are told to do so that they won't lose their jobs.

WHAT THEY CALLED "SALTY WATER"

When I leave my work for the day, I pass a canal. This canal has what they call "salty water." When I'm irrigating, the water goes below ground through a pipe and joins a larger drainage pipe that empties into the canal. So this water in the canal is contaminated water, because whatever I spray or other workers in the area spray—insecticides, fertilizer—it goes into this water that passes into the fields and then into the drainage pipe.

I've seen many farmworkers washing themselves in the canal, bathing themselves in their underwear, washing their clothes. And besides the dangers of the pollutants, I've heard of cases where people passing by called the police on these poor people, because they were in their underwear!

Many people working in the fields have come from far away for the work and don't have a home or place to wash themselves.[13] Everyone who works in the grapes that doesn't have a place to go washes in the canal. This happens all the time!

There was a family that came from Mexicali, a father and his two sons. We met working in the fields, in an orange orchard. We spoke, and the man asked me, "Can I stay out here in the orchard? Will there be any problem?" He had nowhere else to go. I said, "No, there

---

[13] Each summer, thousands of migrant farmworkers arrive in the Coachella Valley to harvest grapes and other fruits and vegetables. Without enough available housing units to handle the surge, many are homeless, living out of their vehicles or sleeping on flattened cardboard boxes in parking lots.

shouldn't be a problem as long as you don't make any problems." He came with a pickup, and he slept there in the camper and cooked his food outside. He and his sons came everyday to the canal to wash themselves. One day the man started to itch badly. He got sick and developed a rash. The bosses sent him to a hospital in San Diego, and in San Diego, the man died. His body was completely covered in blisters and sores. I know this because his sons came back and told me what had happened. And they never knew what chemical it was that affected him.

I HAD THIRTY DAYS TO MOVE

Unlike some of the people that have to bathe in the canal, I've lived with my family on property away from the fields for more than thirty years now. In 1985, I lived in a tiny house on a farm with my wife and children. At that time, I had three kids. The rent was $500 including electricity and water, so I looked for something more economical. I bought a trailer for $5,000 and parked it at a trailer park called Don Juan in Thermal. It was a small trailer, 60 feet long by 12 feet. We paid $250 a month plus the electricity. We didn't have to pay for water.

I bought a doublewide trailer in 1994. By then the inspectors had arrived. They wanted me to put a railing on the steps so you wouldn't fall. We put it in. We put the skirt around the trailers. When I moved into the trailer park, the electricity from the trailer was connected directly to the cable. They said that we needed to buy a circuit breaker, so we bought a circuit breaker.

This went on for a couple of years. All this time the inspectors were asking, asking, asking for more fixes. Finally, in September 1997, when there was nothing more we could possibly change, they declared that the whole trailer park we were living in was illegal and that it had to close. I arrived home from work and there was a note in Spanish on the door saying that I had thirty days to move my trailer.

So I went to look for another trailer park. There were two other trailer parks in the area, but there the inspectors had already done the same thing: people had to take their trailers out because the park was illegal. There was a woman who lived at one of the other parks, Bertha, who worked in the Catholic Church. She told us, "Why don't we form a committee to protest, so they can't make us leave?" She said the bishop would help, and he did. He called a meeting and there were about twenty agencies that came to try and help. And the person who was able to help the most was a lawyer from California Rural Legal Assistance named David Saldivar.[14]

We filed a lawsuit for discrimination—it was discrimination because they were only shutting down trailers owned by Latinos. There was an Indio trailer park owned by an American that had a sewage pipe that ran out into the streets.[15] There were other trailer parks that were worse than ours. But we believed that since those were owned by Americans, the inspectors didn't shut them down.

Shortly after learning about the threatened mobile-park shutdowns from Jose and other residents, California Rural Legal Assistance filed thirty housing discrimination complaints with the Department of Housing and Urban Development (HUD). The complaints accused Riverside County of applying code enforcement regulations in a discriminatory manner, focusing their efforts disproportionately on Latinos. In 2000, HUD approved a landmark settlement between the residents and Riverside County. In the settlement, Riverside County agreed to spend $21 million to build new mobile-home parks, replace aging mobile homes with newer models, construct additional low-income housing, and create the Farmworker Service Center in downtown Mecca. In

---

[14] California Rural Legal Assistance is a fifty-year-old nonprofit that provides free legal services to rural poor throughout the state. Its advocacy work focuses on housing, labor, education, health, and leadership development. For more information, see Appendix IV, page 304.

[15] Indio is a city of 75,000 in California, about twenty miles east of Palm Springs. The word means "Indian" in Spanish.

the fall of 2015, the county met one of their final commitments: the creation of a $1.2 million Mecca Comfort Station. The Station is free of charge and includes restrooms, showers, and laundry facilities. Some 200 farmworkers use it each day during peak season.

One of the things that I put in the CRLA lawsuit was to make sure they give farmworkers washing machines and bathrooms and showers. We won the lawsuit, but they just put a small trailer with showers outside of Mecca, a mile and a half away. People couldn't go, because it was so far away. Some farmworkers could only reach the showers by foot, so it made no sense to have people walk a mile and a half from town in the hot sun for a cool shower. So we returned to sue again to make sure they put it where it is now, which is right in Mecca, next to the highway.

Last October, we were invited to celebrate its opening. It felt wonderful to see it—it's a great accomplishment. People didn't have a place to wash themselves or their clothes. Now they do. So you see a lot of things that are wrong, but little by little we are moving forward.

MARIA AYALA ARROYO, 46
PEDRO AYALA HERNANDEZ, 55
GUADALUPE AYALA ARROYO, 21

OCCUPATION: *Farmworkers—table grapes*
INTERVIEWED IN: *Coachella, Riverside County*
AGRICULTURAL REGION: *Coachella and Central Valleys*

Farmwork is often a family affair. Parents bring their children to labor alongside them in the fields. Workers learn about a job opening and tell their relatives, the word spreading quickly from uncle to aunt to cousin. If a crew sticks together long enough, it may find that most members are related to each other in one way or another.

Such is the case for the crew of the Arroyo-Hernandez family. Maria and Pedro came to the United States in 1994, ten days after getting married in Mexico. Their plan was to stay for a couple of years, save money, and return to Mexico to open a business. Then they had their first child, Guadalupe, and those plans changed. For more than two decades, they have traveled across the Coachella and Central valleys with a grape harvesting crew filled with siblings and cousins. When Guadalupe turned sixteen, she joined them in the fields, adding another family member.

Guadalupe is now completing her senior year of college at Cal State Long Beach; her parents continue to follow the grape harvest. Over several conversations, the family talks about the daily challenges of being a migrant farmworker family, the dramatically different opportunities presented to the younger generation, and how, no matter how much schooling one may have, a day in the fields will always be an important educational experience.

OH WELL, EVERYTHING CHANGES

Maria

I'm from Zinapécuaro, Michoacán, a town about half an hour from Morelia.[1] I was born in 1970. When I was young it was all very beautiful. I remember feeling free. We lived in a big adobe house, but it was really old. One day it rained very hard and some of the walls collapsed. My dad had already started to build rooms with partitioned walls, so we just all lived in the space that was walled off from the collapsed part of the house. Oh well, everything changes. Everything comes to an end.

My mom was a warrior, a great fighter. She fought to make ends meet, to take care of us kids. She'd wake me up to go to the mill to bring back corn dough. Then we'd start making tortillas. She sold them very early in the morning, at 5 or 6 a.m. When I was older and needed to help out, she went to my middle school and talked to the teachers, so that I could study in the afternoon and help her in the mornings.

When I finished middle school I studied for two years to become a commercial secretary. But my parents were always afraid to let us kids leave the neighborhood, so I found a job at a hardware store. And that's where a friend of mine introduced me to Pedro, and we began to talk.

---

[1] Zinapécuaro de Figueroa is a city of 45,000 people in the state of Michoacán, on the central west coast of Mexico. Morelia, the capital of Michoacán, has a population of 750,000.

Pedro

I was born in 1961 and grew up in a small ranch with twenty houses, maybe more. I was nine years old when I started to work, helping my dad look after the cows. During the rainy season we planted corn and beans on cooperative land owned by the community. During the dry season we made salt on land that my parents owned. We used that salt to make cheese, so it wouldn't go bad or get worms.

There's a lot of business that goes on in Maria's hometown, but you have to have your own transportation to get there. People rode horses, donkeys, all that. Or you just walked. To go see her I had to cross a hill, and it took hours on foot. Once I stayed for a dance that was over at midnight. I came down the hill at 4 a.m., got home, got under the covers, and my dad told me, "Get up, it's time to milk the cows."

Back in those days, the ranch had many hot springs with boiling water. Hot pools sprouted from those springs, and if an animal fell into one of the big hot springs it would get cooked. Sometimes we even cooked corn in the hot springs. You didn't need any firewood. When I was sixteen, my eight-year-old brother fell into a hot spring when he was trying to cross it using a mesquite bush. After he fell, they say that he still went to lock the cows in. It wasn't until he got home, dripping from head to toe, that my mom asked him what had happened. "I fell," he said. They tore his pants off and the skin came off as well.

YOU'RE GOING TO JUMP THAT FENCE

Pedro

We got married on January 8, 1994. I was already thinking of coming north. I told Maria, "We're going to get married, and then we'll figure out how you can come with me."

I first came to the United States when I was nineteen. My sister got married, moved here, and then she helped me come. So by the time there was amnesty, I'd been here long enough to get my papers.[2]

Ten days after we got married, we crossed the border. Since I had my documents I didn't cross with her. The plan was for me to wait back in Mexicali, in case she was caught and had to return.[3] And I also wanted to make sure everything was OK—that the coyotes picked her up where they said they would pick her up.

Maria

We found a coyote in Mexicali. He said that I had to wear dark clothes to be less visible in the dark and he gave me directions for how to get across. "You're going to jump that fence," he said, "then run and get under that palm tree and don't come out until I tell you to." And thank God, I did jump and ran and hid under the palm tree. About an hour later he suddenly said, "Now come out fast!" But he wanted me to roll over in the dirt, and I was wearing a nice black sweater. I thought, *How can I get my sweater all dirty?* I didn't listen to him. I just came out and ran. So the coyote scolded me because I hadn't done what he asked.

A bit further ahead there was a line of taxis. The coyote asked me to tell a taxi driver to take me to a particular swap meet. He said, "When you get out of the taxi you'll see a small bench. You'll sit there and you won't move. A blue pickup truck will pick you up."

When I got to the swap meet, the bench was full of men. I thought, *I can't sit there.* A woman was nearby, selling a lot of plants—

---

[2] The Immigration Reform and Control Act, referred to as "amnesty," was passed in 1986 and provided permanent legal residence to eligible migrants, including those who could prove that they'd worked in agriculture in the United States during a certain time period. For more information, see the Glossary, page 286–7.

[3] Mexicali is a city of over 800,000 in the Mexican state of Baja, California. The Calexico-Mexicali metropolitan area is a major border crossing between the state of Baja in Mexico and eastern California in the United States.

I figured it would be a good idea to stay close to her. I started helping her take out the plants to show people, just to blend in. I remember she was telling customers the difference between "the patent rose bush and the non-patent rose bush." Apparently the patent rose bush has an aroma, and the non-patent rose bush has no aroma.

That's when my husband arrived. I was very happy when I saw him. He said, "Don't come near me, because they'll see us together. I only came to see who's going to pick you up." The coyotes didn't know he was watching and he didn't want to get in trouble. Fifteen minutes later, a man arrived. He was drunk, his breath smelled of alcohol, and he couldn't walk straight. He was another coyote. He picked me up and took me to a house with more people. We stayed there for a little while and then they drove us to Thermal, where Pedro's sister paid and picked me up.[4] He'd stayed in Mexicali in case I was sent back, and when we got home, she called to let him know I was there.

Pedro

I was waiting at a hotel in Mexicali. That's when I got the phone call and learned my wife had made it. In these situations you are always afraid, but you will try anything to be together. It was late when she called, so I went to bed and left for the United States the next morning.

THOSE THIRTY DAYS WERE VERY LONG

Maria

We lived in apartments owned by the government in Coachella, built for people who work in the fields.[5] Pedro had a lot of relatives—too

---

[4] Thermal is an unincorporated community of 3,000 residents in Riverside County, located in the eastern part of the Coachella Valley.

[5] Coachella is a city of 40,000 people in Riverside County, about thirty miles east of Palm Springs. The family lived in a cinder-block apartment complex for

many relatives. They'd ask him, "Is she going to work?" And he would say, "No, she isn't." Back then you heard a lot about *la migra* going into the fields, doing raids, setting up checkpoints on the highway.[6] So he was afraid.

About fifteen days after we arrived, the work in the grape fields started. Then another fifteen days went by.

Those thirty days were very long. I was in the house and I'd just keep staring at the clock. It would be 3 o'clock, then 4. Since we didn't have a car, Pedro would walk to the post office. "Take me with you," I asked. He said, "I can't take you with me in case *la migra* comes." His sisters began to notice that I was getting depressed, because I was used to working. That's when they told him to take me to work. I wish he hadn't, because now he won't let me stay home.

From March to July we worked in the grape fields in Coachella. It was all so new to me. I remember the man telling me to "hurry up, hurry up." I couldn't pick them fast enough. My back and hands ached. Even at night, when I got home and closed my eyes, I'd see grape bunches that I still had to pick.

In July we went to Edison, near Bakersfield, to live in a labor camp that had trailers.[7] The trailers were completely empty, except for a stove. Well, sometimes they had a fridge. Other times we'd have to rent one. We slept on the floor and used whatever we could find as a table.

We were at the labor camp from July until October 1994. I was pregnant with Guadalupe—we call her Lupita. At the labor camp

---

farmworkers called the Fred Young Labor Camp—known by locals as "el campo." Today, the 253-units are managed by the Coachella Valley Housing Coalition and are being renovated.

[6] *La migra* is short for an Immigration agent. For more information, see the Glossary, page 287.

[7] Edison is an unincorporated community in Kern County, 7.5 miles southeast of Bakersfield. Bakersfield is a city of 375,000 located at the southern end of the Central Valley, about 110 miles south of Fresno.

we were served eggs every morning, and every morning I was like, "Agghhhh." I was pregnant and I didn't want any. I threw up all the time. And the woman that cooked for everyone *always* cooked eggs for breakfast. The only thing I was able to eat were the grapefruits my husband got for me.

I WANTED TO DO SOCCER AND ACT

Guadalupe

I was born in Indio in 1994.[8] We lived in an apartment complex with over a hundred apartments. Mostly farmworkers lived there. It was a two-bedroom with a small living room, a small kitchen. My cousins lived there, and we're about the same age, so we'd play with Barbies and normal girl stuff. Ride bikes. Go to the park.

In the summer we lived in a labor camp in Edison. The cook lady at the camp was also my babysitter. She had a bell that she used to ring. One of my first memories at the camp was to walk around every trailer and ring the bell to let people know that food was ready. Everybody in the trailers worked for Giumarra.[9] The camp was right in front of the Giumarra office, surrounded by vineyards. There was a trailer full of restrooms, and another trailer full of showers. And then there was a bigger trailer where they set up the kitchen, and that's where they had benches where we would sit and eat.

Our trailer was basically the size of a college dorm room. When I wasn't helping the cook she would send me back to her trailer and I would watch TV or play with my dolls, something like that. When I was eight or nine, my parents decided we couldn't live there anymore, that we had to find something better.

---

[8] Indio, which means "Indian" in Spanish, is a city of 75,000 in Riverside County just north of Coachella.

[9] Giumarra Vineyards in one of the largest table grape companies in California.

Maria

One of my husband's nieces took care of her, but there was nothing for the kids to do at the camp. They could only go out to play in the dirt, throw water at each other. There were no playgrounds in the camp, nothing. We lived for about six years in that labor camp, and Lupita's sister Marlene was born. Then we learned that apartments existed in Arvin.[10] Those apartments have beds. They have things that make living in them possible. Then Arvin's apartments were demolished because they were too old—they were made of decaying wood. So the growers sent us to the labor camp in Shafter. Then my other daughter Jasmine was born. We lived there for three years before going back to Arvin.[11] That's where Lupita began going to school.

Guadalupe

I went to schools in Indio, Shafter, and Bakersfield. They were completely different school systems, so I'd fall behind, because they were doing things that I didn't know how to do, because I hadn't learned them.

When I went into middle school, I lost the electives I had chosen. I wanted to do soccer and art. I wanted to be part of the Associate Student Body program. The school didn't allow me to because I was supposed to be there at the beginning of the year. When I came back, they gave me a new schedule and it was nothing like what my schedule looked like before. I was really upset.

---

[10] Arvin is a city of about 20,000 in Kern County, about 15 miles southeast of Bakersfield.

[11] In Arvin, they lived at the Arvin Farm Labor Center, an 88-unit development for migrant farmworkers, which is open from May to October. The original camp was built in the 1930s and was visited numerous times by John Steinbeck while he did research for what became *The Grapes of Wrath*. He fictionalized the camp as "Weedpatch" in the novel.

I talked to my parents about it. It took a little bit of convincing, because they didn't know how it would work, because we had never been apart from each other. But eventually they gave in. They thought it was the best for me, too, for my education.

Maria

Switching schools made life complicated. The credits can't be transferred, and they lose everything and have to start from scratch, with the basic classes. It's a huge problem. So one year, Lupita would go back early to Coachella with my sister, and then one year with me, and so on. My husband's brother used to say, "I'll be happy if my daughters finish high school." And Lupita would say, "No mami, I want to keep studying." She's always wanted to go to college.

Guadalupe

Ever since I can remember, both of my parents would always tell me, "You have to go to school so you can work in better conditions than what we're working in." So I feel like it's something that they inculcated in me. That there was no way out but going to school.

Maria

From the time she was in kindergarten, I went to the meetings of the migrant program, all the time.[12] They told us about the help that we could get, the financial aid. The migrant program has helped me to be more awake. Because you're basically asleep, you don't know anything, and they kind of wake you up and tell you about these steps that you have to follow.

---

[12] The Migrant Education Program is a federally funded program that provides educational and support services for children of migrant farmworkers.

YOU THINK YOU'RE READY TO WORK?

Guadalupe

We were living in the Arvin camp when I started to work. I was fifteen and saw that most of the cousins that I hung out with, their parents had already taken them to work. They'd come home and tell me stories of how they'd hide from the supervisor, or how they threw grapes at each other. Just funny stories, 'cause most of the crew was family. So I'd hear these stories, and I'd be like, "Oh Mom, take me! I wanna go too!" They didn't wanna take me. They were really hesitant. But I kept bugging and bugging them. They were like, "All right, you think you're ready to work?"

On the first day, my parents tried to teach me how to pick. But I wanted to be a packer, because my cousins were all packers and I wanted to be close to them so we could talk during work. I got my dad mad, 'cause I kept telling him, "I don't know how to do this; I wanna pack!" Eventually my mom gave in. She took me to the table where you pack and taught me. There were a lot of family members and they were like, "Ohhh, watch out for the newbie."

My parents were both picking, and I was packing, and I came out to be really good at packing. When I'd finish packing I'd scream, "Grape!" And everyone would be laughing 'cause they're like, "Oh look—she's a newbie and she's really good."

That day, we sat down to have lunch in the field, and I was so surprised—the workers didn't have any tables, or anywhere to sit. They just had to sit in the shade near the grape vines on the ground and eat. I think that was one of the biggest "wow" moments that I had that day, when I saw my parents having lunch on the ground.

It was probably around two in the afternoon when my legs started getting really tired. And since I had finished packing the grapes that I had, I was like, *I'm just gonna take a seat.* My cousin was the mayordomo. He saw me and he's like, "You know you're not supposed to do that. You can't sit down on the job." I was kinda scared, 'cause I was tired at that point. I just wanted to sit down—it was hot.

That first day was super life-changing, eye-opening for me. Sometimes when I used to stay home I wouldn't clean the house, and my mom would get really mad at me and be like, "Why haven't you cleaned?" And I'd make an excuse, because I was watching TV or something. On that first day, as soon as we got home, I made sure my sister cleaned. I knew how tired my parents were from working 'cause I had to go through it myself. It made me value my parents a lot more. I had no idea how hard my parents' work was. I mean, I knew it was hot, but that was about it.

Pedro

How could I forget that first day? We worked for a little bit, and then I sat down with her and told her, "You see, this is the work." And she liked the work. Like us, she's a hard worker. We don't wait around to see if other people want to work—we're going to do the work that's asked of us.

WE WERE ALWAYS NUMBER ONE

Guadalupe

I've worked six summers in the grapes. Even after I started college, I still came back to work each summer. My parents would keep most of the money I made—they'd give me a $100 allowance every week. And they'd tell me that I had to purchase my own uniform, my own school supplies, and everything with that money.

When I arrive in the fields, the first thing I do as a packer is to wipe down the table and grab a scale. My parents take the wheelbarrow along with five trays, and go inside the grapevine and start picking the grapes while I grab the packing materials. We pack different types of boxes. Sometimes we need bubble wrap, sometimes we need lids. It depends on what type of box we're packing on that day.

After we pick all five trays, my dad sets the trays on the floor and puts two trays on the table and I start packing. My dad takes more trays inside the vines, so he and my mom can continue picking. If I'm done packing before he brings the next wheelbarrow full of grapes, I go inside and help them pick. Just back and forth.

A box is supposed to weigh about twenty-two pounds. You knew if you were good or not based on how many boxes you packed in a day. Like, "Oh, we made 100 boxes?" It depended a lot on the grape. If the grape was really good, we would make almost 200 boxes a day. When they were OK, we would make 150, 120. When the grape was semi-OK, 70. There was a day when the grape was really, really bad, it was *podrida*—rotten, nasty—and we made like 20 boxes that day. That day was horrible.

They divide you into groups of two or three, and they give you a number—that's how they'd keep count of the boxes. We were always number one. We like to be on top. My parents are known for being some of the top workers in the crew, so they thought that with me starting with them, I was gonna slow them down. But they were really happy because all three of us came out on top, even on my first day.

There was this lady called a *chequeadora*, the checker. Every time the truck is gonna come pick up the boxes, she'd count the boxes and write them down on her notebook. And most of the time I would write them down too, 'cause my mom would tell me to. She said that sometimes they'd miscount them, steal boxes, so she'd make sure that I wrote them down.[13]

Honestly, I think like 75 percent of the crew was family. Aunts,

---

[13] Many grape harvesters are often paid an hourly wage plus a bonus for each box of grapes they pack. Other workers—especially in lettuce and berry crews—can be paid piece-rate, according to how much they harvest. In both cases, when companies undercount the amount harvested, it is a form of wage theft.

uncles, cousins, second cousins. Somehow we were all related—or if they weren't related to me, they're from the same place in Mexico where my dad's from. Or they're related to my uncle, because my uncle's wife is related to them. Sometimes I find out some people I've worked with aren't really family, but I've been calling them my uncles and aunts all my life.

When we were packing, we'd always be talking about something. I don't know if you've ever seen a porta potty, but outside it has a lock so that when they're transporting them the doors won't open. When my cousins would go in there, we'd like lock them in there for five minutes after they were done, just 'cause we were jerks, and we thought it was funny. We'd get in trouble a lot. My cousin, the foreman, would always go tell my mom, "Tell them that they can't be doing that."

I FEEL LIKE I HAD HELP EVERYWHERE

Guadalupe

I really enjoyed high school. I was involved in so many things. I went to Indio High School and I was the associate student body vice president all four years. I played soccer, I was a mentor in Big Brothers Big Sisters, and part of a forum called Young Women Leaders.

I feel like I had help everywhere. In the Boys and Girls Club they had workshops on financial aid, they had workshops on when the deadlines were for University of California and Cal State schools. I was part of the Migrant Program and they offered free tutoring when we came back from Bakersfield and were falling behind. I was also part of Upward Bound at College of the Desert. They focused on sending us to college.

We visited UC Berkeley, Stanford, Cal State Sacramento, and Fresno. And then we came to Long Beach. That's where I found out about the CAMP program, and that it was offered only in Long

Beach and Cal State San Marcos.[14] I thought, *Hey, there's the beach, it's two hours' away—not too close to home, not too far away.* It was offering the most money, but honestly I feel like the CAMP program was the thing that made my decision clear. Because I was going to a whole new city, a whole new place, and I wasn't sure what I was gonna be doing. But at least I'd have people with similar backgrounds that I'd be able to hang around with.

Maria

In 2013, we drove her to the university for orientation. My husband can't read—that was our first fear. How were we going to drive along these highways when he didn't have any idea what the signs said? But by then, because of the migrant program, they'd already taken her to visit the university. And she is very intelligent, thank God, so she learned the exits and entrances really fast.

I remember that day well. We were ready to go and she asked her dad to give her the keys to the truck. He looked at her as if saying, *Are you crazy or what?* "Give them to me," she said again. She already had a license. And he had to agree. "You'll get angry if I tell you to take this road, go here, take this exit," she said. "So I'm going to drive." And she took the car and drove all the way there.

Guadalupe

The CAMP Program offered an orientation meeting a few days before they dropped us off at the dorms. At the orientation, my mom and my dad were asking questions like, "Do they have a curfew? Do they not let the students out after a certain time?" And they were like, "No, your kids are free."

My parents were so worried that I didn't have a curfew, that there

---

[14] The College Assistance Migrant Program (CAMP) is a federal program funded by the U.S. Department of Education that provides social and academic support services to students from farmworker families during their first year of college.

was nobody watching me. They would always tell me to not go out by myself, stuff like that. It was interesting to see them so worried. They would call me every single day. Every night. They would ask, "Are you in bed? Are you sure you're in bed?"

Maria

When she left for college, we were afraid. First, because she had never been to the city. How was she going to survive, right? She would be there all by herself. I mean, you have a lot of fears, a lot of things you feel when she doesn't come home to sleep. It was very hard for us to get over it. We'd say, "We are going to bed now, but what about her?"

Pedro

Maria's *still* not over it, because she doesn't go to sleep when she's waiting for Lupita to come home.

THEY HAD WHAT THEY CALLED QUESADILLAS

Guadalupe

I was kind of upset that my parents weren't able to actually drop me off when we had to move into the dorms. They were working and they had already taken a day off when we came to the CAMP Orientation, so they couldn't ask for another day.

But I was excited. I was gonna live so close to a beach, and in a new city. And I was excited because I knew my roommate. We'd been friends in high school.

I hated the food at the dorms. That was the biggest culture shock that I had. I was used to my mom's homemade tortillas and homemade salsas. They had what they called quesadillas, and they had yellow cheese! The tortillas were hard; they were gross. When my mom made quesadillas, they were with mozzarella cheese and homemade tortillas. The school had enchiladas and they didn't taste like enchiladas.

In the morning, I would either have waffles or cereal. I ate French fries most of the time. They also had Chinese food, Vietnamese food, and I'd never tried that. My mom only cooked Mexican food. I wanted my mom's food. We bought a mini fridge so I could store stuff and heat it up in the microwave, because I was losing so much weight.

I got really homesick my first semester at college. I wanted to get a car so I could visit my family, but I needed money. During winter break I went home to Coachella and worked in the strawberry fields. I remember going in the first day and thinking, *Oh, this isn't so bad.* We started at 5:30 a.m. and got out at 4 p.m. The next day I couldn't get myself up. I was so sore from being on my knees the entire time. Strawberries are really horrible. Grapes seemed like a piece of cake compared with picking strawberries.

But I went back to work. I wanted to get a car, so I needed money. I had to continue working no matter how sore I was or how bad I wanted to stay in bed. We made nine dollars an hour, or eight something. And I did get a car.

Pedro

I didn't like to see her working in the strawberries, down on her knees. It's the kind of work where you are stooped over all day, really fast work. I've picked all kinds of fruits, and it's one of the hardest to pick.

Maria

It was January, very cold. When we got to the fields of strawberries they were white, covered in ice. It was really sad to see her, sleeping warmly in the bed, and have to wake her up and see her get into cold car, still covered in a blanket. But she said, "I need money," and so she did it.

That first year was very difficult for her. During the weekends she came home and I'd fill a Tupperware with rice, beans, and chicken— food for the week. But then she told us that she had a food plan and she had to use the money or she would lose it. Little by little she realized that she had to eat more of the food that they offered. Thank God she has managed to survive.

Guadalupe

The CAMP program made me feel welcome. There's a specific build- ing on campus, the CAMP building. When you walk in to the first floor, there's only CAMP people. They have a lounge for the students, a computer place, so most of the time you'll find a lot of CAMP students studying there, waiting for their next class to start, or just chilling there 'cause they want to be there. I've met people from Bakersfield, Wasco, Salinas. One of my really good friends is from Watsonville. They come from all over the place, and most of them have worked in the fields, so it's nice hearing their stories. We call each other the CAMP *familia*.

THINK ABOUT THE FUTURE

Guadalupe

This has been the first year that I haven't gone to work with my parents during the summer. I was employed at the university and they offered me a full-time position over the summer. I started working in October in the Foundation Research Building, receiving donations for the university and inputting them into a database.

I kinda have to think about the future now, since this is my fourth year. I might be walking in graduation this spring, or I might not be walking—it depends on if I'm allowed to go over the limit on my units, 'cause I'm double majoring in psychology and human development.

I know that I don't wanna stay here in Long Beach. I wanna go back home. I have three siblings now—two teenage sisters and a younger brother, who is six.

My sisters are really competitive towards me. Both of them say that they're gonna go to a better university than me, so I encourage them. They say, "Oh yeah, I'm gonna go to Stanford, I'm gonna go here." And I'm like, "OK, you do that." My sister's gonna be a senior this year, and she was telling me about the number of AP classes she was taking, and the AP test that she just took. And she's like, "Ha I got a better score than you on AP History." My other sister is a freshman. She's competing with the senior, and they both compete with me.

Maria

I don't have hopes that anything will change, like that she'll graduate and then help us. No, because her education is for her. She's become an accomplished person, someone who has overcome a lot. And her sisters will see her, that she's not following a path to the fields but doing something else.

Pedro

For me, it was important that she knew what work in the fields was like. More than anything, I advised her to study and that if she kept studying, she'd have a better life than we had. "We're getting older, we're going up to heaven someday," I told her. "But if you study, you're going to have a great future." And up to this very day, that's what she's done. And she's studied so much! We'll see what happens.

Guadalupe

I'd like to work somewhere where I can help students like me. There were various groups that helped me; I'd like to give back. To help students like me reach their goals of going to a four-year university. I'm not sure exactly where I would be able to do that, but I know I want to go back home and do something similar to that. My parents are excited that I want to come back to the valley. We're desert rats. We hate the desert but we still go back.

ISMAEL MORENO

AGE: *17*

OCCUPATION: *High school student, part-time farmworker*
BORN IN: *Visalia, Tulare County*
INTERVIEWED IN: *Dinuba, Tulare County*
AGRICULTURAL REGION: *San Joaquin Valley*

According to the National Institute for Occupational Safety and Health, a division of the Centers for Disease Control and Prevention, every day nearly 170 farmworkers are injured on the job seriously enough to miss at least one day of work. In 2014, the industry category that includes farmworkers—Agriculture, Forestry, Fishing, and Hunting—had the highest work-related fatality rate. Employees within this sector died at a rate more than seven times that of all combined industries, and nearly twice as often as miners and oil and gas extractors.

Despite such well-documented dangers, child labor standards are considerably weaker in agriculture. Youth can begin working in the fields at the age of twelve, two years earlier than in other industries. They are also allowed to perform what the government defines as "hazardous jobs" at the age of sixteen; in other industries, they must wait until they turn eighteen. (In agriculture, such jobs include handling toxic chemicals and operating earth-moving equipment.) Unsurprisingly, young farmworkers face a workplace fatality rate four times that of children in other industries.

I meet Ismael Moreno in Dinuba, a small city 30 miles southeast of Fresno, during a scorching heat wave in late July. On the short walk from my air-conditioned car to his mother's air-conditioned apartment, my face flushes and beads of sweat gather on my face and back. The temperature reached a high of 105 degrees that day—a day Ismael spent outside, picking nectarines atop a ladder. When he opens the front door to the apartment, the first thing I notice is his beaming smile. It's a smile he'll maintain for most of the afternoon. Ismael is freshly showered, and has changed into a clean pair of jeans and a purple shirt. As his twin eleven-year-old brother and sister play in a back bedroom, he sinks into the living room couch and talks about his love of soccer, the deep admiration he has for his parents, and the hardships—and pleasures—of being a teenager who spends his summers in the field.

IT'S ALL ABOUT FAMILY

My dad's really into soccer. When he was a teenager in Mexico, he almost went pro. He's from Michoacán. Morelia.[1] He played for Fútbol Club Morelia, for the youth team. But his family was poor. I remember he told me he had a pair of shoes that were ripped, you could see his toes and everything, and he had to put duct tape around them to keep playing soccer. My grandpa, my dad's dad, he was working and living here in California when my dad was in Mexico. My dad stayed in Michoacán with a man and woman who aren't related by blood, but are like a grandma and grandpa to me now. So my father was in the reserves of his team, getting ready to go pro, but my grandpa came back from the States to Morelia to get my dad and take him to California.

I know it was really hard for my dad growing up here. My grandpa lived in Orosi, so first my dad went to Orosi High for his

---

[1] Morelia is a city of 750,000 and the capital of Michoacán, on the central west coast of Mexico.

freshman year.[2] That wasn't so bad for him, since there's a lot of Hispanics at Orosi—a lot of kids spoke Spanish. But sophomore year my dad came here to Dinuba, and it was more English-speaking kids.[3] My dad would get picked on for his English, 'cause he didn't know much. Some kids would make him really feel bad. He's told me that sometimes he'd come home crying from kids making fun of him. And my grandpa had remarried. His stepmom was also really mean to him, from what I know. My dad worked in the fields, too.

But the thing I admire about my dad is that he's really hard working. Anything he sets his mind to, he's gonna do, no matter what. And he wanted to learn English really bad, so he practiced every day, and eventually he got it. And he tried to play soccer—when he was a little older he actually played with Fresno Fuego.[4]

My dad met my mom at Dinuba High. They were both really into athletics. My mom had a really rough childhood, her parents divorced, it was just really, really tough for her. My mom, actually, was a very smart girl, and she got a full ride to Fresno State. But she just didn't have the support from her parents. Her mom didn't care if she got in or not.

And then before my mom could go to college, I came along. She and my dad had to make money, and school would have been really hard. I know that's something she really wishes she could have done. She had all her classes picked out. And I know my dad didn't want to leave soccer. But when I ask him about it, he's all, "I don't regret it, because it's all about family."

Honestly I admire my mom and my dad a lot. They both went through a lot when they were kids.

---

[2] Orosi is a community of 8,000 in Tulare County.

[3] Dinuba is a municipality of 25,000 in Tulare County, 30 miles southeast of Fresno.

[4] Fresno Fuego is a development league soccer team founded in 2003.

I'VE BEEN INTO SPORTS SINCE
I WAS VERY SMALL

I was born in Visalia, but most of my life I spent here in Dinuba.[5] When I was growing up, my mom worked in a jewelry store, and my dad was a bus driver, then he became a custodian, and then a truck driver.

I've been into sports since I was very small. My dad said that at a young age—like, three—I was kicking a ball, and he supposedly saw it was something I was good at. When I was seven, we moved to Cutler, and we had a pretty big back yard. And I remember my dad bought me these little goals. We'd do drills like high knees. We'd work on my passes with my left and right foot. Stuff like that.

Honestly I was just really proud of the effort my parents would put into me. I got into club soccer, which means I was playing at a high level. At one point our team was first in California and second in the nation when I was thirteen, fourteen. We'd travel all around, down to Santa Cruz, San Jose, Santa Barbara.

Cutler is just a little town, and while we were living there I still came to school over here in Dinuba. Just sort of 'cause of the reputation of the Cutler schools. Some of the kids around there were bad influences. A lot of gang-related stuff. I was always active in sports and kept myself out of that. But walking down the street I'd see taggings on the wall, stuff like that.

So my freshman year, I started at Dinuba High School, where my parents went, and we moved back to Dinuba. I quit club soccer my freshman year, because I was getting into high school sports. I could have done club and high school sports, but with club soccer you have to pay every month to play. It was wasting my money, so I quit. But last summer, my friends on the club soccer team went to Spain for a tournament. They did good over there, real good. They

---

[5] Visalia is a city of 135,000 and the county seat of Tulare County.

placed fourth in the tournament, against teams from Italy, Croatia, Portugal.

I still play soccer for my high school, but I also got into football. With football, I'm a kicker and cornerback. Since I play soccer, I'm a good kicker. I started kicking for football my freshman year. And halfway through my sophomore year, I got moved up to varsity. Usually sophomores are only supposed to be on junior varsity, but the coaches saw how I could kick.

But around that time some family issues happened and it kind of got tough. I guess you could say my family owed some debt. My parents got separated, and we needed some money around the house. I needed to work; I needed to help.

"JUST TRY IT OUT, SEE HOW IT IS"

I remember my first time in the fields, in the fall of 2014. My mom's friend owned some vineyards. He grew grapes for raisins. One Monday before school early in my sophomore year, my mom was all like, "Just try it out, see how it is." I said OK.

After school I had football practice, and we were doing conditioning. For conditioning, you wear your pads so it adds a little weight. And then the coaches make you do up-downs. You're running in place and they blow a whistle, you go down, do a push up and get back up, you run in place—fast. They blow the whistle, you go down, get back up. Then you run 100 yards. Run 50, run back. Run 100, run back.

When I got home my mom's like, "Remember what we talked about? I want you to try it." I was like, "Yeah sure, I'll try it." So I went out to the field, even though I was already tired.

Where we worked, it was a big open dirt field, with the vineyards surrounding it. The other workers called the dirt field the *tabla*. First, the crew set up tarps. Then they took the grapes that had been picked and trimmed and put them on the tarps. There's, like, a lot of grapes, and the harvesters just leave them there in long rows.

I was given a rake. And what I had to do was get into the pile of grapes with the rake and spread them out as flat as I could, make them even. That's so they can all dry out evenly. That first day I had to do five rows, and each row was pretty long: maybe the length of a football field. So I had to go up one row then come back down the other row, trying to flatten out all the grapes.

I kept going back to the fields after practice. Once the grapes were dried a little, they'd get sticky and clump together. So then my job would be to break them apart. Once they were dried up real good and broken apart, I'd help scoop them up and we'd pack them into crates.

So that October, on weekdays I'd go to school from 8 to 3, then practice would be from 4 to 5 or 5:30, then I would work in the field from around 6 to 9. Some days I had to wake up at 6 in the morning to try and get my homework done before school. The good thing about my high school is that the teachers really understand that some kids have to work. Sometimes if you talk to them about what's going on, they'll help in different ways, like letting you get homework done in class. And then that's one less thing to worry about.

But honestly, I did raisins for just two weeks. Two weeks. I couldn't handle it, 'cause it was tiring with football and everything. I told my mom, "I wouldn't mind doing it in the summer when I'm more free." But trying to keep up with school, trying to do sports, and then trying to do that was a lot. I remember the wage was $11 an hour. Some of that money went to me, but anything I could do for the family, like gas money, or just little things like that, I tried to help out.

IT'S TOUGH, BUT AFTER A FEW DAYS YOUR BODY GETS USED TO IT

The next time I worked in the fields was the summer after my sophomore year—the summer after my job raking grapes. I started in July. This time I was working in peaches and nectarines.

I got the job through friends who were already working there. I had a lot of friends already working, but the friend that actually helped me, his name was George. He played soccer with me. I asked him about it, like, "Hey, is the orchard looking for anyone?" He's like, "Yeah, here's the mayordomo's number."[6] That's how I got into it, and so I joined George's *cuadrilla*, which is what a crew is called. The mayordomo is the boss of the cuadrilla. The thing about the cuadrilla is that everyone usually knows each other already because there's a lot of relationships already in place—the crew is made up of a lot of cousins, friends, sons, fathers, stuff like that. The mayordomo I called already had four of his own sons working in the cuadrilla, so he was understanding about young people starting out.

So I started in the orchard. Peaches and nectarines are basically the same thing, workwise, and I'd always work with the same cuadrilla. The shift was nine, ten hours. I'd start at 6 a.m. and end at like 3 or 4 p.m. We worked Monday through Saturday. Sunday's the day off.

The first day, I remember how heavy the ladders were. Just carrying one from tree to tree was hard. The boss gave me a strap with hooks on it, and the buckets have little holes. You put the hooks through the holes, and usually the bucket stays on there when you're up in the tree. The bucket hangs over your shoulder and goes down to the waist, and then you climb the ladder and start filling up your bucket. We fill the buckets three-fourths of the way. We don't fill it

---

[6] A *mayordomo* is a supervisor of a work crew. For more about mayordomos, see the Glossary, page 287.

up all the way, 'cause we have to hoist it onto the back of the tractor. It doesn't take that long, but it depends on the tree. If the tree has a lot of ripe fruit, obviously you can fill up the bucket fast. But if the tree doesn't have that much fruit, you move your ladder around, pick whatever fruit is good and go on to the next tree.

The first day, since I was the new kid, I kinda wanted to show everyone, like, *Oh, I know how to pick.* So I'd go fast. I watched the other workers, though, and they'd keep the same pace, going at their own pace all day. So they kept the same pace all day, never slowing down, but by the end of the day I was exhausted and couldn't keep up.

I also learned the first day to wear gloves, 'cause with the peaches, your hands get really rashy from the peach fuzz. It really makes your skin itchy. I noticed some people would wear sweaters even though it was hot, and at first I didn't understand that, since it was July. But I figured out it was because you need to be covered up or else your skin will get so irritated without protection. I watched what the other workers did, how they carried their ladders and stuff like that that made it easier for them, and so I started copying them.

I also learned a lot the first day from the mayordomo. He was understanding. He said, "We all start somewhere." And he showed me the right way to set up a ladder—it's different if you're right-handed or left-handed. There were all these little details. With the fruit, too. You have to pick the fruit that's just the right color and size. If not, leave it. They always tell you to look closely at the *color*. Like if it's just the right red, red-orange, that's when you know if it's ready. And if it has a little green still or a little white, the fruit's not ready.

When my dad was in high school, yeah, he worked in the fields. Once I started working, he was like, "It's gonna be tough, but after a few days your body gets used to it." And it was true—it was hard the first few days, but I got used to it.

THE HEAT IS THE REALLY HARD
PART OF THE WORK

This summer is my second summer working in peaches and nectarines. I wake up at 4:50. I need an alarm still, but I've gotten used to it already. Let's say I have the day off the next day, and I stay up until 10 or 11, thinking I'm gonna sleep in the next day. I'll still wake up at 6 or 7. My body's wired to wake up early now. On days when I work, I have to be out the door at 5:20.

A guy I work with gives me a ride to the field, which is out by Kingsburg.[7] The guy that gives me rides, we call him Chaba. His name's Jesús but we call him Chaba. And it's me and two other guys that just got out of high school, he gives us rides. We get there, we sign in, and then we get our ladders and set up. Sometimes we get there like 5:40, 5:50, and just relax and everything 'til exactly 6 a.m., and that's when we go to work.

This week was a hot one in the orchard. It gets real humid. And then below all the trees are these reflective tarps. That's so that sunlight can reach the fruit at the bottom level of the tree by reflecting off the tarps. We have those up now, and so there's extra heat being reflected up at you while you pick.

On Twitter, Instagram, social media and stuff, people have been tweeting about how hard it is for the fieldworkers right now. It's been in the hundreds. The whole week was hundreds. And the heat would start coming in as early as 9:30, 10 in the morning. When it's this hot, we work as much as we can from 6 to 8:30 in the morning, and then we get a little ten-minute break. Lucky for us, our mayordomo is really nice. But we work around other cuadrillas, and sometimes their mayordomos are really... First of all, some mayordomos don't really give breaks. Today, for example, we had a break and watched other crews keep working. I felt really bad.

---

[7] Kingsburg is a municipality of over 10,000 about 10 miles west of Dinuba.

Some of the mayordomos are mean, too. There's a worker I saw a few days ago who finished his tree and moved to another, but I guess he'd left some fruit on the tree he'd finished. The mayordomo called him back and he was all like, "Look, you idiot!" Stuff like that. *"Hombre, no puedes hacer trabajo"*—like, "What, you don't know how to work?" Another worker in the crew was getting tired of the attitude. I could tell he didn't like this mayordomo anymore. He started telling the other workers in his crew that he was leaving, that he'd found another job, and that they should all work for someone else. The mayordomo got real mad, and was like, "What are you doing! You can't tell them to leave!" The worker says, "I'm taking them with me. We have a right to leave if we want to." So the mayordomo tells them all, "Fine, leave if you want, but you're not gonna get the money that you worked for. I won't be paying you." So the guy left, but he was the only one to go. The other workers, you could tell they wanted to leave, but they needed the money.

For me at least the heat is the really hard part of the work. My mom is friends with that vineyard owner who had me rake grapes, so she knows the rules through him. And one of the laws is, if it gets to 95 or higher in the morning, then the workers shouldn't be working past 12. It's too hot already, and that's unbearable for most people to work all day in that heat. Like today, by 9:30, the heat started coming in and I was already sweating a lot. I had a long-sleeve shirt over another two shirts, and all of them were soaking wet by 9:30. My sleeves, my shoulders, everything. Soaked wet. So today we finished at like 12, 12:30.

On Tuesday, it was really hot, and with the little tarps under the trees reflecting the sun up at us, it was super hot. We were all sweating; everyone was starting to go slow. And we worked 'til like 2 p.m. that day I think. This whole week that's the latest we worked to. And towards the end, like at 1 p.m. or something, one of the men was blacking out. He was drained, you could tell. He was pale, white. And he was going super slow. He was a little older, maybe late forties, and the mayordomo told him, "Just sit down, relax already, just drink." The mayordomo is a really nice guy.

But there's mayordomos that still make their workers work 'til 4 p.m. From 6 a.m. to 4 p.m. in the heat. They're still working that long when it's over 100 degrees. Other mayordomos don't give breaks. They just won't give breaks. Our mayordomo, he gives us breaks, he's a really understanding guy. And he tells us even when we're working to take little breaks, drink water, make sure to drink water when it's so hot. But some mayordomos are really bad. A lot of workers can't really do nothing about it, 'cause some are illegal here, and they need money, they need to support their families. It's hard.

Talking to the older people on the crew you learn a lot about them. It's one of the things I like about the field. They're very friendly. Like everyone is there working hard, and everyone I guess is really comfortable with each other. They know everyone out there working needs to make money, so they help make sure everyone knows what to do.

On my crew there are a good fifteen to nineteen workers every day. It's a lot of family. There are brothers there, dads there with their sons. And everyone's really outgoing with each other. It's a good vibe I guess. We pick on each other sometimes, but we don't really fight or argue, and everyone respects the mayordomo.

The farmworkers, we drink Monsters in the fields. It's an energy drink. And then sometimes we make bets, like, "Oh, we'll see who finishes this shift the fastest, and the loser has to pay for a Monster for a winner." Stuff like that. Those energy drinks can be dehydrating, but it does give you a lot of energy for an hour or so. Then you have a sugar crash. That's why we only drink them towards the end of the day when we're already really tired.

We get paid every Friday, so yeah, I got paid today. I'm using the money for just back-to-school shopping, stuff like that. That's kinda it. And then whatever my mom needs or something, I'll help her out. Last week, we worked like nine, ten hours a day, but Friday we couldn't work, 'cause there was no work. None of the farms needed our crew to pick. Then we went back Saturday and worked 6 a.m. to 1 p.m. And I got my check right now and it came to $414. From working like nine, ten hours every day. And next week's check, everyone's kind of sad about it, 'cause everyone knows it's gonna be around $300, because we'll have less work.

Working in this heat means working shorter hours. And I'm not gonna lie, I think it's harder working shorter hours with the heat than longer hours when the temperature is OK. You're sweating, sweat gets in your eyes, you're burning, you're all wet, you feel uncomfortable, the peach fuzz gives you a worse rash in the heat—it's bad. We work short hours, but it's just harder, and then our paychecks are smaller.

Now I'm almost done for the summer, since school is about to start. I think the boss is gonna have trouble in a few days, since six to seven people on the crew are high school or college students. The high school students go back to school in a few days and then the college kids a little after that. So they're gonna need new workers. That's what we were just talking about today.

The older people on the crew tell you stay in school, focus on your books. That's the main thing they say. They tell me they wish they had that opportunity. They're like, "We're always here working, and the mayordomo's a good guy, but it's still a hard job." And they're like, "This isn't something you wanna do for the rest of you life. You have choices; make something good out of yourself."

THERE'S TEENAGERS THAT DON'T DO ANYTHING AT ALL

My parents have always told me to go to college. If I could go anywhere for soccer I'd go to UC Merced. I've been to the campus already; I visited when I was in a program that helped high school kids get ready for college, see what classes to take, take us on trips to colleges to see the campuses. And we went to UC Merced. During the tour there was a lot of talk about the soccer team, and I fell in love with the campus. The campus is nice, the dorms are nice. It seems like a good school. And that's somewhere I would wanna go. Also it's not too far from home, which is good because I'm really close with my siblings.

Last June, I went to Stanford for a kicking camp. I did really good out there. You always find competition. There were kids that I met at the camp from Los Angeles, Texas, some guys from North Carolina, others from Las Vegas. I was just talking to them, getting to know them. And I wanna say that for field goals I was top three. After that, just a few days ago, I got an email from a coach. I guess he's been a recruiter and college coach for twenty-five years and he told me that he saw me at the camp and he's really interested. That he could recruit me, help me go to college. So I'm trying to do that with football, even though my main sport is soccer.

There's teenagers that don't do anything at all. There are teenagers that I know personally, like friends, on Snapchat and stuff, that are going to bed at 5, 6 a.m. because they were up playing video games. That's when I'm waking up already getting ready for work.

I'm not really jealous. I mean, that's their life. Honestly, I feel like all that's happening right now, it's hard, but I'm also taking it as a great learning experience. I feel like this or that could happen if I don't work hard. I need to work hard, I need to be at school, stuff like that.

But when I'm not working I like hanging out with friends. Going to the movies. A lot of those friends also work to help out. My friend—his name's Luis—he does cross country. He's a really cool guy, but he's actually one of the guys who's been working the whole summer, since June, like right after high school. I think he does it to make money for himself, but I think he does help his family too. My friend Gustavo—they're cousins, Luis and Gustavo—they work to pay for their own phones and stuff like that, 'cause their parents can't afford it.

Life in Dinuba is just simple, I'd say. It's friendly around here. But then again, sometimes there's nothing to do. There are no beaches around here, there's no stuff like that. We do have a bowling alley. But there's nothing like going to Visalia or Fresno, where they have the big SkyWalk trampoline place.

Sometimes I'll go practice soccer on my own. We live by a water tower, and there's soccer fields right there by it. So I'll kick the ball, do some drills. And then the weekends I play in an adult league. Sometimes Sundays we do work, and sometimes we don't. Like I know two weeks ago we did work on Sunday. It's rare though. I got off work at 2 p.m. and then the game was at 6 p.m. Yeah, I went to go play. I was tired, but it's something I love to do.

I used to play video games, too, but I don't much anymore. At the beginning when it came out, I was into Pokémon Go. But when I saw the distance I had to go and the work I had to put in—like for example I had to walk all the way through town just to catch a Pokémon—I was like, *Nah, this game isn't worth it, it's too much.* So I just deleted it. I don't have time for that kinda thing.

SILVIA CORRERA

AGE: 47

OCCUPATION: *Farmworker—wine grapes*
BORN IN: *Puebla, Mexico*
INTERVIEWED IN: *Stockton, San Joaquin County*
AGRICULTURAL REGION: *Napa Valley*

Silvia Correra lives in a low-slung apartment complex near the shore of the San Joaquin River, which cuts through Stockton's west side before reaching the San Francisco Bay. Aside from a brief trip to harvest crops in Oregon, since coming to the United States she has spent her entire life in this sprawling city, which is surrounded by rich farmland but filled with poor people—many of whom work that land.[1]

We meet on a crisp Sunday morning, the sole day off for most of the farmworkers in the complex. As the hours pass and the temperature rises, a crowd of Silvia's friends and relatives gather on the front lawn to grill chicken, their laughter occasionally reaching us through the walls. Inside, seated at the kitchen table, Silvia tells her story in bursts. At times she pauses to gather herself. Other times we are interrupted by a pet iguana, which climbs up to the table and demands to be fed bits of iceberg lettuce.

---

[1] In 2008, Stockton, with a population of 300,000, became the second-largest city in the country to declare bankruptcy.

Much of Silvia's life has been defined by the deep trauma caused from a multi-generational cycle of domestic violence. It is likely that domestic violence among farmworkers is significantly underreported. Partly this is because of the fear of deportation: at least half of California farmworkers are estimated to be undocumented. Victims may also be economically dependent on partners when away from family and other support systems and worry about how they would survive on their own.

Silvia shared both of these concerns, but she was also one of the few to break the silence. She has begun to move away from the trauma, slowly. As we speak, her youngest daughter, twelve-year-old Jennifer, darts in and out of the kitchen, flashing a shy smile. A whiteboard hangs on the wall with a handwritten message: HAPPY BIRTHDAY ABUELITA—TE AMAMOS MUCHO. *(Happy birthday Grandma—We love you.)*

"I have arrived at a good place, finally," she says. "But it wasn't easy."

YOU ARE TAUGHT TO WORRY
WHAT PEOPLE WILL SAY

People back home tell you that if you marry a person, you have to stay with that person, you have to put up with that person. Otherwise what is your family going to say? What are your uncles going to say? What is your mother, mother-in-law, father-in-law going to say? And so you put up with beatings, you put up with everything, because you are taught to worry about what people will say. But I said, "Enough." I don't care what anybody says. I don't care. The only thing I want is life. My husband told me, "Don't ask me for nothing. I'm not going to help you with anything." Each time he hit me I thought about separating from him, but I didn't have the courage to do it. I endured it for some twenty-five years. I thought, *How am I going to be able to survive with my children?* But you don't realize what you can do, too.

MY MOM WAS ALONE, AND SOMETIMES
WE HAD NOTHING TO EAT

I was born on the outskirts of Puebla, Mexico in 1969.[2] When I was seven years old my mom separated from my dad. She took us to a village with my grandma, about an hour and a half by car from Puebla. The village was very small, with only about 200 inhabitants, and we had to survive on the farm. She raised us and worked in the fields planting corn, so that we could eat.

We stayed with my grandma for a few years, but after my grandma died, we had to return to Puebla. In Puebla, my mom worked cleaning houses and washing other people's clothes. My mom—how should I say it? My mom was alone and sometimes we had nothing to eat. Sometimes my mom was gone all day and I had to take care of my younger brother. I had to wash all the clothes and do all the chores in the house.

I attended school for only two years because my mother didn't have money. From my school years, I remember that my mom would buy me these small notepads with twenty pages, and I had to show her that all twenty pages were full, or she wouldn't buy me another one. We couldn't waste one single page. I didn't learn much. In two years of school you can't learn much.

Eventually, my dad started coming around again. By the time we moved back to Puebla, my dad had started another family, but he still went to see my mom. He would arrive drunk and say, "How are you Maria? Are you well? Give me some food." Then he would kick my mom and beat her. My dad beat my mom a lot. This had been going on when I was younger, but I didn't recognize it then. It was only when I was almost a teenager living back in Puebla that I understood what was happening.

---

[2] Puebla is a city of 3 million and the capital of the southern Mexican state of Puebla.

Once, my mom was with a good friend—they were both standing and chatting in the house. My dad arrived at like three in the afternoon, didn't say anything to my mom, just gave her a kick and then another. I was angry, and I suddenly felt brave. Without thinking I grabbed a broom and hit my dad in the back. Then I took off running, because my dad said I was going to pay for that. I was about twelve years old. I remember it well, when I hit my dad. Since that time my dad never beat my mom again.

MY PROBLEMS WERE GOING TO BE SOLVED

In 1983 I got married, at the age of fourteen. My husband was nineteen, also from the same town as my mom. When I told my mom I was getting married, she didn't say anything—she accepted it. She went to sign the marriage certificate because I was a minor.

My husband made it easy to go with him. I thought, *I'm not going to fight, I'm not going to have to wash so many clothes, I'm not going to have to do so many things*. I had many problems with my mom. I thought I was going to marry someone and my problems were going to be solved, but it wasn't so. I moved in with him, but his mom was very mean. She would hit me, call me names.

I had my first child when I was fifteen. We named him Antonio. When he was five months old, we moved to Mexico City. My husband found work downtown, selling tacos on the street. But his parents didn't want us to be together. They sent him letters saying I wasn't good enough for him. That's when he left me. He took me back to my mom in Puebla. I thought, *I can't stay here, I'll have problems with my mom.* So I decided to return to Mexico City.

I didn't know anybody there, and I had to find work in order to survive. I got a job in a market, selling coffee at a cafeteria. I woke up at midnight to make the coffee, and I sold it from 2 a.m. to 7 a.m. I talked to the owner, and she said I could stay there, so I slept under a table with Antonio. He was seven months old then.

If I left the store to sell coffee outside, another person would keep an eye on him. And if that person left, then another one arrived. And that's what it was like until the earthquake in 1985. I had finished my work and laid down to sleep with my son. At about seven o'clock in the morning I felt the earth moving. I grabbed my son and ran outside, and by then the earthquake was over. The earth had parted, cracked. Everything in the street was rubble.[3]

After the earthquake, Antonio's father returned, and we got back together. In Mexico City, he'd find jobs, and I'd stay at home all day with my son. I got pregnant again. I didn't have anything in the house—no stove, no bed, nothing. He left at five in the morning and came back at nine or ten at night. When he came home, he'd ask me, "Where'd you go? What did you do? Who did you go out with?" He'd hit me for everything.

He didn't drink much back then, but he started drinking more as the years went by. Once a week, then twice a week, then three times a week and so on. I would tell him, "No, don't drink. Why are you drinking?" I told him, "I like our lives, even if we're poor." And he'd say that he was going to stop, but he kept on drinking.

So many things happened. One day in 1989, I was down by the river washing clothes. I was six months pregnant at the time. Suddenly my husband appeared and began attacking me with a machete. I remember while he attacked me, there was a woman there who couldn't speak well, she was a mute, but she made sounds like "ta-ta-ta," screaming at him to leave me alone. That's why he stopped. At that point I said I don't want this life anymore and swallowed a bottle of pain pills, like twelve of them. Days passed and I felt nothing.

When my girl was born, her body was purple. We baptized her on her fourth day. Her name was Rosio. After four months she was

---

[3] On the morning of September 19, 1985, an 8.1 magnitude earthquake shook Mexico City. The quake killed 10,000 people, injured another 30,000, and destroyed 3,000 buildings.

still unhealthy. When I'd breastfeed her, she seemed as if she couldn't breathe. I took her to a doctor, and the doctor said that my daughter had a heart murmur. That was a Saturday, and on Sunday I took her to the hospital. She stayed there Sunday, Monday, and Tuesday. On Wednesday she died. They tried to do a test on her, and she couldn't withstand the testing.

I asked the doctor why she was born like that, if it was due to some medicine—because I had it in my head that it was my fault for swallowing those pills. "It wasn't because of the pills," he said. "It wasn't because of the pills." He asked me if I had any more children and I told him that I had two sons. He said, "Ah, well then, take care of the ones you do have."

We didn't have money to bury her, so I had to beg for money on the streets. My husband was a hard worker—I've never said the father of my children wasn't a hard worker. But he was a womanizer, he drank too much, and everything he earned he spent on his vices.

That was how it went until 1998, when he decided to buy fireworks and sell them in Acapulco. He and Antonio, who was fourteen years old, rented a room in Acapulco with other guys. One day they went out, and when they came back all their money had been stolen. That's when he decided to come to the United States, because that was money he'd borrowed.

INSTEAD OF TURNING RIGHT, WE TURNED LEFT

My husband went to Stockton in April 1999. His sister already lived here. In August, Antonio came. The rest of us came to Stockton in December. By then it was five children and me. My girl, the littlest one, was a year and a half. The others were five, seven, nine, and twelve. Two daughters, three sons.

My husband's sister asked me, "How are you going to go with the children? You could be raped; it's very difficult." I was brave and told her, "I am going because I don't want to be here, with so many needs. Nobody is going to tell me what to do—neither those that live here or those that live there."

We flew from Mexico City to Juárez and crossed to El Paso using fake documents. But we had bad luck. We were going to take the plane from El Paso to San Jose or Los Angeles. We gave our documents to the coyote, because at this time they didn't ask for any real documentation to fly, just a Mexican ID.[4] He gave us American clothes to wear, American shoes for the boys, a stroller for the girl, and sunglasses for me. The coyote bought the tickets, told us where to go in the airport, and which plane we were going to board. When he left us at the entrance, he said, "Go up the stairs, turn right, and go straight ahead."

But we didn't understand, so instead of turning right, we turned left. That's when an airport worker saw us and told us that the entrance was on the other side. And I saw that all these Immigration agents were sitting near the stairs, at a table. Instead of crossing in front of the agents, we tried to sneak behind them, and when they saw us do that, they became suspicious. That's why they caught us. The Immigration officers even told us, "If you hadn't passed behind us, we wouldn't have thought you didn't have documents." We were deported back to Juárez.

I returned and talked with the coyote. This time, they only had a fake ID for a girl who was four years old, and my little girl was a year and a half. He said, "Now I'm not going to be able to get you past the border patrol. We'll have to go through the river." The first obstacle was a small river, but it was sewage—we crossed floating on tires. Then we went through the Rio Grande, and the water was up to my shoulders. The men we were with carried the children across. I never thought the river was so dangerous. But afterward people said to me,

---

[4] *Coyote* refers to a guide who helps migrants illegally cross into the United States. For more information, see the Glossary, page 284.

"How did you dare cross the river? It has whirlpools and sometimes it sucks people in."

Then we went to the airport in El Paso again, but we no longer made the wrong turn.

IN THE TIME IT TAKES TO FORGIVE

We arrived in Stockton in December 1999. In January, my husband started to hit me again.

He worked at a warehouse. One day in March, before he went to work, he gave me money so I could deposit it for his dad in Mexico. I didn't have a car, so I had to get a ride from Pedro, the brother-in-law of my sister-in-law. I was with my two daughters and my son Eduardo, who was twelve years old. When I got home, my husband picked a fight with me. He said, "You went out with your lover; Pedro is your lover." I told him, "Don't start. I took my children with me—how can you even think that I would go out with him?" Antonio said, "Dad, mom is telling the truth, why won't you believe her?"

My husband said, "Ah, you're covering for her because you want Pedro as a father and not me." Then he took out his belt and started hitting my sons. My son Antonio has scars on his back from the beatings. Eduardo has marks, too.

I told him, "I've had it with everything you've been doing. I'm going to call the police." He thought I was bluffing. I took the phone and went out and called the police. He was hitting them while I made the call. When I finished talking to the police, I went inside and thought, *Whatever happens, happens now.* My kids were crying. And when I looked, I saw the reflection of the lights outside—the police had arrived. They got there really fast. They arrested him and deported him to Mexico.

The following day, his sister asked me, "Do you want to destroy my brother's life? Is that why you're doing all this?" She frightened me. Everything my sister-in-law told me got in my head and I never did anything again to endanger my husband. He was in Mexico for a month; he told us that he was sorry, that he was going to change. We sent money to Mexico so he could come on a plane to Tijuana, and in Tijuana he got a coyote to bring him across the border. The coyote charged $1,500 or $2,000.

It took a little while for him to start hitting me again. Later, when I went to the women's center, they explained to us how domestic violence works: how men beat women and the next day they bring you flowers and say, "Forgive me, I won't do it again." And in the time it takes to forgive them, they're beating you again.

HE SPIED ON ME EVERY DAY

In October 2004, my daughter Jennifer was born. The next year I found a job at a company that made mops. The father of my children worked in the afternoon at a lumberyard on El Dorado Street. He started to spy on me; he spied on me every day. My coworkers would tell me that he was outside sitting in his car. Sometimes I would be sent outside to get cardboard from a bin, and when I would get home he would ask me, "Hey, what were you doing outside?"

One day I didn't take lunch with me. I left for the store, and one of my coworkers yelled, "Mrs. Silvia, I'll go with you." We walked to the store, and I ate my burrito on our way back. I hadn't noticed that my husband was following us. We were chatting—just coworkers going to get some food. When we were almost back, just outside the factory, my husband appeared and he started screaming. "So this is your lover? You're a bitch!" The guy went inside to work and I stayed there dealing with this problem.

My husband took the car keys from me, so a friend drove me home in the afternoon, and she took me to work the next morning. At around nine o'clock I was called into the office. They told me that they were letting me go. They said, "You're a good worker, but since your husband has been spying on you, we're afraid that he could come one day with a gun, shoot you and shoot somebody else."

I thought, *I won't take this anymore.* I got home, grabbed the keys of the pick-up truck that we have, took my four youngest kids and left. We went to sleep in the parking lot of Walmart. I parked where I saw that there were other cars, and said, "We're going to stay here." I threw some blankets over them and we slept sitting up. It was very uncomfortable.

The next morning I went to the Women's Center.[5] We stayed first in Stockton for two weeks, but then he found out where I was, so they moved us to Tracy.[6]

My son Jorge stayed at the apartment. He was fourteen or fifteen. He didn't want to come; I think he thought, *I love my mom, I love my dad; I don't want to be apart from either of them.* He would call me crying, and tell me, "My dad says that he's going to be different. Mommy, come back with dad, he says he's going to change." So I told him, "Listen, your dad has done a lot of bad things to me, some you know and some you don't." He said, "Give him another chance, please. And I promise that if he fails again, I will stay out of it." That's when I went back with him. And everything was different, for a while.

THIS ISN'T GOING AWAY

I started selling corn and ice cream on the streets out of a cart. I did that from 2007 to 2008, until the economy plummeted. The same employment agency that found me the job at the mop company got me a job at a company that makes pots for plants. The woman said,

---

[5] Founded in 1976, the Stockton-based Women's Center–Youth and Family Services is San Joaquin County's only provider of free, confidential services and shelters to meet the needs of homeless and runaway youth and victims of domestic violence, sexual assault, and human trafficking.

[6] Tracy, California, is a city of 90,000 located 20 miles south of Stockton.

"If you have problems like last time…" I said, "My husband says he is going to change."

But he still spied on me every day. What I didn't realize was that sometimes he'd be in the trunk of my car with a camera when I drove to work. When I realized that he was doing this, I said no, that's too much. This isn't going away; it goes with him.

My husband no longer slept. I don't know if he used drugs. He walked around the apartment at night, thinking that he saw things that weren't there. Sometimes at night he went outside the apartment and peered through our windows. One time my daughter saw him and began to scream—she said that it was something evil. "Don't be afraid, it's your dad," I said. It was very, very traumatic.

We fought day after day. One time, my son Eduardo came home and saw us fighting. He arrived right when his father said that he wanted to hit me. Eduardo told him, "You know what dad? We're tired of you. Get your things, get in your car, and leave this house."

My husband said, "Fine, I'm going." He took his clothes and what did he do? He moved to the apartment of his sister who lived next to us. One night, two weeks later, he was drinking beer. It was 2 a.m. He came over and knocked on the window and told me that he wanted another beer and another cigarette. I said, "I don't ask you for anything. I don't need anything, and if I want it, I buy it myself." He opened the window, jumped through it, threw me to the chair and pulled my blouse up. I got scared; it was awful. I managed to shout. My son who was sleeping heard me and came out. "What's going on, Mom?" he asked.

"It's your dad," I said. "I don't know what he wants to do to me." My son told him to leave, but my husband promised that he wasn't going to do anything. "No, dad—go away," he said. He left and I closed the door, but I kept thinking, *He's going to come and kill me one day.*

The next day I took my children and left.

I SAW A LOT OF LITTLE STARS

I went back to the Women's Center and they helped me fill out papers for divorce and for custody of my children. We spent another night in the Walmart parking lot and then I found a one-bedroom apartment for $550 a month.

My children were very young and I had nowhere to leave them, so I couldn't work. Sometimes I went to the food bank. Other days I got welfare—I had to take money from welfare to pay rent. When we separated, my husband took away the car; he took everything. I even had to fight for the pans. Sometimes I made tamales to sell and also to give to my children to eat.

I didn't know what to do with my life. I worked one day in the grape fields, tying vines. They paid us piece-rate—I don't remember what they paid us per vine.[7] I left for work at five in the morning and came back at five in the afternoon, and only made $27. My son Antonio said, "Stay here and take care of the kids, and I'll give you money." He was living with us and working in construction. So after that I didn't work and besides, looking back, I was kind of depressed. I didn't want to go outside.

I didn't really start to work until 2011. One of my friends told me, "Let's work, Juanita." She worked in the grape fields. She arranged a ride to the fields for me for a week, but then the van we were commuting in broke down. Another guy sold me a car for $800. I had just gotten my check and I said, "OK, I'll give you $400 and pay the rest later." And I started going to work by myself.

I started in July, on a very hot day. I knew nothing, really. At about one in the afternoon I got really dizzy and crouched down.

---

[7] Farmworkers are either paid hourly or by the piece (in Spanish: *por contracto*). When paid piece-rate, they receive a certain amount based on how much they harvest. If their piece-rate earnings fall below the minimum hourly wage—as they did for Silvia—then an employer is legally obligated to pay the minimum wage. For more on California farmworker legal rights, see Appendix III, page 289–303.

When I stood up I saw a lot of little stars. The supervisors never tell you about overheating or that you should take a break to go drink water. They don't tell you that. They say, "Do the work like this, like that." Nothing more. The next day, someone came from the state who gave information about protecting ourselves from the sun. They described the symptoms of sunstroke. It was exactly what I felt the day before.

I worked in the grapes for a month, and then there was a break. One day a young man asked if I wanted to work in the chili fields. I told him, "Let's go." They said we were going to make the minimum wage. I don't remember how much the minimum was at that time, I think like $70 for the day.

With chilies, the harvester machine goes down the rows and you're behind the machine, picking the chilies and putting them on a conveyor belt. You're bent down the whole time. At the end, the boss said that the work was for only one day. That night I was so tired that I couldn't get up or bend down. I swear that even going to the bathroom was difficult. And I had a fever.

I called the young man who told me about the job: "Hey! Did the boss give us the money?" He told me no, and that the boss had changed his phone number. I say the worst job I've ever had was picking chili, because I couldn't bend down for a week afterward and I never even got any money.

A LOT OF PEOPLE WERE ARRESTED

In May 2011, I went to Mexico because my dad died. My dad, may he rest in peace, died from drinking too much. I came back to the United States through the desert. The group I was traveling with walked three days and three nights. I looked at some of the crosses, even found some of the bones that no one had seen. It's very, very ugly when crossing through the desert. The coyotes were howling and I remember somebody said, "The coyotes are going to eat us." I didn't sleep well.

We arrived in Tucson, and from Tucson we went to Phoenix. The coyotes had us in an apartment, like we were kidnapped. They didn't let us bathe, they didn't allow us to talk, nothing. Only lying there in the dark with the windows closed for four days. They had people with guns. Say I made a deal with the coyote for $3,000 to get me across. When you arrive, then they charge you some $4,000. The man who was responsible said to a niece of mine, "Well if you want to hear from her again you have to send more money." My niece sent the money.

I returned to Stockton in June. In July I was assaulted. My friend and I were coming home from a store at 9 o'clock at night. There were five or six men; they put a pistol to my head. They took our two phones and stole my friend's wallet that had $200. A Chinese man passed, and he called the police, who arrived and arrested the men who had robbed us. I went to court as a witness and learned that the pistol was loaded—if we hadn't given them our things they would have shot us.

Right now I'm trying to fix my papers because I was the victim of an assault.[8] But deportation is always a worry. On July 22, after my assault, two of my sons were arrested for selling pirated CDs. Antonio worked with another man at the flea market—at this time there weren't many other jobs. The police came and arrested Antonio. They arrested my son Rafael too. He didn't work there, but he arrived to give Antonio a ride, so they arrested him. A lot of people were arrested at that time for selling CDs in the stalls. Rafael was in prison for one year, but they let him out because they didn't have any proof of his involvement. Antonio was in for a year and a half, and then they deported him. It's a federal crime to sell pirated CDs.

---

[8] The U visa, which allows undocumented immigrants to legalize their status, is available to victims of certain crimes who have suffered mental or physical abuse and are helpful to law enforcement in the investigation or prosecution of criminal activity. Victims of domestic violent can also petition for legal status under the Violence Against Women Act. Because Silvia made only one complaint, which focused on the violence her husband directed towards her children, she didn't pursue this option.

In November, they arrested my son Eduardo for driving without a license. He was driving home from church with his wife and two young girls. I think they were nine and five. He was in jail for eight days and then they deported him. He had to return, because he had to support his family. He came back in a group with six people, including a couple from Oaxaca. My son said that the coyote raped one of the women in the group.

That year, 2011, was a very, very difficult year.

SHE NEVER YELLS

When I got back from Mexico, I found a supervisor in Stockton who was a good person. He taught me how to tie up wine grapes, how to work with the wine grapes. After two or three years, he was moved to Modesto.[9] He invited me to Modesto, and I would go there for a couple days each week. Then I tried to look for a job closer to Stockton, but couldn't find anything. Last year, in 2015, I called a friend who said he knew someone that needed help. He gave me the phone number of a lady supervisor. That's who I work for now, in Napa.[10]

She's been a supervisor for almost eight years. The supervisors are usually men. In other places men might have problems with a woman telling them what to do, but they're used to it here. When she tells us what we're going to do, she says it in a nice way. She never yells, or even says hurry up. No, she speaks in a nice way. She says, "Let's do our best." She might get an agreement from a farmer that if we do our best we can leave an hour early. She never calls us names. There are fifteen people in our crew, almost half men and half women. Only Mexicans—there's not going to be an American working in the fields, no.

---

[9] Modesto is a city of over 200,000 located 30 miles southeast of Stockton.

[10] Napa County is over an hour's drive from Stockton.

I get up at three in the morning and come home at seven at night. It's a long drive, four hours round trip. But here jobs pay $10 an hour, and there I make $14. I can't live in Napa because rents are more expensive, food is more expensive. Over there, a burrito costs $10.

It's hard because I have to leave my children the whole day. I hit the shower, I eat something, I sleep. I do it for them; I want the best for them. I don't want them to go through what I lived. I don't want them to spend a day without food. I told my older children and I tell the younger ones and they understand. I know they understand.

If Immigration catches me, I maybe won't be able to get back to my kids. In 2011, I had more strength to make the journey, but times get harder. Now the coyotes ask for as much as $10,000 or $12,000 to cross. We don't have this money. In 2009 they stopped a van driven by the supervisor's husband as he picked people up to take them to work. They hit the lights on him and he thought they were the cops. It was Immigration. They followed him until he picked up all the people and they deported everybody. Even her husband. He got back just one year ago, but he tried many times to cross and he wasn't able to. They took him just like that.

Right now, I'm driving a car that I think Immigration won't recognize. It's an Infinity. So, they won't think I'm carrying immigrants. Many field workers drive Astros, and they get targeted. If you follow the rules and drive the speed limit, and if the car is insured, there's no problem. We try to take care of ourselves so that we don't look very suspicious.

VACATIONS? VACATIONS?

My ex-husband is in Mexico. He was deported. He started to sell fake movies on the street, so the cops caught him.

He bothered me for a while. He bothered me *a lot* for a while. We got divorced in 2010, and he would call me just to insult me. He would say that nobody would marry me with so many kids. "Well, that's my business," I would tell him. The first man I had couldn't see that I was worth it. I'm not going to wait for another man to care about me.

I thank God because I've lived through many bad things, but in the end there must be something good. I've been with my new husband for two or three years now. My friend got to know a friend of his. One day the friend gave the phone to my husband and he asked me on a date. He's a good person, very reliable. He drives a tractor in the afternoon, and takes my kids to school, buys lunch, pays the bills. He understands me and I understand him.

Before I felt a lot of anger towards the father of my children. A lot of anger. I went to church and told God that I was leaving him my problems, that I don't want to have this weight forever. And with the grace of God, when the father of my children came here from Mexico, I saw him like any other person would see him. Sometimes I cry because I remember; it makes me sad, but I don't hate him anymore. No more hate.

I take my son Carlos to the psychologist. He says, "But I'm not crazy." And I tell him, "We don't go to the psychologist because we're crazy, but because we need to learn how we're going to organize our life, what we should do when we're upset." The state gave me a psychologist, one for him, a different one for my daughters, and a family psychologist for all of us. We've learned a lot from this.

Now I am doing well. My children don't have to witness any violence, my grandchildren either. They come to my house and hear ... *tranquility*. Last week was my birthday. I went to work and when I got back they had a surprise, with balloons here and there, and they jumped out to surprise me. Me, I didn't know anything.

I look at my kids when they gather here and feel comfortable. I feel good to have all my kids close to me. Like they say, once you get here you only want to work, work, work, and work. So that your kids don't go through the same struggle you went through. That's my goal. Vacations? Vacations? No. Well, when my two youngest kids are grown up I'm going to go out and have some fun.

HAROLD MCCLARTY

AGE: 65

OCCUPATION: *Grower*

BORN IN: *Parlier, Fresno County*

INTERVIEWED IN: *Kingsburg, Fresno County*

AGRICULTURAL REGION: *Central Valley*

In the office of HMC Farms is a deed from 1887. That was the year that Harold McClarty's great-grandfather purchased 40 acres in Parlier, a small town twenty miles southeast of Fresno. As a kid, Harold worked those acres, harvesting grapes and peaches, but when he left for UC Santa Cruz in the 1960s, he didn't plan on coming back. Farming was a hard, seven-day-a-week job, and the pay wasn't great.

But Harold missed the quiet fields of the Central Valley. After college, he returned to Parlier and worked a string of agriculture-related jobs. In 1987, with partner Mike Jensen, he founded HMC Farms. What began as a small farm has grown into one of the largest stone-fruit operations in the country. Today, HMC Farms grows 4,000 acres of peaches, plums, apricots, and nectarines, along with 2,500 acres of table grapes. One sign of the company's growing influence occurred earlier this year, when Harold was elected chairman of the California Fresh Fruit Association, an industry trade group. Today, HMC farms is one of the many family-operated farms that contribute the bulk of Fresno County's $6 billion or more in annual agricultural *sales—by far the most productive farming county in the United States (and more productive even than most states).*

HMC's headquarters is located just west of Highway 99, reached by driving down a dead-end road lined on either side with peach orchards. When I visit, on an afternoon in late July, Harold is wearing a white collared shirt, khakis, and brown leather shoes. "I had to dress up for a meeting today," he complains. Behind the small office is a hulking packinghouse and cooling station, where more than two hundred workers—nearly all Latina women—briskly sort and pack thousands of peaches and nectarines harvested just hours earlier. It is late July and the temperature is 109 degrees, so we retreat to a conference room, where he talks about the path he took to become a successful farmer, the farmworkers he employs, and why, despite the rapid growth of his company, he still considers HMC a family farm. Though California's meat and dairy industries are increasingly operated as large-scale industrial farms, today, much of California's fruit is still grown on mid-sized family farms much like Harold's. That may be slowly changing, however, and Harold explains that many of his neighbors have sold off their fields in recent years.

IN HIS ENTIRE LIFE, I NEVER
HEARD MY FATHER COMPLAIN

My father's people came in the 1860s or '70s after the Gold Rush and worked in the mills up in Tuolumne.[1] They came from outside the Montreal area. Good little Scotch-Irish. Then they settled around here in the Parlier area.[2] It was a forty-acres-and-a-mule type of thing. They were part of the history of Fresno County, the CID, "Church water," and all that.[3] Their roots go back that far.

---

[1] Tuolumne County is in eastern California and today includes the northern half of Yosemite National Park.

[2] Parlier is a town of over 15,000 located 20 miles southeast of Fresno in the San Joaquin Valley.

[3] The Consolidated Irrigation District has overseen irrigation management in the

My mom was one of those people you read about in *The Grapes of Wrath* where she, at eight or nine years old, was one of twelve children in the back of a Model-T coming to California from Oklahoma. Her family came out in the 1930s, and she was the youngest of the twelve kids—a twin. They all came out here for the same reason. There was opportunity. I'm not trying to be sentimental about this. It was, OK. *I can't make a living here in Oklahoma, and I've got a family, and I've got to move to where I can make a living.*

My mom and dad met after the war.

I grew up in the house my grandfather built and on the 40-acre ranch that his father first purchased. The house looked like any house built in the late 1800s, 1900s in the area. It was built from redwood that they brought down from the mountains, and it was originally probably two bedrooms, a living room, and a little kitchen. At some point they added on two more bedrooms. When indoor plumbing became popular, they added on a bathroom. When I was growing up, we had no heating, other than just a little oil heater. It was just a regular old farmhouse.

I had three sisters. We all worked from almost the time we could walk. It was one of those things where your work ethic was instilled in you at an early age. There were always jobs to do and there were always chores, and there was always that work ethic ingrained in you that you made your own way, you did what you had to to be responsible.

On our 40 acres we had peaches and raisin grapes. In the summer, we'd cut the grapes and put them on the ground on a tray to dry, and then in the late summer we'd box them. I mean, if your mom's out picking grapes, you're out there with her and you're carrying trays or doing something. If you're old enough to sit on a tractor

---

San Joaquin Valley since 1921. "Church water" refers to water rights granted to farmers in the San Joaquin Valley since irrigation of the region was spearheaded by Moses J. Church starting in the 1870s.

and just keep it going down a road when boxing raisins, that might be what you did.

During the off-season, my dad also worked at Del Monte. He was one of the guys who drove a forklift and managed some of the raisins at their receiving plant. You couldn't make enough just from 40 acres to support four kids and a wife, so that's what he did. And we were careful about money, careful about saving. As kids we made sure to finish everything on our plates. You don't lose that just because you get older and things are better. When he was seventy, my dad bought a used refrigerator that didn't have a handle. I said, "Hey, Pop—it's your last refrigerator." He said he'd ordered a handle and was going to put it on. He goes, "Hey, I didn't grow up the way you did."

In his entire life, I never heard my father complain, nor my mother: "Woe is me," or "I've been mistreated." For them, that's life. Life isn't fair. Growing up on the ranch, if you want to learn about responsibility, you stick a twig in the ground and three years later you've got a tree or you've got a vine. That's reality.

WE NEVER FELT WE WERE
BETTER THAN ANYBODY

I went to a small K-8 grammar school that had 300, 400 people. It was all farming kids and farm laborers. One thing that the school did that I thought was kind of neat was, starting in first grade, we had two-person desks and the teacher would pair English speakers with kids who didn't speak English, and it was our job to help them learn. Looking back now, that was just a great way for us to learn—a great way to learn is to teach. It makes you kind of understand what you're trying to learn, because you've got to tell somebody else what you're doing. I thought it was a great concept.

We never felt we were better than anybody. We worked alongside these people. I mean, you know, when you're out cutting grapes, whoever's out there are the people you associate with as your friends. For whatever it's worth.

We worked during school, but after school we were free and played sports and did other normal kid stuff. But we all had weekend jobs. We all had summer jobs. Finding a good summer job was a real challenge, and finding one that made a little money was very important to us.

During summers at our ranch we had a little peach-cutting shed where I'd help cut peaches and dry them. Then if the neighbor needed something done, I'd go and do it—drive a tractor or something like that. Basically, as kids we worked seven days a week. When we were teenagers, maybe we'd work at Hunt Foods and load bins onto trucks, and we picked fruit all summer because it was steady work. None of these jobs paid well. My first job was 90 cents an hour. I got $1.10, $1.18, $1.29. I think it followed the cost of beer. I mean, a six-pack of beer was $1.29, and that's about what you got paid hourly. By the time I was done with high school and ready for college in 1969, I'd saved $4,400 at $1.18 an hour. So you can tell how many hours I worked and saved.

IT WAS INCREDIBLY EXCITING

There's a family I grew up with, and we all worked together every summer: the Hanson family. I spent most of my summers and a great part of my youth growing up with them. We all played sports together and stuff, so we were pretty close friends. The mom was a great influence on a lot of what I did, because she was a true intellectual. The family was pretty bright. The mom was a judge and the dad was a college teacher. It was because of their influence that I went to school at UC Santa Cruz at the end of the 1960s, beginning of the '70s.

So that's where I ended up, in the dorms with one of the Hansons as a roommate. We were pretty tight, and in the summers, we'd pick fruit together—peaches, nectarines, and plums. It actually was a pretty good job, because you could do that and you could play baseball at night. We'd usually be done with work at 3 or 4 p.m. We were seventeen, eighteen years old. We could party all night and work all day. I mean, come on.

UC Santa Cruz was a cultural extreme, to say the least. I mean, where I grew up and the people that I was around, we worked. We never felt deprived of anything because we were all the same. Then I got to UC Santa Cruz and I saw some incredibly wealthy people, people with incredible educations. There were people on my floor of the dorms who had pretty substantial backgrounds, and their parents were well known.

I never viewed education as a way to get a job after college. I was looking to get the best education that I could get, and to me, education's a state of mind. The job isn't the reward at the end, because there were better, cheaper and easier ways to go get a job. I always felt like it was fun to be around enlightened, intelligent people that were so different. There was a bigger world out there that I needed to see, and I was in no hurry to work towards any kind of a career.

I went into environmental geography as a major. I worked in city planning as an intern in Santa Cruz. I really wanted to do something that made a difference. This was the time of the Vietnam War, the draft, rock'n'roll. I believed that our generation was going to make the world a better place. I mean, I swallowed that one.

MY EDUCATION IN MY
MIND WASN'T OVER YET

I graduated from UC Santa Cruz after four years, probably in 1973. After I graduated from college, I came back to the area, but I wasn't going to live at home. So I looked around for a place to live and found an old farmhouse around Parlier. If you know anything about Parlier, it's basically just a labor camp.[4] The house was out in the country, because I decided that I'm a country guy. Then I went up to visit my best buddy, who was going to Cal.[5] I told him, "You're done here. Let's go. I got a house for us." So he came, and we moved into the farmhouse. I remember it was $75 a month, and that included utilities. But the front door to the place wouldn't shut, it had no heat or electricity or anything.

We did odd jobs like field labor, suckering trees, whatever. Then we got a job with my buddy's stepdad who worked for a cannery. We got hired by the cannery as field guys for tomatoes and worked all the way up to Stockton.[6] Being a field guy is where you represent the canner and you're out there and you're making sure the crops get picked right and the trucks get dispatched correctly. We'd live in a little motel and work 12-hour shifts. I'd work from say 4 a.m. to 4 p.m.

After that, I worked in citrus and frost protection, cutting oranges to avoid frost damage. The next summer I worked as an inspector, inspecting stone fruit in the packing houses. What I wanted to do was have a couple months off in between jobs so I could do my traveling. I did the whole hitchhiking through Europe, and then I went across the United States. I went to San Francisco, I went to Haight-Ashbury. Because, I mean, my education in my mind wasn't over yet. Then all of my local friends were getting married and getting real jobs. So I decided, *I've got to find something.*

What I wanted to do was find something that was interesting, something that offered some opportunity to travel and would allow me to use some of my abilities. So I went into the marketing part of produce. I knew produce, obviously, very well, and I went down to Los Angeles and got a job with a fruit broker there and represented

---

[4] For more on labor camps, see the Glossary, page 287.

[5] "Cal" refers to the University of California at Berkeley.

[6] Stockton, California, is 150 miles northwest of Parlier.

him up in the Valley, buying fruit for different wholesalers in the United States.

I did that for a couple years, and then I got a sales job for a citrus grower. I was around twenty-nine, and I got married around the same time. We also moved to Reedley. This all happened around 1979.

It was a good job, but eventually I felt it had run its course. When I'd started, it wasn't a huge company, but it had grown very, very large and corporate, and for me it had just become a *job*. I wanted to try to do something on my own. But during the eight or nine years I was working there, my wife and I had had two kids, so I had a family to support. I talked to my wife about it. "Can we take a chance on this?'" She agreed, since I was miserable at my other job. My wife had a degree from UC Davis, but we'd decided early on that she wasn't going to work, that she was going to stay home with the kids. But there's no way I could have been even remotely successful without her confidence in me and willingness to forgo a few things while the business got off the ground.

I WAS SCARED SHITLESS

For whatever reason, I still think I had some of my school left in me, some of the old "I want to make a difference." So what I did was, I started my own little company with nothing, and I worked out of my living room trying to broker fruit. I met up with an old friend of mine, a guy I'd known since I was five years old, and he had a little packing house with stone fruit—peaches, plums, nectarines—and we decided to go into business together. I had my dad's forty acres at that time. So I planted stone fruit trees on it. I moved into this little rented room in downtown Reedley, and brought in a grape guy that I'd done work with. So we started the company.

We had nothing to lose, and I was scared shitless. I didn't know how I was going to make a living. I just knew I had to try. There are easy ways to survive and exist. I'm not an exister. Both my partners and I were—I wouldn't say naïve, but we didn't really realize that we were competing against generational families who maybe had someone to mentor them or to get them through some tight spots, and to not make some of the classic mistakes. And we trusted people that we should never have trusted. One of the biggest things we learned is this business is not Kumbaya, I can tell you that. We were living off our wits, just like when we were kids.

A lot of it was luck, the timing was right, and a few good things happened. At the end of the first season, I told my partners, "Guys, if we want to be real, if we're going to take this to the next level, we have to build our own cold storage." So I went to Production Credit, which was, you know, interesting. I said, "Hey, where do I get a loan? I need three million dollars, but here's the thing: it doesn't make sense, collateral-wise, on paper. I've got 40 acres, Mike's got 80, and the grape guy's got a little bit. But you have my word that you can have anything and everything for the rest of my life if we ever default." They absolutely took a chance on us. That was a long time ago in another world. And we pulled it off. We built the beginning of a storage facility.

We became a real player at that point in time. Mike and I, the stone fruit guy, every year we just put every penny we had back into the operation, and we worked hard at it. We just made good decisions and worked hard and always knew we could think our way out of problems. And we didn't have any real fights in thirty years.

Our company is now one of the largest operations in our industry. We have operations in Chile and Peru and Mexico, and we employ thousands of people. There are eighteen people on the phones and computers, moving product all over the world. We're the largest supplier to Australia—right now we're flying 103,000 pounds a day of stone fruit to them. Singapore, Malaysia, all through the Pacific Rim. We're meeting with a Chinese delegation this afternoon.

I'VE NEVER HAD AN OFFICE

I've never had an office. I sit in a doublewide cubicle with my quality-control guy. Everybody else has their own little cubicle. I choose to sit with him. He's a youngster, about thirty-four, and we've hired a lot of the young kids that worked during the summers. We gave jobs to as many summer kids as we could, and I kind of picked the best and the brightest of all of them and tried to get them to come to work for me.

We picked a lot of good Valley guys, because you can't get them from along the coast anymore. They won't come and work in the Valley. We got a good strong group. One of the sales guys is like a son to me. His dad's in Florida, and I'm taking care of him; he's my boy. The other one, the quality-control guy, lived with us when he was a senior in high school. It's a true family operation. My entire family works with me—my son and daughter and their spouses. My daughter married a guy from Tahoe who was a civil engineer in the Bay Area, and I brought him down here. He runs my entire grape operation now. My son John's wife was a CPA down in Southern California. Now she's up here and one of the people running the books for us.

The biggest reason I'm still in it is that my family's in it, and I want to make their lives comfortable. They don't need me, they're very intelligent—more intelligent than I am; they really are, seriously. I like working with them. Most of the time, you know?

We understand we're all in this together. My guy that runs the stone fruit part of my farms doesn't speak very good English. He goes, "You leave your 'eggos' at the door." Which means, "You leave your egos at the door" when you come in here. We're all the same and we all work together. And I don't want to tell ya that it's perfect, by any stretch of imagination, but it's a family business and it's a way of life. I'm sincere about that. I've taught the kids that you do the right job and money shows up. I mean, don't do it to make money. You're providing a piece of fruit that people like to eat. You're doing something that is in the ground, that you can see what you've done. Not to get overly philosophical, but every day is different. You can fail or succeed on a daily basis, hourly basis.

YOU CARRY A LADDER, YOU
CLIMB UP THE LADDER

There's a whole story about farmworkers. It's hard work. It's hot out there. They have ladders and bags and they work early in the morning till probably mid-afternoon, when it starts heating up. You carry a ladder, you climb up the ladder, you pick fruit, and you put it in the bin and at 2:30 or whatever you go home. It's an entry-level position for people with not a lot of skills or education, and it provides some opportunities if you're good. In my opinion, there are a lot of opportunities in agriculture. We need good people, but like I said, it's hard work.

We can't automate this. You need the human eye to determine it's round enough, it's colored all the way through the stem, it's got the right shape and, you know, it's gonna be 10, 11 percent sugar. You've gotta have a tree-ripened piece of fruit. It ripens on the tree; it's not an avocado. It doesn't get any better once you pick it, so you gotta be careful how you pick it. These aren't tires or something. People eat 'em.

We try to make sure we manage our labor force so they have a job six days a week for as much of the year as we possibly can. My ultimate goal is to make sure my people have work eleven months out of the year. You don't want people to have to worry about being laid off or anything like that. I've got a core group of people that have been with us forever now, decades. What I call the crew bosses. Individuals within the crews will come and go and come and go, but the people like my tractor driver and the irrigators, they've been around a long time. We have a tight little group of people down here; we get along with each other.

One day I had an NPR lady come out to the farm, and she wanted to do an interview in the fields. That's fine, I don't care, we've got nothing to hide. It's a little different out there than you journalists believe. We went out to one of the ranches when the crews were picking. The reporter talked to one of the crew bosses, a guy named Jose, who's been with me twenty, twenty-five years. We get along great—he loves baseball, and I always give him extra tickets to the local Fresno team's games when I have them. She was looking for a story, asking him, "How do you like it here?" And he says, "Well, we all love it here, there's my brother, there's my dad, we've been here over twenty years. The guy treats us right, gives us raises without us asking; we'll be here as long as we can." Obviously, that made me feel real good.

I'm not trying to paint over a dent or something. There are hot days, and there are long days, but it's what we do. People are trying to make something out of this that it really isn't. It's hard work but it's good, honest hard work, you know? And we don't complain about it and we don't sit here and moan and groan. And that's the point that is hard to get across to people: this is our way of life. There's very little exploitation here, of anybody or anything, because it's not sustainable if you do that. Does that make sense? You exploit the land, it's not gonna be around. You exploit the workers, they're not gonna be around. Everything finds a balance.

My best friends are in the field. And my best friends are people that have just good values, that don't politicize this. And all of us need to be at least responsible enough to understand the world is changing and people need more money and they need health care, they need all these things. But just like with the drought, these things get politicized, and you take a situation like overtime pay, or this and that, and by the time it gets legislated, it ends up worse for the workers.[7]

---

[7] Assembly Bill 1066, passed in September 2016, created a framework for mandated overtime pay for many of California's farmworkers. Growers throughout the state

There's people that want to do something but are uneducated about our industry—I don't even want to say ignorant—and a lot of times they're hurting the workers. These are important things. If we can provide these things, why don't we do it? I mean, there's no reason not to.

IT'S GETTING ROUGH OUT HERE

We do a ton of scholarships for the workers. Any one of these kids that wants to go to junior college, I make sure they get to. You know, I'm not Hispanic but I could have been—I mean, what's the difference? There are still opportunities for people who wanna work hard, who wanna risk.

This isn't some dreamland out here. I mean, it's getting rough out here, let me tell you. It's gotten a lot, lot, lot rougher in the last ten, twelve, fifteen years. The gangs are out here. You've got the same problems here, maybe even worse, than you have in a lot of places.

When I was growing up, agriculture was the driving force behind all these towns. When I went to my little Selma High School, the town had 5,000 people; well, now it's 28,000 people. Reedley was 6,000 people; now its 35,000. They're still all ag towns, but now you're into second generation and in some cases almost third generation. I'm not quite seeing the same willingness to work in the fields as the earlier generations. That's obviously having a cultural effect upon the towns.

And not to put all the blame on the kids, your crops followed the school cycle almost, to the point where school ended about the time you're getting really busy in fruit, and school started back up about the time you're about finished. Now the schools start not in

---

lobbied heavily against the bill, arguing that the overtime rules would force them to hire more workers at fewer hours to avoid losses due to overtime pay. For more on farmworker rights and wages, see Appendix III, page 289.

the middle of September, it's the middle of August. In August, well, you're in the middle of your season. You can't be a big part of the harvest and keep up with school at the same time.

Working in the fields is like a training ground. Part of my success was I had to work my ass off when I was little. Everybody wants to be vice president when they graduate. They tell 'em, "You graduate from college—boy, the world opens up." It doesn't. You gotta work hard at it. The culture in the small towns has changed. I'm doing my best, because I live in these communities, to contribute and to give back, and I believe that they need more opportunities. I would love to see more than agriculture come into these small towns, but I don't see it.

YOU JUST GET TIRED

There are no Monsantos here.[8] Every owner in stone fruit is an owner-operator that works in the business. With grapes, there's at least one company around here that's a little more corporate, but these aren't industries that lend themselves to remote management. We've had big corporations start up around here and then walk away two years later. As a grower, you've gotta be out there every day making decisions that could make or break your business.

As independent farmers, there's a lot we can deal with. We can deal with the drought. If we can't plant one thing, we can plant another. But what we can't deal with is the manipulation of our labor, our water, new rules and regulations all the time that don't really make anything better for anyone. That's why we're losing farms.

I always tell this story about the reason we've lost so many small farmers. One day I might get a call from a Japanese neighbor—and I say Japanese because Parlier had a lot of old Japanese farm

---

[8] Monsanto, based in St. Louis, Missouri, is one of the largest multi-national agri-businesses in the world.

families—and he would say, "I wanna sell my farm." So I'd sit down with the old guy, he's eighty years old, and there's no negotiation. He knows what it's worth, I know what it's worth. We're fair and we shake hands. And you see on the wall pictures of his kids. And I go, "None of the kids...?" And he goes, "Well, he's an airline pilot; he's a CPA; she's a nurse; and this one's an eye doctor, and it's just gotten too hard. I work all day, all night, there's government paperwork, and my kids don't wanna work that hard. And they don't have to. This little farm put all four of 'em through college, and it's time to move on."

I'd say, "Well OK, that's fine. You gonna live here?" "No, we bought a house." I'd say, "Why don't you just do me a favor. You stay here as long as you want, move when you want."

I had two or three former owners die on the ranches they sold me. They'd been there since the twenties. They couldn't leave. I have thirty-two ranches, and well over half of 'em were done just like that. Neighbors calling me saying, "Hey, I'm ready to leave, ready to get out of this mess." The government is driving small farmers out of business, even when they're thinking they're helping farmers.

I'm optimistic 'cause I have to be, not necessarily because I am. I just have to be, and it's kind of a front. I could lose all the money I've made in one year. And every year you roll the dice and at some point you get tired, you know? You just get tired. I'm sixty-five, and it's not nearly as much fun as it used to be, but like I said, I'm here to do what I've done. It's all I know. Nothing I do is gonna change my lifestyle now.

MARIA ELENA DURAZO

AGE: *63*

OCCUPATION: *Vice President for Immigration, Civil Rights,*
and Diversity at UNITE HERE
BORN IN: *Madera, Madera County*
INTERVIEWED IN: *Los Angeles, Los Angeles County*

According to a USC professor interviewed by the LA Times, *Maria Elena Durazo is "probably the single most influential individual in Los Angeles politics." As the head of the 800,000-member-strong Los Angeles County Federation of Labor, Maria Elena dramatically expanded the power of workers—especially immigrant workers—in a city that has long been hostile to organized labor. During her tenure, the LA County Federation of Labor, or "County Fed," helped push through numerous living-wage ordinances, elect labor-friendly politicians, and was the major force behind the city adopting a $15 minimum wage in 2015.*

That's quite a legacy for a woman who spent her childhood crisscrossing the state with her migrant farmworker family. It was in California's fields that Maria Elena, who had ten siblings, first witnessed and experienced the exploitation of immigrant workers. But it was only later that she fully understood that not all families are forced to survive on such low wages, or to live much of the year in a tent, or to pick cotton until their hands bled. Over several phone conversations, she spoke about the structural challenges that farmworkers face when trying to organize, her own journey from child farm-worker to national labor leader, and how her time in the fields helped push her into what became her calling: organizing and advocating for immigrant workers.

FOR ME, MY FRIENDS WERE MY BROTHERS AND SISTERS

My father came to this country in the early 1940s, after my two oldest sisters were born in Sonora, Mexico.[1] He was from a town whose name is a little embarrassing. It was called Oputo.[2] Every time I'd say it, people would laugh at me and I'd be like, "But that's really the name of it, you know." My mom was from Cananea, the mining town nearby.[3] They met and that was the start of the family.

My father first came over by himself and connected with an uncle who was already working in the fields in Madera.[4] The uncle was a *mayordomo*, a supervisor. I don't know what my father's status was when he came, but at some point he was able to get a green card. Maybe it was because he volunteered for the army. He never went abroad during World War II—he talked about peeling potatoes, doing that kind of stuff. So he was able to get his papers and bring my sisters and mom, and that started our whole journey in this country.

I was born in 1953, the seventh of eleven brothers and sisters. There were eight kids in my family, including me, who worked in the fields—five girls and three boys. We started as soon as we were able

---

[1] The state of Sonora is in the northwest corner of Mexico and borders Arizona and New Mexico.

[2] There are multiple translations of the word *puto* in Spanish; the least offensive is a male prostitute.

[3] Cananea is a city of nearly 35,000 in Sonora.

[4] Madera is a city of over 60,000 in the San Joaquin Valley, 25 miles northwest of Fresno.

to help out. I was carrying water around to my family in the fields when I was five years old.

We all were born in different towns in California. I was born in Madera; Elizabeth and Ricky in Fresno; Johnny was born in San Jose. Our family would go from field to field in our truck, and a couple of us would sit up in the front with my mom and dad, the rest in the back with our clothes and stuff.

We went as far south as Calexico and all the way up to Oregon. Peaches, plums, apricots, walnuts, tomatoes. Of course grapes. Every year was a different school. I certainly don't remember having a lot of friends, because we'd start and then have to leave, start and have to leave. For me, my friends were my sisters and brothers.

We'd try to make do with what we had, with what was around. I played marbles in the dirt with my brothers. Among the sisters, there were four of us working in the fields, and we became notorious for singing, like karaoke style. And dancing. We'd put on our own little shows for each other. In San Jose, next to our house was a sort of a ranch, and they had horses in it. We'd try to sneak off and jump on the horses when the owners weren't around. I remember once, my siblings threw me up on the horse bareback and slapped the horse, so the horse went galloping away. I was holding on as long as I could before he threw me off. What the heck? That's how we entertained ourselves.

Our brothers, they got to do a lot more things than the girls. My dad sort of trusted the boys to go off on their own. That's how they learned how to swim: they'd go into the canals. No way we girls could go out there, or go to the swimming pool or anything like that. Part of it was my dad was, you know, a big prude. But the other part was that he felt like the boys could take care of themselves. So the boys learned how to swim and I didn't, and it's really embarrassing, when you're my age and you don't know how to swim.

Many times we didn't have housing. I'm not exactly sure why. I think my dad was trying to make the most money that he could during the key harvest times, so that in the winter, when there was less work, he'd be able to carry over. We'd just park the truck down near a river. What do you call it? Squatting. One time we were down by the river, and suddenly there was a helicopter overhead. The helicopter shone its lights on us and we were ordered to get out. I remember scrambling to pack up. Other times we lived in the barn of the grower, where the tractors and equipment were kept.

I remember the different towns. But sometimes I don't remember the schools themselves. What is clearer is the crops. That's really clear in my mind, the crops we picked. And I remember San Jose. We were living in a tent in San Jose when my infant brother died. I was maybe four or five. My mom couldn't get him to the doctor in time. He was burning with fever. A church heard about it and the priest took up a collection to be able to bury my brother. I'll never forget the little white casket for his funeral.

PICKING COTTON WAS
THE ROUGHEST OF ALL

In order to incentivize us, my dad would give us a quota of buckets or boxes, whatever it was that we were filling. If you did more, you'd get ten cents or whatever. The quota was based on age—he was pretty fair about it: he didn't expect the younger ones to pick as much as the older ones. And that was neat, 'cause you knew you'd get ten cents if you worked really, really hard. We'd use the money to sort of enhance our lunches with candy or other sweets like Snowball cupcakes.

Picking cotton was the roughest of all, because of all those little buds. It's very prickly. You have to pull the cotton out of the little bud, and every time you get pricked at the tip of your finger, so by the end of the day your fingers have all these little pricks of blood. Not gobs of blood, but just constant.

I remember my dad saying that we had to be really careful, because on top of how little the foremen paid, they'd also cheat us.

We had a long sack that we'd drag, and because cotton was so light, you had to pick a lot in order to make it worthwhile. So you dragged it over to the truck and the supervisors would weigh it. They'd write something down as to how much you brought over, and empty it and give your sack back. You couldn't trust these foremen. You didn't know how well the scale was working. And it always seemed like you were getting less than you were owed. My dad would do the best that he could to watch them, but we didn't have any control. Unless a bunch of people didn't like it and were willing to speak up, it was pretty much you had to take whatever they paid you.

In the fields they never had bathrooms. We'd go out, at least two or three of us girls, and find the furthest possible place. We always wore layers, and we'd take a shirt off and cover ourselves, make like a little tent around us, so we could go to the bathroom.

My dad preferred for us to work as a crew. For example, the plums in San Jose—he'd negotiate with a grower over a certain amount of money, and then our crew, our whole family, would do the orchard. But there were a number of times where there was so much work that we were just mixed in with other groups.

Our dad always kept an eye on us girls, making sure that guys didn't get near us, that sort of stuff. He was extremely strict with the girls. Some of my sisters disagree, but I'm grateful now. Because what he was really saying was, I don't want you to get in the cycle of being young, getting pregnant, and then what happens in your life? He was doing it for a lot of good reasons, reasons that he didn't explain to us. All we knew was that he wouldn't let us talk to guys. He knew the dangers, right? He knew that foremen would take advantage of young girls. He knew the foremen would use sexual favors.[5] That was going on, and we just didn't pay attention to it. For us it was like, *Hey there's a cute guy, why can't we talk?*

---

[5] For more on sexual harassment and sexual abuse of workers in the fields, see Appendix V, page 310–18.

"I WISH I'D BEEN ABLE TO DO MORE FOR YOU"

When I was in sixth grade, we came back to Fresno for good. My older sisters didn't want to move around in a flatbed truck anymore. Part of the reason we settled down in Fresno was that grapes provided year-round work. There's always something to do related to the grapes—you prune, you tie, there are the different phases. We could settle in at school and work on the weekends. We worked whatever was within an hour or two from Fresno, but we weren't moving from town to town anymore.

With me, my dad was very pushy about going to school. Unfortunately, we just didn't have enough to survive on, so my older sisters didn't finish high school. Not because they weren't smart enough— dad just needed them to work and help support the rest of the family. So I benefitted from that because I was younger. My older sisters went back to school later and got their GEDs, and one got her teaching credential and her BA.

My dad loved to read. He was always reading a book, always reading a newspaper. He'd send away for projects, to learn how to do this and that, how to fix electrical appliances. So he really was self-taught. We didn't have that many books around the house, but he'd sit down with me in the evenings and teach me where to put the accent marks in Spanish, how to write in Spanish, or he'd do projects with me.

That was influential. But I have to say one of my main motivations to study was that work in the fields was so awful. We'd pass the day and try to make the best of it. You always had your transistor radio to listen to. That's why Cesar Chavez was so smart in developing a radio station, 'cause everyone had their transistor radios in the fields.[6] So you'd try to figure out ways of getting through the day. But

---

[6] In 1983, the United Farm Workers launched its first radio station to reach farmworkers. Today, the Radio Campesina network consists of nine stations in three states—California, Arizona, and Washington—with a listener audience of 500,000.

bottom line, I wanted to do whatever I could so as to not have to do that the rest of my life.

One of my older brothers, Ben, went to Fresno State. This was the late sixties, and he became a real activist. He burnt his draft card, there was the Chicano movement, the farmworkers movement—all this activity was going on.[7] Ben took me to my first protest, against the Vietnam War. And then when I was in high school, he took the time to help me navigate the system, so I got exposed to college, even though it was around the activism. He also had friends who would talk about how to apply to college, how to apply for financial aid. All those kinds of things helped a great deal. I applied and I got accepted at several colleges. There was this one, Saint Mary's in Moraga, and when my dad saw that it was a Catholic school he said, "OK, you can go to that one."[8]

I remember when I left home to go away to college. I'll never forget this. When I left home, my dad packed a little box, a care package. Remember the care package days? And like a typical farmworker, it was in a little cardboard box, wrapped up in twine. It had tortillas and a bunch of stuff to take away to school. Anyway, he pulled me aside to give me the package—I still get all choked up—and he says, "I want to apologize to you." And I thought, *Well, this is really something.* He never sat down and had a nice conversation about this or that. He was always the disciplinarian in the family.

So I said, "What do you mean?"

And he goes, "I wish I'd been able to do more for you."

I thought, *How is it that someone who worked day and night, and never abandoned his family, could feel that somehow he failed us?* It sticks to me to this day. There was no reason for him to feel that he'd failed

---

[7] The Chicano movement of the 1960s sought to ensure equal rights and increased power for Mexican Americans in the United States.

[8] Moraga is a town of 16,000 people ten miles east of Oakland. Saint Mary's College is a liberal arts college connected to the Catholic Church.

us, when in fact he'd done so much to protect us. He always believed that if he worked hard he'd get rewarded for it. And he never was. I think that moment had more influence on me than almost anything else in deciding what I was going to do. Something very strong hit me. Things shouldn't be that way.

I WANTED TO DO SOMETHING
ABOUT IMMIGRANT WORKERS

I went away to Saint Mary's in the early seventies. Back then it was easy to get attracted to the activism that had just started to happen on the campus. It's a very small school, but we were influenced by what was going on at Berkeley, and I'd been influenced by my older brothers' activism in the Chicano movement. We had teachers from Berkeley and other schools that were real hotbeds of activity, and we recruited them to teach classes at Saint Mary's.

Part of what we were trying to do was make it easier for Chicano students like me to come to college and make the transition. Within a year or two, I was in the middle of organizing on the campus to recruit more Chicano and black students. We didn't have enough black students to form a Black Student Union or Chicano students for MEChA, so we had a Third World Center, and we did things together—black and brown—which was a really good experience.[9]

I was a sophomore when we took over the chapel on the campus for a week and fasted. What we were demanding was services for better retention of minority students. We'd done all this recruiting to bring black and brown students to campus, but it was difficult for many of us to stay in school, because of a lack of financial aid and that sort of thing. So we wanted better services to not only attract

---

[9] MEChA, the *Movimiento Estudiantil Chicano de Aztlán* (Chicano Student Movement of Aztlán), is a Mexican–American civil rights organization that was founded in the 1960s.

students, but to keep them in school as well. So we took over the chapel and started our fast. Well, I actually fasted. I found out later that some of the students didn't really fast, that they were cheating. That's something we all laugh about now!

Activism became so important to me I almost didn't finish college. I was driven by what my father had said to me when he sent me off to college, how much he had worked and how little he was rewarded. So my activism started out focused on campus, but by my third year some of us campus activists got involved in things that were going on in Oakland with Bert Corona, who was an incredible immigrant-worker organizer.[10] There was a strike at a *tortilleria* factory in Richmond, and being involved in that was one of my first steps away from activism on campus to activism within the larger immigrant community. I made the connection between workers and immigration. It wasn't a union issue for me, it was about immigrants working in bad conditions and fighting back. That's what became in my heart the key thing—I wanted to do something about immigrant workers.

I graduated from college in 1975, moved to Oakland, and got married. My son Mario was born a year later, in Oakland. When he must've been six months or so, we moved to San Jose for about a year. Corona had started a CASA chapter in San Jose, and so I got active with them.[11] What hit me the most about Corona was that he was very, very supportive of women in leadership roles. He was very open-minded about decision-making, and you could tell that his approach was just much more respectful of the rank and file workers than some other labor organizers. That was really impressive to me.

---

[10] Humberto Corona, known as "Bert" Corona, was a major civil rights and labor leader and an inspiration for young Chicano activists in the 1960s and '70s.

[11] CASA, or the *Centro de Acción Social Autónomo–Hermandad General de Trabajadores* (Center for Autonomous Social Action–General Brotherhood of Workers) was founded in Los Angeles in 1968 and operated for a decade as a vocal and active political group within the Mexican American community.

I was only in San Jose for about a year when my husband and I separated. Then I moved to Los Angeles, in late 1977. I always had a full-time job to support myself. So in San Jose I worked full-time as a translator for the public health nurses. In LA, I worked for the *LA Times* as an ad taker, and then I did my CASA work. I mean, to me it was like, *OK, how do I support myself and my son?* But my real goal was to be a community organizer or worker organizer.

MY SON SAYS THAT THE PICKET
LINE WAS HIS NURSERY

In 1978, I became an organizer with the International Ladies' Garment Workers' Union.[12] The union had enormous resources they were putting in Los Angeles to try to organize the garment industry. Like today, it was all immigrant workers back then. The union was very aggressive. They had militant actions, strikes, picketing, boycotting. I mean they were open to creative and innovative ways of doing things. We sued the INS for the way they would drive right up with green vans and go into workplaces and round people up and deport them.[13] We said you can't walk into a workplace without a warrant and without specifically naming the people that you think are undocumented. That was a big, big issue. I was very proud that the union was incorporating the realities of what undocumented immigrant workers went through every day.[14]

---

[12] The International Ladies' Garment Workers' Union (ILGWU), founded in 1900, was for a time one of the county's most powerful and radical unions. Union membership began to decline in the 1960s, however, and in 1995 it joined forces with the Amalgamated Clothing and Textile Workers' Union to form UNITE, the Union of Needletrades, Industrial, and Textile Employees.

[13] Immigration and Naturalization Services (INS) was the federal agency responsible for immigration enforcement prior to the passage of the Homeland Security Act in 2002. For more on federal immigration agencies, see the Glossary, page 286–7.

[14] In 1982, a coalition of unions filed a class-action suit against the INS claiming that immigration raids on private businesses without warrants or consent of the

I was proud and excited to be making a difference for the workers, but it was also very difficult, because I was a single mom with a young son at home. My son Mario, who is forty years old today, says that the picket line was his nursery. I learned how to do this work and take care of a family. You always have this sense of, *How do I do both?* But you end up doing both out of love of both. You don't abandon one or the other. Sometimes one gets more attention, and the other one less, and then it goes the other way.

After several years with the Garment Workers' Union, I went to People's College of Law.[15] Way back in high school I thought that I was going to be an attorney. While I was at People's College I interned at a labor law firm for a couple of years. While I was there, in 1985, I met someone at HERE Local 11, and got offered an organizing position.[16]

Working with hotel and restaurant employees was quite the opposite of my experience with the garment workers. The union was very disconnected from the work force they represented, which had become largely immigrant. They were disconnected to the extreme of not translating materials or contracts into Spanish, not conducting any membership meetings in Spanish or having a translator. The culture of the union, of representing the workers without interacting with them, was a complete contradiction and it wasn't getting any better. The union leaders were unwilling to make the changes. It was extremely, extremely controlled; they never negotiated with a committee of workers. That's what pushed things to a head. My choice

---

business owner were violations of the fourth amendment guarantees against unreasonable search and seizure. In 1985, a U.S. district court ruled against such INS raids, barring warrantless arrests or questioning of suspected undocumented workers on the grounds of private businesses, including farms.

[15] People's College of Law is a small, progressive school geared towards working adults in downtown Los Angeles.

[16] HERE stands for the Hotel Employees and Restaurant Employees Union. In 2004, HERE merged with UNITE—the Union of Needletrades, Industrial, and Textile Employees—to form a new union: UNITE HERE.

was either to walk away or to try to do something about it. A number of people, outside organizers, kept nudging me: "You should work to change things, take on a leadership role." So I finally did. I organized a group of folks and we took on the leadership, took 'em out. I was elected president of HERE 11 in 1988.

We had to start from scratch. Now that's a big culture shock, to say to workers, "You're the union. We need you to be involved and we need you to become leaders in your workplace." And a lot of them kinda looked at us like, "What are you talking about?" You know, "We pay you dues, that's what you're supposed to do, not us." But there was a mix of attitudes, and from some of the hotel workers I'd hear, "Yeah, that's right, we're gonna make our union stronger, I'm gonna be a part of this."

We decided that we were going to raise the issue of being immigrants in this industry. We started to negotiate contract language to offer protections for immigrants. For example, once you were hired, the employer shouldn't have the right to re-check your immigration papers whenever they felt like it. 'Cause that was just an environment of intimidation. In '86, even before I got elected, we went out and did a lot of work around Reagan's amnesty, helping our members process their applications.[17] Which was a really big deal, 'cause this was the opposite of how immigrants had been treated before. So rather than exclude immigrants, we openly welcomed them as a core part of what we were.

After three or four years of fighting, we had our first really big victory, against Hyatt in '91. The next year we had to prepare for a citywide hotel strike. We thought we were gonna have to go out on strike. We produced a video called "City on the Edge," and our message was that there was poverty in Los Angeles in part because of

---

[17] The Immigration Reform and Control Act, passed in 1986, provided permanent legal resident status to eligible migrants, including those who could prove that they'd worked in agriculture in the U.S. during a certain time period. For more information, see the Glossary, page 286–7.

how the industry was treating workers. The city could continue to just use PR with palm trees, you know, to get tourists, but eventually it had to deal with real content, and substance, and had to treat workers in this industry better. And we won that citywide contract short of having to strike. So that was very important, and it raised standards to a much higher level.

Developing that first generation of organizers was very difficult, and some made it and some didn't. It was a real mix: we won some fights with employers, we lost some. It took a lot of years. We just kept at it.

TO FEEL AND TOUCH WHAT THAT WAS LIKE

I met my second husband, Miguel, when we worked together at Local 11.[18] We got married in 1988, and after that he got hired at the Federation as the political director. He made a lot of changes in the labor movement as far as making organizing a real priority, reaching out to Latinos and immigrants, to say labor is about everybody.

When Miguel died in 2005, he was the executive secretary-treasurer of the LA County Federation of Labor, AFL-CIO. In 2006, his successor resigned, I was named the interim secretary-treasurer, and I ran in the election to become the permanent secretary-treasurer. The challenge for running for the position was that I wasn't known. I didn't personally know most of the leaders of all these different unions that made up the Federation. So I didn't know about construction unions and their issues, I didn't know firefighters. But they knew about me and about Local 11 being a fighting union. And I knew about fighting back. I was also committed to making sure the labor movement wouldn't become, as Miguel said, the "ATM of

---

[18] Miguel Contreras had his first organizing experiences with the UFW, and grew to become one of the most important Latino labor leaders in the country. He died of a heart attack in 2005.

the politicians." I did have that reputation, so we were able to pull together the support I needed to win the election in 2006.

The first thing I really needed to understand were the specific issues certain parts of the labor movement had. I spent time with construction unions, half a day in the shoes of a worker. I went to an industrial laundromat, you know, to feel and touch what that was like. I went with a sanitation worker on a two-ton garbage truck.

The second thing I did was to try to find points of unity. After a couple of years, in 2009, we did something called Hollywood to the Dock. It turned out that in that year, contracts covering like 350,000 workers from the Screen Actors Guild and other unions were gonna expire. So this group of unions did a walk across the county, from Hollywood to the docks of San Pedro. It was all about connecting our unions to each other, to give the sense of the power of the labor movement. We spent the night in different places: two nights in a church hall, one night in a union hall. It was important to show our power and to send a message to the industries and the employers that we are going to back each other up.

The next year, there was a lockout at this borax mine in the Mojave Desert.[19] That was a test for us. We specifically picked it because it was two hours away from Los Angeles, but within LA County. The workers were locked out, and we challenged our union to show that solidarity. So we did a caravan of 200 cars, taking food and money to them. And marched with them. We did a really big action in support of them in West LA. So the idea was to pick out certain struggles and really throw down for them. Nobody would be isolated or left on their own.

---

[19] During a lockout, an employer prevents union employees from entering their worksite, and replaces them with temporary employees. The hope is to force concessions during labor disputes. This particular lockout was begun by the international mining conglomerate Rio Tinto against its employees in Boron, California. The lockout is described by narrator Terri Judd in the Voice of Witness book *Invisible Hands*.

WHAT DO WE DO? HOW DO WE DO IT?

Now I'm the Vice President for Immigration, Civil Rights, and Diversity at UNITE HERE. I think of this chapter of my career as focusing on ways a union of primarily immigrant workers can have an impact on passing comprehensive immigration reform. That's one task. And to lift up the stories and struggles of immigrants as workers. I didn't go into union organizing for just any group of workers. I really wanted to make that connection between what my family experienced, you know, working in an industry that is highly profitable and yet where the workers live in complete poverty. That's what inspired me.

There are a lot of similarities between the workers in our union and farmworkers. Undocumented status, for example: you have to get past that particular fear. There is so much at stake. You're not just worried about losing your job—it could go so much further than that. So when undocumented workers do commit to organizing, they really put a lot on the line. It's a level of courage that is just so inspiring.

Organizing takes an enormous amount of resources. That's a big challenge for the farmworker union. It takes millions and millions of dollars for a single campaign. What is the pot of resources available? If you're not organizing in a number of geographic areas at the same time, and making gains, then it's really hard to sustain. For example, if you get only one sector of the industry, then it becomes an island. Now you're competing with a majority that is not organized. That's a challenge for organizing farmworkers. How are you going to build up the resources to the scale that is needed for organizing? It's easy to say, "The conditions in the field are awful; we should do it." Where are the massive resources that you need to do it?

The structure of the industry is also a huge challenge. You have all these little contractors that actually hire the workers, but contractors are not the ones making decisions. You've got to aim at much bigger targets. In our industry, if we didn't have the resources to research the industry and employers, we'd be fighting the wrong target. We'd be fighting someone who's not the decision maker. Who owns the Sheraton? I don't just mean the name on it, but who actually owns it, who calls the shots? That's a very complicated question, and it takes a lot of resources to figure it out.

I continue to hold up the farmworker union as a wonderful example of a movement union, and not a conventional business organization. There are advantages to having institutions with resources battling side by side with housekeepers and dishwashers. But what continues to inspire me is this: *How do we create a movement union?* You can't lose sight of the enormous contribution that Cesar and Dolores and all those farmworkers made in teaching us what a movement union looks like. What do we do? How do we do it? To this day, I use them to help answer those questions.

RAFAEL GONZALEZ MERAZ

AGE: *58*

OCCUPATION: *Mayordomo*

BORN IN: *Colima, Mexico*

INTERVIEWED IN: *London, Tulare County*

AGRICULTURAL REGION: *Central Valley*

London, California, is one of those places that outsiders can drive through without realizing they've done so. A plot of land measuring seven blocks by five blocks, London is an unincorporated community that is home to fewer than 2,000 people, a couple of churches, and a single general store. Several miles west is Highway 99, the main thruway of the Central Valley. Twenty miles to the southeast is Visalia, the nearest big city, with a population of 130,000.

More than 40 percent of residents live below the poverty line; the homes are modest but well-kept. One of those homes, a three-bedroom painted dark green, belongs to Rafael Gonzales Meraz. His migration story began at the age of ten, when he left his family's house in Mexico to venture into the world of full-time work. A large man with a dry wit, he explains how his journey transformed a boy without enough money to buy sandals into a mayordomo, or crew leader, in the California fields.

I ALWAYS DREAMED OF HAVING
A BIGGER MOTORCYCLE

I was born on a *rancho* between lime orchards. My dad would move from one ranch to another, and every time he changed ranches we'd move. My sisters and I never went to school while we were moving from ranch to ranch. When I was seven or eight, my dad moved to the city, to Tecomán, Colima.[1] Then he had rent to pay, and he said he couldn't pay all the bills, so my sisters and I had to go to work at the ranches. We helped by cutting limes in the orchards.

Eventually my whole family moved into a place in Tecomán, but things weren't the same with our whole family together. There were a lot of problems at home, and I didn't feel welcome, so I left. I was ten years old.

I ended up getting taken into another family. It was a family with three young daughters and no sons. The man would take me to work with him every day to cut limes, and the woman would feed me. I lived with them until I was thirteen, but then the man kicked me out. He said he was afraid I was going to steal his wife. I said, "How's that possible, I'm only thirteen!" But he'd heard a story about something similar happening to a guy he knew, so he kicked me out.

Then I ended up living with another family. The woman was alone, because her husband had gone to the United States to work. While I was with this third family I also worked in the lime orchards. But instead of cutting limes, I learned to drive a truck. I remember how boring it could get, and how there was always a cloud of dust that the tractor would kick up in the orchards. Sometimes when I got too bored, I'd go find other work, like cutting coconuts.

I saved up enough money to buy a little motorcycle. But I always dreamed of having a bigger motorcycle. There was also a girl I was

---

[1] Tecomán is a city of 115,000 in the central-west coastal state of Colima. It is the self-proclaimed "lime capital of the world."

interested in. Vanesa. She was one of the sisters in the house where I'd lived before the dad had kicked me out. I'd visit her, but she told me she didn't want me because I was too poor to even have sandals to wear. "Well, fine," I told her. But that's when I decided to move to the United States. I'd always heard people do well up north, and I wanted to make money. So when I was seventeen, I decided to cross over.

I DIDN'T WANT TO BE BY MYSELF

I had a cousin that I hung out with, and we talked about crossing. We had an uncle already up north, so we sent him a letter asking for help, but he never wrote back. So my cousin and I decided to do it on our own. We saved money, my cousin and I, and he came first. He arrived in Tijuana and he was there for about six months. Then he crossed the border, saved money, and sent me a letter telling me where he was. I sold my motorcycle, and then paid a coyote $250 to take me across.

This was 1978 or 1979. I crossed by Tijuana. In Tijuana, there's a neighborhood called La Libertad, in the north of the city. That's where I crossed, and there were no Immigration officers, or I didn't see any at least. The coyote brought the group I was with to London, where my cousin already was, and I started working as soon as I arrived. Back then around London there were not as many tree fruits or grapes as there are now, so I was working with carrots, squash, cauliflower.

Then, after one year, I went back home to Tecomán. I wanted to see Vanesa, the girl who didn't want me because I didn't have any sandals on my feet. But now I was wearing boots and nice pants. I actually had another girlfriend in town at the time, but I really wanted to see Vanesa instead. And now she was interested in me. I told her, if you come out with me, I'll leave my girlfriend, but if not, that's it. So we went to the movies, and I left my other girlfriend.

Vanesa and I were together for a year in Tecomán, got married, and we had a daughter. That was in 1981.

After my daughter was born, I came back north to London to work and send money home. But I didn't want to be by myself. Back then it was easy to cross, so I crossed back over and went to visit my family. I asked my wife if she wanted to come with me. I told her, "If you do want to come, let's go now, but if not, then it's over. There's no point in me being up there working and you here happily getting the money I send you." She said she would come.

I remember we crossed as a family in Tecate.[2] It was raining really hard, and so to keep her dry we put my daughter in a black plastic bag with just her head sticking out. I carried her over the border on my shoulder. My wife was pregnant at the time with our second child.

A PLACE FOR MY FAMILY

When my family first moved in with me to London, I was having trouble finding enough work. It was winter, and so there was less work, and the other problem was that I didn't know many mayordomos at the time. None of them trusted me to know how to prune and things like that, even though I knew how. So my family lived in a little shelter made of wood planks, and that was all we had. After my son was born there wasn't enough money for the whole family. I ended up having to send Vanesa and the kids back to Mexico while I stayed and kept working. Fortunately I got to know more mayordomos, and I started making a little more money.

I lived and worked by myself for another year, and then I went back to get my family. By this time, I was renting a room from a mayordomo I knew that had his own family. So my family moved

---

[2] Tecate is a city of 65,000 in the state of Baja on the U.S. border. Tecate is about 40 miles east of Tijuana–San Diego and a smaller, more isolated border crossing.

into my room, but it didn't last long. The mayordomo's granddaughter was living in the house, and the girl didn't get along with my daughter. The granddaughter was always tripping her. Then one day my daughter bit the girl, and the mayordomo got fed up and kicked us out.

Luckily I had a friend that lived across the street. I told him what happened, and my family stayed with him a while. From there we eventually found a small house to rent, and that's where my second daughter was born. We ran into more problems at that house, so we had to move again. That's when we moved into the trailers for farmworkers run by another mayordomo. I ended up becoming friends with the manager, and we finally had a place where we could stay for a long time. We lived in that trailer for five years. But the manager, my friend, he retired and his son-in-law took over, and we didn't get along. The son-in-law wanted to overcharge us for everything, and even charged us to patch a hole in the trailer. We ended up getting into a fight, and he kicked us out. From there we lived in a hotel and then another house that we rented and fixed up, because it was really filthy when we got it.

We lived in all these places around London. Finally, in 1993 I had the chance to buy a house. I'd saved up around $13,000, and I used that for a down payment and fees. All my friends who were renting, people back in the trailers, told me not to buy a house. Most of them rented and saved to buy a house in Mexico, where you could get something more for less money. They said I'd probably die before I ever paid off the mortgage, but I said, "If that's true, at least I won't have to have paid the full amount!"

So it took over ten years in the United States, but I finally had a place for my family to stay. It was expensive, though. I remember getting the first electric bill for $50 or $60 when I was used to paying $15. After that, I unscrewed all the lightbulbs in the house but one. That one was enough.

I'D GO INTO WORK ON A SUNDAY. I'D WORK IF IT WAS RAINING

During the whole time that we were moving around, I always worked. I learned to prune, to harvest, to dry, to plant, to mark, all the different jobs in the field. I never failed at my job. If there was work to do on Sundays, I'd go in to work on a Sunday. I'd work if it was raining. And if it kept raining, I'd just keep working. The employer I worked for saw all that. Around 1993, around the time I bought the house, the mayordomo I was working for came up to me. "Hey Rafael, there's going to be a meeting, and the boss wants you there. I don't know why, but let's go."

I thought, *What could this be about?* But I went, and the meeting was in a big warehouse on the ranch. It turned out to be a meeting of all the mayordomos to plan for the coming year. In the middle of the meeting we stopped to have a barbeque, and people grilled chicken, steaks. I still didn't know why I was there. But afterward, my boss David, the labor manager, came up to me and asked if I was ready to be in charge of a crew. *Me?* I thought. I told him, "But I can't read or write. I don't even speak English. What do you want me to do with a crew?"

He was like, "What do you need to know English for?" He asked me if I wanted to do it or not. Except he swore a lot. "Are you up for it or not, asshole?" I told him I'd think about it, but he said he needed to know right then. So I agreed.[3]

I had to pull my own crew together. So I started gathering people I knew, mostly friends that I'd worked with before. Eventually my crew reached about forty people. We were sent by the labor manager to work at a ranch owned by an older couple named the Jacksons. The problem was that I didn't speak English and they didn't speak

---

[3] Wages for mayordomos vary, but it is common for them to make as much as double the wages of the field workers that they supervise.

Spanish. They followed me around, giving me instructions, and I just nodded and pretended to know what they were saying and started pruning. At one point I tried hiding behind a tree, but the old lady just followed me. "Blah blah blah blah." I was nervous. I knew how to do the job, but I'd never been a mayordomo before. I had a group of guys there looking on and the old couple just staring at me, and I wasn't used to that. But luckily I had a very good crew and everyone knew what to do already. They were good workers so there were no problems.

After the Jacksons' ranch, I went to another one for a week, and then my employer sent us to a place in Hanford[4] to do suckering and cutting.[5] We were one of about six crews working for the boss. I had a very good crew, we did a good job, and everyone could see that.

YOU KNOW WHAT? PEOPLE CAN'T WORK THIS HARD EVERY DAY

I worked with my crew for the Jacksons for about twelve years before Mr. Jackson retired. I'd arrive with my group of about forty workers, bring the tractor, and we'd do whatever we had to do.

But then Mr. Jackson was getting older, and after he had a pacemaker installed he retired and divided his ranch in two between his two sons. The older son got help through his father-in-law, who ran a fruit-packing business. So my crew and I worked with the younger son on his ranches.

Things were different with the son. This son, Eric, he'd be checking on us constantly. He'd be watching me, clocking me in when I left for lunch and when I came back, and then when the day was

---

[4] Hanford is a city of about 60,000 and a major agricultural and commercial hub in the south San Joaquin Valley.

[5] Suckering refers to pruning branch buds from growing fruit trees.

over as well. So I told him, "Hey, if you don't trust me, and you're always here watching the crew, why would you want me here? You're always here, it's your farm, but you make people angry. We can't even have lunch in peace. If you don't think I'm good for this job, then I won't come anymore. But stop pressuring us so much." We were paid hourly, and he let me know he didn't like paying people, and he wasn't going to pay a minute more than he had to.

Eric would always complain that we weren't working fast enough and always pressure us to go faster. We'd work very fast in the mornings, but after 11 or 12 p.m., when it was hot and workers were tired, we wouldn't be as fast. That's when Eric would come into the fields. He'd come at 2 p.m. and then mark out the territory he expected us to finish—maybe six more rows. We weren't working piece-rate—we weren't paid based on the amount of fruit we picked. We were paid hourly. And what he demanded we accomplish wasn't possible.

It went on like that for years. One day he came in the afternoon and pushed us to work faster. It was like 100 degrees. None of my workers were complaining, but I could tell that they were all sweating, exhausted. Nobody would ever complain, because they were too afraid of losing their jobs. So I said, "You know what, Eric? People can't work this hard every day." I reminded him we were working by the hour, and he couldn't force us to finish extra rows.

Eric didn't say anything in front of the other workers. He just told me to come with him to his house. He took me to his garage, and that's where he started yelling at me. I remember he said, "Are you working for me, or are you working for your employees?"

I told him, "I'm working for the job, and making sure everyone does their job. But I won't have people killing themselves every day. No." I wouldn't let him criticize me. "You can't do anything on this farm without the farmworkers."

Then I went back to my crew. Eric's ranches weren't the only place my crew and I worked. There were some other places where we didn't have to work as fast and as hard. One of the workers in my crew said, "You know Rafael, let's not go back and work with the Jacksons; let's stay at this other ranch." I just told them all, "We'll quit one day, but we still need the work."

You see, I didn't want to give up on the Jacksons' farm because it was very close to my house. Only five minutes away. I didn't want to have to drive a long way to and from the fields every day—it could get expensive, especially transporting equipment and crew. So I kept taking my crew to work for Eric, even after we'd had the fight.

After the fight, though, he didn't really talk to me. He'd just give me dirty looks. Then he started bringing in new crews to compete with mine. He'd drive them very fast as well.

Finally, in 2008, I got a call from another supervisor that worked with Eric. The supervisor said, "Hey, Eric says that there will be no more work starting tomorrow." I asked what he meant. "He says he'll call you if any more work comes up."

He didn't call. When I called the supervisor to ask about work, he said, "Nothing more this season." So Eric had fired me, right? He hadn't even told me in person. I'd been with his family for nineteen years.

I knew I'd been fired without him giving me a reason. I had a friend that knew my situation and said, "Well, that's not right. I know a place we can go to report this. I'll go with you, and you can tell them everything." I wanted to sue. So my friend and I went to visit the Labor Commission in Fresno. There wasn't much I could do, but there were waiting-time penalties since we'd gotten paid late for our final work on Eric's farm.[6]

I told my story and filled out the paperwork, but at the last minute, the lawyer told me there was a problem. Eric wasn't officially my employer, and so I couldn't go after him for the money. You see,

---

[6] California's labor code stipulates that when an employer dismisses an employee, the employee must immediately be paid all wages due. If the employer fails to do so, they pay a penalty equal to the employee's daily rate of pay for each day after they are fired and not paid, up to thirty days.

I had worked directly for the Jacksons with my crew for many years. But about three years before letting me go, Eric had started paying me and the crew through a labor contractor named Yolanda. He did it so he wouldn't have to take out insurance as our employer. But since he wasn't directly paying our wages, I couldn't go after him.[7]

It was already the end of the harvest season, so I had to drop it and go find work elsewhere. Since it was October, I took my crew up to Washington to harvest apples. I met some workers there who had also worked for Eric. They told me they'd been hired to put me out of work.

After I came back to London, I started working again at different ranches. I worked with my crew for another labor contractor for years. Eventually I quit, though, because I was spending hundreds of dollars in gas every week going from ranch to ranch.

Now I work for a company called Family Tree Farms. They're happy with me and my crew, and we're happy working with them.

WHEN MY PEOPLE ARE WORKING, I'M RIGHT THERE WITH THEM

Today was a typical day. Well, I did wake up a little late—4:25 a.m. I don't like being late to work. After I got ready, first I drove to the store to get the ice, which I put in the gallons of water I bring. Then I picked up some of my people, and we arrived in the fields at 5:30. I have my coffee while I wait for everyone else to arrive. The workers

---

[7] Farm labor contractors are used by growers who don't want to directly employ or manage farmworkers. The grower pays the labor contractor, who agrees to furnish and supervise a certain number of workers and carry workers' compensation insurance. In such cases, the farmworker's direct employer is the contractor, not the grower. In the past, contracting out a labor force could be used by growers to shield themselves from penalties for workplace violations, as this was the responsibility of the contractor. In 2014, however, California passed a new law that holds employers and contractors jointly responsible for labor and health and safety violations. For more on laws protecting farmworkers, see Appendix III, page 289–303.

in the crew signed in and I chatted with them, joked with them. Sometimes I try to have the people showing up do exercises to get ready for the day. But some of the people that don't want to stretch make fun of everyone else, and it's a disaster, so I don't force anyone.

I have two guys that drive the trucks with all our gear. They showed up by 6 a.m. They get paid half an hour extra every day for the time they're picking up and dropping off the vehicles.

When my people are working, I'm right there with them. I do whatever I have to do. First I might distribute the boxes that the crew uses to gather fruit. I might stack or organize the boxes as they come back. I might drive the tractor to where it needs to be. If someone's tired and can't carry more boxes, I might help them out. When I have a minute I might drive and examine the rows of trees to see which have ripe fruit. And if I have nothing to do, then I just jump in and harvest with the others. I take my box and work with them, chatting.

And I have told them, "You know what? I'm the mayordomo. But that doesn't mean that I think I'm better than you. I'm a worker as well. I make your reports, enter your hours, pick up your checks, but I'm just like you. Don't think that because I am a mayordomo supervising work that puts me in a higher position than you. No. We're all the same. And if anybody has a question or something tell me, ask me, tell me how you feel." I tell them that because there are people who have been working with me a long time—one person for fifteen years. Right now the youngest person working with me is about twenty. The oldest is sixty-three.

We get three breaks a day. We get thirty minutes at 9:30. Then half an hour for lunch. At twelve we can take fifteen minutes. We're supposed to take ten minutes for a break, right? But we take fifteen. They don't press us at Family Tree. Then at 2 p.m. we get another fifteen minutes. But we don't take them: we work during those fifteen minutes. Why? So we can leave fifteen minutes earlier. So then we're usually done at 2:45 or 3 p.m. We sometimes get extra hours as well, and they're not stingy about it. If we work twenty minutes past 3 p.m., they'll pay us for an extra half hour. Because of that, my crew doesn't mind putting in a couple of minutes of extra work now and then.

I'm able to work at Family Tree Farm almost all year round now and stay close to home. There aren't many times of the year when there isn't something to do on the farm. Most of the harvest last year was over by the end of September. We had about twelve days with no work and then pruned plums and peaches through the winter. We didn't stop until January, and that's around the time I usually go back to Mexico to visit. By February I'm back at the farm getting ready for the growing season.

I'm about five years away from retirement, but I don't talk about it much. I'm not really looking forward to retirement, because I'm happy here. Joking with other workers, you don't ever get bored. We can work and have a good time.

I haven't had much trouble with any of the workers in my crew, because I try to take care of them. I remember one young guy in the crew that was injured once. We were pruning peach trees, and this young guy was up in a tree pruning a branch when he fell off his ladder. He didn't fall far, but the pruning shears nailed him in the hand when he hit the ground. He had a big cut. I had him raise his hand above his head and not look at the blood while I bandaged him up. Then I drove him to Fresno to get stitches. I remember he was happy with how I took care of him, and he said, "Boss, no supervisor has ever done anything like that for me." I told him I took care of him because it was my duty.

There are mayordomos who don't know their people at all. I always make sure that we're chatting, that we're happy. There are some mayordomos who never leave work dirty. That's not me. I'm dirty all the time, because I work with the others.

Every company has its rules. But usually you can talk to bosses as a mayordomo and come to an agreement that works for everyone.

Because a good mayordomo has to know how to do the job, first of all. Second, he has to be respectful, respect the worker; and the worker has to respect the mayordomo as his mayordomo. If there's no respect with a worker, then he won't do a good job: he will just play games. You have to know how to treat people. Know how to talk to people so that they don't get upset and decide not to finish their job. If you don't know how to talk to a person then he won't work and that'll be on you as the supervisor.

If a mayordomo is grumpy, if a mayordomo thinks he is better than everybody else, then that will make things hard. You have to be gentle with people. They are workers and you are a worker as well. If you push them, they get angry and don't do anything. If you can get along with them, they'll work and they'll laugh while they're working.

JIM COCHRAN

AGE: 69

OCCUPATION: *Grower and founder of Swanton Berry Farm*
BORN IN: *Orange, Orange County*
INTERVIEWED IN: *Davenport, Santa Cruz County*
AGRICULTURAL REGION: *Santa Cruz County*

From San Francisco, Highway One meanders down the Pacific Coast, tracing a stretch of the state that is breathtaking for its rugged beauty. Bluffs rise and fall to reveal largely empty beaches, while the sun occasionally peeks through the fog to turn slices of the ocean from gray to emerald green. High overhead, a flock of seagulls flies in circles; down below, a lone pelican glides just inches above the water's surface.

It is morning, early August when I head down Highway One to the outskirts of Davenport, an unincorporated community of 400 residents just north of Santa Cruz. At the first turnoff, a yellow truck is parked on the highway shoulder, a large wooden strawberry mounted on its bed. On the other side of the driveway is a tractor long overcome by rust. Jim Cochran bought the tractor for $2,000 in 1983, animated by what many considered a foolish dream: to grow organic strawberries. Today, his company, Swanton Berry Farm, is going strong, with more than two-dozen employees who tend 85 acres of berries and vegetables.

One only needs to step foot inside the roadside store to realize Jim isn't your average grower. There's no employee behind the counter, just a hand-painted sign that reads, "Honor Till—Make Your Own Change," along with a front-facing wooden cash register. The walls are covered with flags and memorabilia from the United Farm Workers. Next to a sign-in sheet for guests is an ancient typewriter that sits atop a book entitled Fatal Harvest: The Tragedy of Industrial Agriculture.

Jim is tall and stocky, and greets me with a firm handshake before ushering me into his nearby office, part of a collection of wooden structures on the property that once housed Mexican braceros—*or guest workers—in the 1950s and '60s. With his feet resting on his desk, he talks about what caused him to go organic, the many lessons he's learned along the way, and why, although he strives to respect his employees, he refuses to call them family.*

HOUSES WERE CHEAP; JOBS WERE PLENTIFUL

My dad was sort of a traveler, a wanderer. He bummed around South America in the thirties, got drafted and went into the Navy in '41, and got discharged in '46. He met my mother when he was still in the Navy, and they got married. I was born in Orange in 1947, so I was definitely the post-war baby.

When I was twelve, we moved to Carlsbad.[1] At that time, Carlsbad was a small town, sort of evenly divided between military families—the Marine Corps was at Camp Pendleton—and small farms. My parents had a number of friends who were small farmers, a lot of the little one- or two-acre flower or cherry tomato operations. A lot of those are still around today.

California then was really idyllic, in the sense that all the men had just returned from the war, and they'd returned alive! And there they were, living in Southern California, with a tenth or a fifth of the population it has now. Houses were cheap; jobs were plentiful.

---

[1] Carlsbad, California, is a coastal city of over 100,000 located just north of San Diego.

I remember my best friend's dad used to love to go out fishing and diving for abalone. He'd come back with a big sack full of giant abalone, a big sack of half a dozen different kinds of fish. Life wasn't fancy like it is now, but everybody was so happy.

My dad didn't have any land in Carlsbad, but he belonged to the Rare Plant Society, for people who grew unusual crops, like macadamias. I remember there was something called the Macadamian Society. They would have a meeting once a year or twice a year, and every once in a while it would be at our house, and there'd be donuts covered entirely in macadamia nuts.

When I was a kid, my dad and mom went to the state of Veracruz in Mexico and bought a small piece of jungle land up in the hills, where they planted macadamia nuts.[2] It's perfect weather up there, that's where you want to be. On the coast it's terrible, mosquitoes and hot and humid all the time. You get up to 3,000 feet and the weather is perfect. The land was on a slope, a volcanic area with big rocks and boulders and grasses. You had to go with machetes and chop it back because it takes over. You cut a trail, and three days later, the trail's not there anymore.

Our parents took us three kids down to Mexico every summer from about when I was ten until I was fifteen. It was a nice mix of working on the farm and traveling around, because my dad became friends with a guy who ran a missionary school and had indigenous kids from villages all over Mexico. The school was sometimes a six- or eight-hour drive from where the kids lived, and my dad's friend would take them back to visit their family twice a year. So he was constantly headed out to some remote part of Mexico, oftentimes only accessible with a four-wheel drive on a dirt road. We also had a four-wheel drive truck, so we'd follow. We'd go to these places where people didn't speak Spanish, and the kid would translate for the parents. It was really, really wonderful. The rest of the time we'd

---

[2] Veracruz is a Mexican state on the southern Gulf coast.

spend pruning Macadamia trees or digging irrigation ditches to get the water to go a certain way.

IT WAS A TIME OF TUMULT

I lived in Southern California until the age of sixteen, when I graduated from high school and went to university. That was 1964. It was a time of tumult.

I started out at the University of California, Santa Barbara. The year I got there, kids had just come back from marches in the South. Everybody was freaked out, not only about the civil rights movement but the Vietnam War. We were all mandatory drafts, no lottery numbers. It was a very heavy time. Things took on a lot of importance, because the stakes were high. I was in school for a year and a half, and it was difficult to concentrate on my studies when all this stuff was happening in the world. I did fine in school, but I just found my mind wandering off to the issues of the time.

I originally wanted to be a CO, a conscientious objector, but I wasn't a religious person so I couldn't at that point. I went into the army in 1966. I'd taken biology at the university for a year and a half, so I said, "I'm thinking about becoming a doctor, what about the medical corps?" I was in training for about nine months, and then worked in surgery in the emergency room in an army hospital in Huntsville, Alabama. I never actually had to go to Vietnam.

After the Army I went to UC-Santa Cruz. In 1970, I was living in a house full of Chicano students, the only Anglo in the crowd. There was some guy down in Watsonville[3] who was recruiting Chicano students at the university to come work for him on this project to set up farmworker-owned cooperatives.[4] Strawberry cooperatives.

---

[3] Watsonville is a coastal city of 50,000 in Santa Cruz County.

[4] Agricultural cooperatives are established by a number of independent growers to help market their products, purchase and share supplies, and achieve better

Everybody was talking about this job and people said, "I don't want to take that job, it doesn't pay all that much." And someone said, "Jim, what about you?"

My Spanish was pretty good. I'd taken four years of Spanish in high school and I'd spoken it in Mexico every summer. When I was in the army, I was certified to be a Spanish speaker as well as an English speaker. I said, "Well, shit. OK."

I went down there and they hired me. It was my first time working with strawberries. I was basically the helper of this guy named Ralph. We're still good buddies, forty-six years later. Ralph had been organizing independent black farmers in the South into a cooperative through VISTA, doing his CO work as a VISTA volunteer.[5] He got chased out of Alabama or South Carolina or something, by the white folks who didn't want some kid causing trouble. Ralph knew something about co-ops, and he came to California and found a suitable place where he could do his work. He was a year and a half older than me, maybe twenty-four. There were three or four people in the organization.

I was doing the administrative part, one of the guys who sat there with an old-fashioned calculator with white-out and a pen or pencil and did spreadsheets by hand. It was amazingly slow. Sometimes you'd look for forty-five minutes for the mistake in a column. I helped figure out the financial planning for a loan package that we were going to submit to Wells Fargo, which was sort of a big deal— we were asking for a quarter-of-a-million-dollar loan.

I did that for at least six months, maybe nine months, in 1970. I dropped out of college a second time, and then my money ran out and I thought, *Well, the co-op field is right next to the local migrant*

economies of scale. Some of California's best-known and largest produce cooperatives include Sunkist (founded in 1893 and now representing over 6,000 citrus growers) and Sun-Maid (founded in 1912 and representing nearly 900 raisin growers).

[5] Volunteers in Service to America (VISTA) was established in 1964 as a domestic wing of the Peace Corps.

labor camp. So I became a nursery teacher, an aide, at the labor camp in Watsonville, while I stayed in touch with Ralph and the co-op members. I did that for a year. There still wasn't a job for me, and I had to do something, so I came back and got a job up here at the University Children's Center at UC-Santa Cruz, taking care of the kids of students and staff. And I graduated and got my degree in '73 in Child Development.

REALLY INTERESTING PEOPLE

I bought a piece of land up here in Swanton in 1970—10,000 bucks bought you six acres.[6] It had trees and shit all over it, covered with poison oak and stumps, so I set about cleaning that up and I built a little shack on it.

In that period of time I also built my house. I had people help me, but nobody knew how to do any of it, we just figured it out. I used $14,000 worth of materials to build my house. Today I rent it out to my production manager and live in a trailer just down the road. My tendency is to build really nice things, and then I can't afford to live there, so I have to rent them out and go on to my next project. Rentals are so tempting, if you're willing to go live in a little shack. I own the land, I can live in the little shack on it; I can rent out the nice place for a lot of money.

I was looking at alternative economic systems. At the time there were co-op buying clubs around California that later evolved into huge businesses. Some of them evolved into stores, some into distribution companies. The nursery school at the university where I worked was a co-op. I was on the credit committee of the local co-operative credit union. I helped some weavers that formed a co-op. I was still interested in all that stuff.

---

[6] Swanton is a small unincorporated coastal community in Santa Cruz County, approximately 30 miles northwest of Watsonville.

Meanwhile, the strawberry co-ops in the area had grown to be a big deal. There were seven or eight co-ops between Watsonville and Santa Maria: 200 families, 1,000 acres, millions of dollars in sales.[7] They had their own cooler, their own marketing association. Growing strawberries is a very technically demanding crop; it's not an easy crop to grow, it's not an easy crop to handle, and it's very competitive. There was a technical assistance arm of the organization that provided agronomists to help with financial planning, business management, and basic business literacy. In 1979, I went to work for that entity, which provided technical assistance to these eight or nine co-ops. I did that for a year and a half or so.

The people we were competing against had a hotshot manager or a hotshot farmer who knew what to do and didn't have a board of directors contradicting what he said. If you're a big independent farmer who doesn't share decision making, bingo, whatever you want to do gets done. In a co-op, there's a debate about it. Sometimes it works out great and sometimes it doesn't. Some member of the board of directors drinks a little too much and says, "Well, goddammit, I'm on the board of directors, I can drive the tractor if I want to." So he gets on a tractor and screws up the clutch! Now the farm's tractor doesn't work.

The families in the co-ops were really interesting people. There's a full range. Some of them really didn't have a clue, and others were actually pretty accomplished farmers. Everybody was really good at mental calculations of the cost of things, because everybody was thinking about that all the time. This was their livelihood, not just this little consumer co-op they belong to that's a little part of their life. They watch every nickel. They may not even be literate, but they know how to calculate stuff.

But we didn't all have the same ideas about things. I remember one meeting when I was arguing with a grower about something or

---

[7] Santa Maria is a city of 100,000 approximately 175 miles south of Watsonville. It is one of the state's largest strawberry-growing regions.

other and he took me outside after the meeting and said, "Jim, just to let you know …" and he's got a .45 there on his side. I mean, he wasn't going to shoot me or anything, I think he was trying to tell me that next time I was trying to make a point I shouldn't make it quite so strenuously. I said, "OK."

A man named Mark, who later became my partner, had been the manager of that co-op. He told me that once it had been getting dark during a board of directors meeting and all of a sudden rats started running around, and these guys pulled out their pistols and took turns shooting them.

The co-op members also varied widely as to their performance as employers. Each family was a unit and they'd hire two or three, four, five people to work for them. Some of them were decent employers and some were terrible employers.

There are a lot of chemicals that go into growing most strawberries. I got pesticide poisoning a number of times when I was working with the co-ops. I was out in the field doing the stuff along with everybody else; I saw how much all the workers were exposed to it. To do fumigation in the strawberry fields, someone comes out with a Caterpillar tractor that forces pesticide gases fourteen inches underground in rows, and then the whole field is covered with a tarp. The guys helping to weigh down the tarp wouldn't have any protection then, and there wouldn't be any protection when they removed the tarp a few days later. You're pulling off the tarp and all this gas is coming out, so you're breathing the stuff in. And then the guy goes in with a tractor afterward, digging it up, and more and more of it is getting vented to the outside air. So I got that. You get jittery and shaky, and you get thirsty.

Another time or two I walked into a field that had been sprayed that I didn't think had been sprayed, and got into the middle of it. I felt jittery and dizzy, but it was my fault for walking out into that field. The fumigation is a highly refined process. The pesticide people were really conscientious. For all the bad PR they got, they were trying hard to make it safe. It's probably a lot safer today than it was thirty-five years ago.

But still, I just didn't like working around it. I subscribed to *Organic Gardening*, but I was never a good gardener. I'd read *Silent Spring* in '62 when it came out.[8] The crew tended to be very cavalier about it. Meanwhile I'm reading all this stuff about how bad it is for you and they're saying "Oh, don't worry, it's not going to hurt you." And I'm thinking, *We'd be better off to just stay away from it altogether*, and eventually, that's what I did.

Most of my work during this time though was helping to renegotiate loans with banks. Through that work I learned about one co-op in Salinas that was a big basket case. It was made up of about 200 acres managed by nineteen families. These families had taken over the acreage from a different co-op made up of fifty families, and these new families were just in over their heads. They were in deep financial trouble. They needed help, so I went to work for them trying to get their finances in order. I remember thinking, *OK, I'm going to quit my cushy job with the guaranteed salary and go work for this co-op that's about ready to go under and leave the bank with a half-million-dollar loan not paid.* We did OK, reduced the debt from $500,000 to $240,000. Still, it was really rough. But I learned more about the business, and pretty soon I thought, *I just want to go out on my own and do this.*

My friend Mark and I formed a partnership. He'd managed two or three co-ops down in Santa Maria. We came up here and rented land in Swanton Valley and we got the farming bug.

GET OUT THERE AND SELL PRODUCT

By the time I started farming myself, I'd been around the business for four years, so I knew a little bit about the strawberries—how to

---

[8] Rachel Carson's book, *Silent Spring*, was published in 1962. The book documented the negative effects pesticides had on the environment—particularly on birds—and forced the banning of DDT and spurred major changes in the laws that affect our air, land, and water.

grow them conventionally, how to market them, post-harvest handling and all that stuff. I wasn't particularly good at it, but I had a pretty good idea of how that worked. Same with Mark.

We bought an old tractor. I paid $2,000 for it in '83. We farmed four acres of strawberries for two years. Mark and I leased the land, and I was more inclined to organic and he was more inclined to conventional, so we did a half-assed version of conventional and a half-assed version of organic side-by-side.

We leased a piece of land on the edge of Highway 1 and set up a little stand. We'd pull out a little wagon and get out there and sell product. The best sales were to restaurants and independent grocery stores at high-end places and over the hill in the Las Gatos and San Jose areas. We had a very high-quality product and they could afford to pay a little more. It worked out OK. We paid all our bills, but we both had outside jobs. My outside job was being a construction laborer, or going back to work at the children's center. Low-paying jobs, you know, $3 an hour, $6 an hour.

Then Mark got married, and that was not enough money to live on. For me, it wasn't so bad because I lived in my little shack, I rented out the big house, so I had income from the big house. I could live pretty cheaply. But Mark needed to find another way to make real money.

When Mark left in '86 I bought a piece of land out here that was an old farm labor camp on two acres of land. It was just a bunch of old buildings like where we are now, precisely like this old labor camp. You'll see them all the way from Northern California to the South. They were old military barracks, then they became a labor camp after World War II, and then they sold them off to farmers after World War II for the Bracero Program.[9]

---

[9] The Bracero Program was an agreement between the United States and Mexico beginning in 1942 to grant guest worker visas to Mexican agricultural workers. For more information on the Bracero Program, see the Glossary, page 283.

Anyway, there was a piece of land that was really cheap on the coast, because it was basically an abandoned camp and they were not habitable buildings. It was just a junk pile. I borrowed money on my house and bought it. I put an acre of strawberries down there and, God, I can't believe it, I coaxed 5,500 trays an acre out of that plot down there, which was really very high production.

THE UNION DOESN'T WANT TO
PUT YOU OUT OF BUSINESS

After I went out on my own, I wanted to stay organic. As far as I knew, the only person who actually had experience in production of organic strawberries was Gene Kahn up in Washington State, who founded Cascadian Farm.[10] But he grew cannery berries, so they're a little bit less exacting because you don't care about the shape or the size of the cannery berries. But with the fresh market berries, customers want a certain strawberry. Some customers are happy with the small strawberries, but many aren't. There was really nobody to turn to if you wanted to learn how to grow organic strawberries at a commercial level, because the answer was always to use chemicals, fertilizer, or pesticides. The organic farming movement was making a lot of strides in general organic farming: it just wasn't about strawberries.

The farm happened to be next to the house of Steve Gliessman from UC-Santa Cruz, and he was a soil biologist. He took a lot of interest in what I was doing, and he and I put our heads together about a lot of the soil issues. He brought in somebody about insects, and over six or seven years we came up with a system. The university wrote it all down, and they brought in other people who by that

---

[10] Cascadian Farms was started by grower Gene Kahn in 1972 and is now one of the largest organic foods producers in the United States. It has been owned by General Mills since 2000.

time had started growing organic strawberries, and those people put together a guide for growing organic strawberries, put out by the University of California.

One of the things that we learned was to look for general soil fertility, rather than to try to dose the soil one way or the other. You're trying to build soil health: that means biological health, that means soil structure, that means the right nutrients. I add compost, always some sort of kelp material. You should see the list of stuff that's in kelp from what it picks up in the ocean. And rock phosphate and gypsum, lime. Then do crop rotations, add compost, do cover crops every year with a really high-quality cover crop. I do a mix that is put out by one of the old organic people—it's got two or three kinds of grasses and four legumes. It grows up real tall and nice and you disk it all into the ground, and it's good for the soil.

For me though, it wasn't just about setting up an organic farm. I wanted to create a good work environment. Some people are just fiercely independent and really aren't going to be happy unless they're an independent farmer. Other people just want a fair place to work, where they get paid reasonably well, they get treated well, and they get, in the best of cases, asked for their opinion about different parts of the job that they're doing, instead of having the manager come in and say, "This is what we're doing and I don't care what you think." The kind of place where people say, "Well, what do you think? Have we been giving this too much water?" or "Why in the world do you think we're having this bug problem now?" And they say, "Well, it's because we've been watering too much and all the extra moisture has given us this particular bug ..." People like having their opinions valued.

I'M SORT OF A SYSTEMS GUY

I came to the whole farming thing first from the larger economic justice issue, and then from the agricultural perspective on how to help improve the conditions for farmworkers. For me, the big influence during the '60s was not Martin Luther King and it was not the anti-war movement. It was Cesar Chavez. When I was working for the co-op, it was the same time that the United Farm Workers was in Salinas, and us co-op people were sort of outsiders in the farming world, in the same way that the union was.[11] So we would socialize together.

The UFW was organizing in Watsonville in '95 or '96, not making a lot of headway. I was organized in the California Certified Organic Farmers group, the CCOF, and it was very clear that they did not want to deal with labor issues. So I said that I'm going to take a similar approach: the union label is a labor certification, it's an outside body and you have to do a whole bunch of things to fit into the program, just like you do with organic farming. You know, there's materials you can use, materials you can't use. And there's philosophy behind it. Well there's also philosophy with the union movement, and I was favorably disposed to the union.

Arturo Rodriguez, the President of the UFW, gave a speech at EcoFarm, which is a big organic farming conference. This was around January of '97 in Monterey. There were a whole bunch of organic farmers there and he said, "Listen, let's work together. Cesar believed in organic farming practices. It's a logical thing. We want to protect farmers from these pesticides. We'd be happy to talk." I was one person who took up that invitation. Arturo came over here to my farm. At that time I had only maybe seven or eight employees. We had an initial conversation, and the union came back to me and said, "OK, this is the point, legally, where we take a different track and we're going to go talk to your employees."

There are a lot of laws built into the legislation that created the

---

[11] Salinas in the early 1970s was a major site of UFW strike actions, as the organization was seeking to raise wages and create better working conditions for lettuce workers.

Agricultural Labor Relations Board.[12] There are certain things that you can talk about, and other things that you can't talk about. Everything we did was by the book. I had legal advice on exactly how to do it, because you have to be very careful. In fact, I had the election challenged shortly after I signed the contract, by Rob Roy from the Ventura County Agricultural Association.[13] I've never met him, but he challenged it once or twice. I don't remember what the basis of the challenge was. Fortunately I'd done a good job of following the rules.

Our contract started in '98, I think. It was a big deal. Not only had I bolted from the conventional strawberry world and become the first conventional grower to go organic, I'd also bolted into the union world. I did get flack from some of the Salinas growers. The wife of a prominent farmer was pretty curt with me when we were at some event. She said, "God, I'm surprised you have the guts to show your face around here." It was alright, she was sort of a hot head. I ran into her husband half a dozen years ago at this little cafe and he said, "Oh Jim, how are you doing? I'm so glad to see you." Everything was fine. I was a pariah for a long time, because of the union, because of organic, but not now.

There was sort of the implicit thing with organic that those farmers were doing something wrong, right? Same thing with the union thing—*they're doing something wrong.* Just like organic, many growers saw the union in an adversarial manner. Arturo, when he gave his talk, said, "Look, it's a partnership. The union doesn't want

---

[12] In 1975, under pressure from the UFW, California passed the Agricultural Labor Relations Act, which created legal protections, along with a general framework, for farmworkers to unionize. (Such rights were codified for all other workers—minus domestic workers—in the National Labor Relations Act of 1938, but excluded farmworkers.) The ALRA created the Agricultural Relations Labor Board, the body that oversees elections to make sure both unions and growers follow the established rules.

[13] Ventura County on California's Central Coast is one of the state's major producers of strawberries; the Ventura County Agricultural Association represents the interests of strawberry growers.

to put you out of business; they want to make the business get much better and share the benefit with the workers. It's not the model that you think of, that our job is to extract every last nickel out of you and put you out of business."

Working with the union has been really good. One of the benefits that you have when you sign a union contract is a written contract. It explains in great detail what procedure you follow when you have an employee that's unhappy about something. Grievance procedures, breaking out the pay so everybody understands who's getting paid what and why, that there's some rational reason why something is done, which is a good thing.

A lot of times somebody will say that such and such happened, and they say, "What do we do?" And I'll say, "I don't know, let's look at the contract." And you've got it lined out, and you just follow what it says and everything's fine. I like that. I mean, I'm sort of a systems guy. I don't believe in the sort of patronizing, "Oh they're all family; I take care of them just like my family." I'm looking at the larger picture of California agriculture and what kind of system would have better results for a larger number of people.

BUT WHAT ABOUT THE WORKERS?

Today I have twenty-six full-time year-round people, and then probably some part-time workers—those are the people that work at farmers' markets or U-picks. We're harvesting something every week of the year. We do nine farmers' markets a week, the farm stand, and U-picks. Between 'em, that's three-quarters or more of our sales. The rest we sell direct to retail, mostly in the Bay Area.

We operate a farm-labor camp right on the other side of this office wall, actually. The kitchen and recreation room is here. There's barracks and individual rooms in those two buildings over there. We probably only have six guys in the barracks and everybody else has their own room. A few workers don't live on site, the ones that are married and have families live in town. But I don't know most of them as much anymore. Of course, I was involved in everybody's lives. The newer ones I don't know as much. I mean, I'm sixty-eight, I'm going to be sixty-nine in a month, and I'm OK with that, you know: I'm not trying to be their family.

I don't do any work anymore. I'm a good delegator, so I delegate. Especially when my son was born—he's twenty-four now, and I started delegating then. By that time I'd already been in the business for over twenty years and had run myself ragged. One person is in charge of production and one person is in charge of farm sales. Then production has a harvest crew, which is about fifteen people, and a crew leader for that, and then half a dozen other people drive tractors, make deliveries, do irrigation, set up and do the more complicated tasks involved directly in production.

Some folks have been here a long time; thirty years is the longest. The younger ones, both with the farmers' market and the people working the farm stand, come and work for a few years and then go. The newer organic, farming youth movement is a different business model, because there are farms that are set up to absorb people like that, and they are more like training places. We are not set up like that. We're more about production than educational.

The farm where we are now is owned by the Trust for Public Land, so it's protected forever. South from here, I lease from State Parks. North, I lease from a family that's owned the land for 100 years. We lease about 140 acres or so, but we only have water for just a little under 90.

About twelve or fifteen years ago I started thinking about ESOP, an Employee Stock Ownership Plan. Reading books, going to meetings. The ESOP is sort of my way of getting to the notion that a really ideal system would be a system in which farmworkers own some percentage of the business. There are 11,000 companies in the United States that are partly or completely employee-owned. Southwest Airlines is 15 percent employee-owned, UPS has a significant amount. Who would've thunk? Except it doesn't exist in agriculture. I'm the only company in the country that's a farm and food production ESOP. It's a way to share the wealth and still be able to have a management system where you can keep good management in place and not have a crisis every time the Board of Directors meets and decides to throw somebody out. Unfortunately, the scale I'm at is too small—my administrative costs are $20,000 a year. So now I'm looking at alternatives that resemble the formal ESOP structure but with lower costs.

I've been doing the union for eighteen years, the ESOP for ten years. It has cost me a lot of money. My job is to get the price to pay for all this stuff. I mean, people have to pay for what it costs to do this. The only thing that irritates me is people who are riding along on the coattails of the price that I charge, charging ever so slightly less but they have 30 percent lower costs than I do. Because union benefits are $3 more an hour per person. That's not the wages, just the benefits.[14]

That's something that nobody else has, at least not in the organic world. They're undercutting me without the sacrifice. People don't know anything at all about the labor practices of this wonderful looking farm that has a great little story, and a nice little this and a nice little that. Maybe that's all true. But what about the workers? What are they getting out of that? Well, they're not doing so well.

About six years ago we started working with a group on the East Coast that wanted to develop a certification process in the US that was parallel to what was happening around the world with coffee, tennis shoes, and lots of other stuff. Why did US producers get a free ride, without scrutiny by a third-party certifier? So these people developed a certification program that looked hard at labor practices

---

[14] Though contracts vary, unionized farmworkers in California often make about 30 percent more than non-unionized workers.

and other stuff. It's called the Domestic Fair Trade label.[15] We were certified a couple of years ago. It's really quite comprehensive.

What I'm trying to do is create a model that says to people, "Well, you know, it seems to work for Jim, maybe I'd be willing to try something like that too." It definitely worked that way for the organic part, because now there are 100 or 200 organic strawberry growers in the state. We're still around, still in business, doing OK. And the labor set of issues is more in the public discussion now than it was ten years ago. People are more conscious of workers now. Organic was where it was all at. And now that organic's established, people are starting to say, "OK, let's really think about the people who are actually doing the work, that are growing the food." I think that's hopeful.

---

[15] The Domestic Fair Trade Association (DFTA) is a membership organization that includes farmworkers and their organizations, farmers and farmer groups, retailers, NGOs, and food distributors, processors, and manufacturers.

BEATRIZ MACHICHE

AGE: *58*

OCCUPATION: *Head Start manager*
BORN IN: *Sonora, California*
INTERVIEWED IN: *Thermal, Riverside County*
AGRICULTURAL REGION: *Coachella Valley*

One of the most difficult challenges farmworkers face is finding good-quality childcare. First, there is the question of money: childcare is expensive, and farmworkers often already don't make enough to cover other basic needs, like food and housing. Work schedules pose another obstacle. Shifts in the fields can start as early as 5 a.m.; if those fields are a ways off, they might need to leave home two hours earlier. Traditional daycares aren't open at 3 a.m.

Many migrant workers find unlicensed providers—typically a relative or neighbor—who watch their kids for about $10 a day per child. Some of these caretakers are attentive and capable, but others simply plop kids down in dark rooms to watch hours of television. Many of these children arrive in kindergarten far behind their peers. This ground can be hard to make up.

Beatriz Machiche manages a Migrant Head Start Center in the Coachella Valley, where the children of migrant farmworkers are provided, at no cost, educational programing, hot meals, and loving teachers. We first meet in May at her office, where she sits behind a large desk surrounded by stacks of paper. But Beatriz isn't really an office person, so we head out for a tour of the local fields, stopping as well at several of the local home-based centers that she oversees. Inside these homes, children sing the ABCs, draw with crayons, and listen to books being read aloud—in short, all the kinds of activities that Machiche, a former farmworker, never got to experience as a kid.

EVERYTHING GROWS HERE

These are lemons growing over here, and everything on this side of the road is strawberries. We have quite a variety of things growing. The only thing I can think of that we don't harvest here is apples. We've got peaches, almonds and other nuts, mangos. There used to be a lot of oranges and lemons, but not as much anymore. Right now the corn is being harvested. The families around here work at night harvesting corn and then get up early in the morning to harvest peppers. The cabbage and cauliflower have already been picked. Everything grows here.

With all the different growing seasons, there are some families that are able to stay here and work on farms year around. For those families, we have the Early Head Start program for kids from newborn to three years old, and it goes for eleven months out of the year—other than the month in the winter when there's no work in the fields. But we also work with families that move around a lot. Some go to Bakersfield or Arvin for the harvests there, others go to Texas for part of the year, others to Washington to pick apples. That's why we started the Migrant Head Start program. The schedule is more flexible for families that move often to follow the harvests.[1]

---

[1] Head Start is a federal program operated by the Department of Health and Human Services. It offers early childhood education, childhood health and nutrition services, and services to parents for nearly 1 million low-income families. Migrant Head Start focuses on children up to five years old and offers longer service hours per day but fewer months of program enrollment per year than many other Head Start programs.

We don't ask for papers or anything like that. Still, some families are afraid of the Migrant Head Start program because of the name—*la migra* is the name given to Immigration officers. We provide information about what we do, that we offer education and childcare, but we're often told, "We're not interested." Some parents think we're linked to Immigration. But we tell them, "No, we just want children to be cared for and safe." Still, many are afraid.

PEOPLE STARTED TO SHOUT, "LA MIGRA IS COMING! THEY HAVE DOGS!"

My dad was Yaqui, and he was born and raised in Sonora.[2] My mom grew up all over, since her dad worked on the railroads. But my parents met in Sonora, and my two sisters and I grew up near San Luis Río Colorado in Sonora.[3]

My dad was traditional. He thought women should either work at home or work in the fields, and that there was no point in girls studying past the basics. My mom wanted my sisters and me to study as well, since she hadn't had the opportunity. But to my father, it was only important that women learned how to cook and clean.

When I was nine, I started crossing into the United States with my family to do the lemon harvest around Mesa, Arizona. We had guest-worker permits, and we'd go back and forth between Sonora and Arizona every day. On days when we worked too late to cross back, we'd sleep under the lemon trees, and just start working again after we woke up.

We also started working in California, harvesting lemons and then grapes. It was around that time that I first started to hear about

[2] The Yaqui are an indigenous people that have traditionally occupied the parts of what is now the state of Sonora in Mexico as well as what is now the southwest United States. The Mexican state of Sonora borders Arizona and New Mexico.

[3] San Luis Río Colorado is a city of 150,000 on the Arizona-Sonora border. Across the border is the city of San Luis, Arizona, which is home to 30,000.

Cesar Chavez in the fields. In 1968, my mother took me to Los Angeles, where there was a rally for grape harvesters. That year there was looting and shooting in LA, and I remember my mom telling me to stay close to her, and I remember the sound of gunshots and people yelling as we walked through the city streets.

Then in 1973, when I was fourteen years old, my mother decided she wanted to stay in Coachella for good. She took me and my two sisters with her. My aunt invited us to sleep in her garage.

That was the year I first saw Cesar Chavez up close. He was in the fields talking to workers about what his organization was fighting for—better wages, an eight-hour work day, breaks. He encouraged us all to strike until we had a new contract, but he was also having a dispute with the Teamsters.[4]

The Teamsters had already been making us angry, even before the strike—they'd wait until the grape harvest was over and then call *la migra* on the workers. I remember one day in the fields harvesting grapes, and people in the fields started to shout—"La migra is coming! They have dogs!" There were about five or six cars that pulled up, and Immigration officers got out and started chasing people. They grabbed a few. My mom got some boxes out of our car and hid people under them. Immigration would come back day to day to grab a few more people. They would jump out of their cars and start hunting people.

We continued to live in my aunt's garage for two years, and my sisters and I were able to go to school. And then we began building a house of our own using a new Self-Help Housing Program, and a community of us worked together to build ten new houses. It was

---

[4] Starting in 1966, the UFW (then the United Farm Worker Organizing Committee, backed by the AFL-CIO) began competing to represent farmworkers with the Teamsters, a much larger union. A dispute over management of labor contracts between the two unions led to violent confrontations in the Coachella Valley in 1973, with Teamsters targeting UFW farmworkers. For more about the conflict between the Teamsters and the UFW, see Rosario's narrative, page 45–57.

a busy time. My sisters and I were going to school and then helping out with the home building, working forty hours a week putting together the ten houses, digging, nailing, whatever needed to be done. My mom would have ten-hour shifts at a carrot packing plant, and then she'd come help on the houses as well. I was in Coachella High School at the time, and I was able to keep up with my studies. In fact, during the harvest season, my mom would take my sisters and me out of school some days so we could help in the fields and make some extra money. We'd rotate, so we weren't all out every day.

Still, I got pretty good grades, and in 1977 I ended up graduating thirty-seventh in the class.

I ENDED UP GETTING MARRIED TWO YEARS OUT OF HIGH SCHOOL

I'd met the man who would become my husband while I was still in high school. I met him through a friend that worked with him in the grape fields. She said this guy had beautiful eyes, and she set us up for a date to the movies.

I ended up getting married two years out of high school in 1979. We got married here in California, and then in 1981 we moved to Mexico, to Colima, and we had a civil ceremony there as well.[5] We lived in a trailer beneath the palm trees. My husband planted sugar cane, corn, and rice, and we'd come back to California every year for the date harvest.

In Colima, I worked for an organization called Desarrollo Integral de la Mujer, which sought to integrate women into political, social, and business life. I'd work with a lot of indigenous families that were in the area to help with the harvests. I'd help train them how to use local resources and encourage them to send their children to school.

---

[5] Colima is a small state on the central Pacific coast of Mexico.

I had my own children as well, and we lived like that in Colima for over twenty years until my children were older, from 1981 to 2003. When we came to stay in the United States, my son was twenty-one and my daughter was fifteen.

When I first moved back to the United States, I worked in the fields. But I was getting older, and my feet and hands were hurting badly with arthritis. I couldn't keep up with the work. I told my husband I couldn't do it anymore, and went to look for work in a store. I ended up working at Walmart arranging clothes and working the cash register. Then after a year I worked in customer service, then managed a bakery until they couldn't afford me anymore. Then I went back to grapes.

When I was forty-nine, I went back to study at the College of the Desert.[6] I'd go to classes at night and work in the grape fields during the day. I was training to be a pre-school teacher. That's when I started working at the Head Start program. They helped me get my teacher permit, and I've been with Head Start ever since.

Now I'm a manager—I'm like the principal. I check on teachers, I do class observations, manage payroll and staff, manage incoming students. I manage a center in Thermal that takes kids from Oasis, Coachella, and Indio. We also have providers who care for children in their homes. We have over 100 children, and a wait list of over 200.

I ASKED THE KIDS WHAT THEY WANTED TO BE WHEN THEY GREW UP

Through Head Start, we offer a number of services to fieldworker families, aside from just education and childcare. We refer people to medical and dental services, and we work in mental health as well. We refer children with special needs to clinics where they're

---

[6] College of the Desert is a community college in Palm Desert with 10,000 students.

observed, and then we provide strategies to parents. We also work with the schools—for instance we have one child who has problems digesting certain proteins, so we worked with her school to provide a special diet through their cafeteria. We provide food—breakfast, lunch, and a snack before we send them home. For the younger children we provide diapers.

We want to expand to provide more services, so that children have a better quality of life and can excel. We want to create more programs and scholarships so that our kids can go to college. Part of that is offering services so these families can stay in one place. I don't want these children to do what my siblings and I had to do— travel back and forth every day, sleep in the fields, not have a place to shower or have a warm, fresh meal.

I'm proud of our children. Kids will bring in their report cards and say, "Look how I'm doing in third grade!" Or "I won an award at school," or "Now I can speak English!" That makes me really happy, because I know they care, and because of that they have a good shot of making it to college. They won't stay in the fields their whole lives.

But it's not easy for every child. One day I asked the kids what they wanted to be when they grew up. One girl said, "I want to be a nurse, because I want to heal my grandmother who can't see anymore." Another child said, "I want to be a teacher, because I really like to teach." Another wanted to work in grapes, and another wanted to work on date trees and get to climb up to the top of the trees and see how small everyone looked below. Then the next kid says, "I want to drink like my father and go around saying, 'Hey, give me a cold one.'" All the other kids laughed, but I thought it was really heartbreaking. Another boy said he wanted to join la migra "so I can take all of you away," because his father had been taken away. So I tell parents to be careful of what their children see and hear at home.

But *la migra* is just a fact of life for many of these children. This is the time of year, too. As soon as there's less work in the fields, that's when la migra comes out looking for people. They're waiting to see if you're missing a taillight, or maybe they'll stop you for some other reason. These children are losing family members all the time.

The question people around here want to ask this guy, Mr. Trump, is: who is going to do the jobs if it's not Latinos? Who is going to put fruits and vegetables on their tables? Who is going to clean houses and hotels, if it's not Latinos? Not only Mexicans, but also Central Americans, from El Salvador, Nicaragua, Venezuela. This work isn't easy, and someone has to do the job. People with education just aren't going to do it. You don't have to step on the Latino's head. I always hear that machines are going to replace workers in the fields. But I've been hearing that for decades, and now there are more workers out there, not fewer. You need a good eye to judge beautiful, healthy fruit, and machines can't do that.

I MISS WORKING IN THE FIELDS

I've always liked work in the fields. You're free, it's sunny, filling up onion boxes, chilies, grape boxes. You bring your radio and you sing; you eat on the ground with your colleagues.

Of course, here in California it's hard to get that paycheck and know how much is going to go to the car, insurance, your cell phone. After all that, not much is left. But at least we can have those things here—in Mexico, it can be difficult to get a car, and you have a TV only because someone brought one down for you from the north. Here at least there's opportunity.

And there are so many other good things about working in the fields. You can be yourself. You aren't afraid to get fired because you're not dressed properly. And you're the same as all the other workers, you can laugh and joke around. In an office job, you have to make sure to always be professional and deferential to your many bosses. You respect your coworkers in the fields as well, but there everyone is on the same level, nobody looks down on you. And the food is great. There's no comparison between rushing to eat at the office versus sitting down with friends under the lemon trees to eat. It might be exactly the same food, but it tastes much better under the trees.

I miss working in the fields. But I've always loved working with people. From a young age I wanted to be a leader like Cesar Chavez, and I've always wanted to love what I do. That's my philosophy— always love what you do. That's why I work on holidays, weekends. When I'm not working, I feel like there is something missing. I need to remain active and helping people, and when I am stressed I like to cook things for my neighbors, to feed people, serve the community.

Sometimes I tell the families, if you have work for me, on Saturday I want to work the fields, I want to cut grapes. Some mothers once asked me, "Do you really want to work the field?" I said, "Sure, if I get paid! I like the work."

APPENDIX I.
TIMELINE OF LABOR
AND AGRICULTURE
IN CALIFORNIA

The following timeline is offered to provide some historical context on California's unique relationship to agriculture, labor, and migrant communities. It is by no means comprehensive. For a thorough look at California's history of farmwork, we recommend Trampling Out the Vintage: Cesar Chavez and the Two Souls of the United Farm Workers *by Frank Bardacke (Verso)*, The Crusades of Cesar Chavez *by Miriam Powel (Bloomsbury) and* Bitter Harvest: A History of California's Farmworkers, 1870–1941 *by Cletus Daniel (University of California Press).*

Before recorded history: Before contact with Europeans, the land that is now the state of California is inhabited by hundreds of thousands of people representing over seventy distinct cultures and numerous languages. Local abundance of food resources helps make the region one of the most densely populated in North America. Nearly one third of Native Americans in what is now the United States live in what is now California.

1492: Christopher Columbus arrives on the island of Hispaniola, beginning a wave of European colonization in the Americas.

1510: Spanish explorers first apply the name *California* to the Baja peninsula. They name it after a legendary Amazonian homeland described in a contemporary novel as "an island near the Terrestrial Paradise."

1529: The Spanish crown grants conquistador Hernán Cortés the entire Oaxacan Valley in Mexico as personal property. Spain considers all native inhabitants in the valley to be the property of the state. Indigenous Mexicans are forced to work in plantations that grow sugar cane and other crops for export.

1542: Juan Rodríguez Cabrillo explores the coast of what is today California. Though numerous European explorers map parts of California over the following two centuries, there is little European settlement in the region.

1769: Spain begins colonization of what is today the state of California. Franciscan missionaries establish permanent settlements along the coast, starting with Mission San Diego de Alcalá in present day San Diego. Diseases introduced by European settlers begin to decimate the native population of California.

1776: Spanish missionaries found San Francisco.

1821: Mexico obtains sovereignty in the treaty of Córdoba.

1824: California is claimed as part of the newly established Republic of Mexico. Native inhabitants in the San Joaquin Valley rebel.

1836: Residents of California declare California a republic and revolt against Mexico. Mexico regains control by deciding to make

California a department rather than a territory and makes the leader of the revolt the governor.

1844: The United States and Mexico go to war over disputed territories.

1848: In January, James Marshall finds gold on the south part of the American River at Sutter's Mill. This starts the gold rush and thousands of non-natives flood the area. In February, the Treaty of Guadalupe Hidalgo surrenders land belonging to Mexico north of the Rio Grand to the United States.

1849: The Chinese immigrant population in the United States doubles from the previous year, from 325 to 650. As the gold rush continues, more and more Chinese immigrants arrive in California. American citizens of California are told to form a government by military governor Brigadier General Bennet Riley. A California constitution is drafted and officials are elected.

1850: In September, California becomes the thirty-first state.

1852: Since the start of the gold rush in 1848, the population of Chinese immigrants in the United States has increased from a few hundred to 25,000.

1850s: Many former gold prospectors purchase land and begin growing grains such as wheat and barley. Because of ideal growing conditions for these crops, a large surplus of grain is grown and exported, including to Europe. California agriculture becomes a profitable business. Innovative, large-scale farming methods that rely on new technology make California farmsteads distinct from smaller-scale, more traditional farms in the east.

1859: Plans for building a transcontinental railroad are made in San Francisco. By this year there are 19,000 farms in California.

1860s: Several droughts and floods hit California and the livestock industry struggles.

1862: The Pacific Railroad Act finalizes plans for a transcontinental railway. In May the Homestead Act is signed by President Abraham Lincoln. The act promotes westward migration by making it easy for the heads of U.S. households to file applications for 160 acres of surveyed government land in the west. The conditions are that the family must live on the land for five years and improve it by at least "building a 12´-by-14´ dwelling and growing crops."

1869–1889: Intensive irrigation begins throughout arable regions in Central California.

1870s: Fruit develops as a prominent California crop. Transcontinental railroad is completed, with Chinese laborers making up much of the rail construction workforce. During this time Chinese migrants also make up much of California's farm labor population, and Chinese immigrants make up 10 percent of California's total population. Many nativist Californians blame Chinese immigrants for depressing wages.

1880s: A time of major farming expansion in California. Chinese immigrants remain a critical farm labor force but face increased discrimination, violence, and forced displacement. They are barred from acquiring U.S. citizenship.

1882: The Chinese Exclusion Act is passed and signed by President Chester A. Arthur. The act bans Chinese laborers from immigrating to the United States.

1884: Migrant Chinese hop harvesters stage a major strike in Kern County, demanding wages of $1.50 a day.

1886: Fruit crop production in California grows rapidly. In this year alone, the state exports around 27 million pounds of oranges and lemons.

1889: "Bonanza" wheat farms (large-scale wheat producers) grow 40 million bushels of wheat a year, making California the second-largest wheat producer in the United States. California is also the nation's leading wool producer.

1890–1914: A major shift occurs in state agricultural practices from large ranches and grain fields to smaller-scale fruit production.

1890–1897: Another major expansion of irrigation begins, with a focus on accessing California's reserves of groundwater.

1892: End of Chinese Exclusion Act. The Geary Act is passed and requires Chinese immigrants to carry identification with them at all times or they may be deported.

1896: The California Development Company is formed with the purpose of irrigating California's southern deserts with water from the Colorado River.

1900: California's population reaches nearly 1.5 million. California farmers are early adopters of agricultural heavy machinery, and surpluses continue to drive a robust export market.

1901: The California Development Company completes construction in the Imperial Canal. For the first time, water from the Colorado River is diverted to farmland in the Imperial Valley.

1902: Congress signs the Chinese Exclusion Act again in 1902 and it lasts for another ten years. Congress establishes the Bureau of Reclamation. Part of the bureau's mandate is "water conservation," which is then defined as making best use of fresh water resources before they flow to the sea. California, among other states, begins cooperating on a number of irrigation and damming projects in order to turn arid regions into arable lands.

1905: A mistake made by irrigation engineers causes the Colorado River to flood a dry lakebed known as the Salton Trough in the Imperial Valley. Flooding over two years results in the formation of the Salton Sea, now the largest lake in California.

1906: Major earthquake and subsequent fires destroy much of San Francisco.

1910: California becomes one of the world's leading producers of citrus, grapes, and other fruits. The state also has success with cooperative/collective farm distribution. The California Fruit Growers Exchange begins marketing 60 percent of citrus shipped from the state under the Sunkist label.

1912: The California Associated Raisin Company (CARC), a raisin grower coop, formed. It would later become known as Sun-Maid Raisin Growers of California.

1910–30: The number of well pumps doubles both decades.

1913: The Alien Land Law is passed. Immigrants ineligible for U.S. citizenship cannot own land. This mainly affects the Chinese, Japanese, Koreans, and Indian immigrants.

1914–1918: During World War I, California increases cotton growing as the price of cotton surges.

1917: The United States joins the fighting in World War I and drafts 2.8 million soldiers, greatly impacting the labor force needed for industries such as agriculture. The same year the United States begins the first Mexican guest worker program. Mexican guest workers are known as *braceros* ("manual laborers") and participate widely in California agriculture until the first guest worker program is curtailed in 1921, partly because Mexican officials respond to reports of low wages and abuse in U.S. fields.

1920s: With the Mexican guest worker program on tenuous footing, California growers begin hiring Filipino farmworkers, many of whom have previously worked on sugar plantations in Hawaii. Between 1920 and 1930, the number of Filipinos living in California increases from 3,000 to 30,000. Every year this decade, as many as 62,000 Mexican citizens enter the United States for farmwork legally, and as many as 100,000 a year enter without documentation.

1922: The Capper-Volstead Act passes. This exempts grower coops from anti-trust prosecution.

1926: Growers continue to lobby for a guest worker program in order to keep wages low and develop a surplus labor supply of workers willing to take on physically demanding work. The American Farm Bureau reports that "California's specialized agriculture [requires] a kind of labor able to meet the requirements of hard, stoop, hand labor, and to work under the sometimes less advantageous conditions of heat, sun, dust, wind, and isolation."

1927: A group of Mexican farmworkers in the United States start a "mutual aid society" and develop a list of demands for improved working conditions in the fields. In March, Cesar Chavez is born outside of Yuma, Arizona.

1928–1934: Major drought leads to significant water rights reforms in the state.

1929–1939: The United States experiences the Great Depression, and the plains states are afflicted by drought and dust storms partly caused by agricultural erosion. Tens of thousands of families flee the "Dust Bowl," with many migrating to California in search of work.

1930: In the Imperial Valley, 8,000 farmworkers strike due to low wages and rough working conditions. In April, Dolores Huerta is born in Dawson, New Mexico.

1931: In the Santa Clara Valley, 2,000 cannery workers go on strike.

1933: Ten thousand cotton pickers strike in San Joaquin Valley.

1935: The National Labor Relations Act is passed, allowing for collective bargaining between companies and their employees. Farmworkers, however, are excluded from these new labor protections.

1934: The Salinas lettuce strike is started by Filipino farmworkers. They protest a wage reduction.

1939: *The Grapes of Wrath* by John Steinbeck, *Factories in the Field* by Carey McWilliams, and *An American Exodus* by Dorothea Lange and Paul Taylor are published. The conditions of farm labor in California become the subject of greater media and governmental scrutiny.

1941: Pearl Harbor is attacked and the United States enters World War II. Anti-immigrant "America First" rallies take place in Los Angeles and San Francisco. The following year, some 120,000 Japanese and Japanese–Americans are forcibly evacuated from the West Coast and moved into internment camps. Many were skilled farmers. During the expulsion, ethnic Japanese lost nearly a quarter million acres of land, worth an estimated $73 million.

1942–1964: Growers argue that the war creates another labor shortage in California fields. The Bracero Program is enacted after negotiations between Mexico and the United States for better working conditions for guest workers—conditions that were routinely violated. The Bracero Program creates special exemptions in the U.S. immigration code for "native-born residents of North America, South America, and Central America, and the islands adjacent thereto, desiring to perform agricultural labor in the United States." Between 1942 and 1964, approximately 4.6 million Mexican citizens are admitted to the United States as farmworkers.

1943: The Bracero Program drains labor from large Mexican farms, a problem exacerbated by a large number of Mexican farmworkers crossing to work in the United States without work permits. Mexican landowners petition their government to demand the United States tighten border security and prevent undocumented immigration.

1945: Mexican and U.S. governments cooperate in deporting undocumented Mexican immigrants deep into Mexico to prevent easy return to the United States. The two governments develop infrastructure to more easily deport immigrants back to Mexico by trains, boat travel, and air travel.

1946–1952: During this time, a number of unsuccessful attempts are made to organize farmworker unions. One of the most notable is the campaign of the National Farm Labor Union, led by Ernesto Galarza, which in 1947 led an unsuccessful strike against the powerful DiGiorgio Fruit Corporation in the San Joaquin Valley.

1949: The number of independent farms in California peaks at 137,000.

1950–60: Labor unions help drive wages for packing-house workers to twice that of field workers. Packing-house jobs are increasingly sought out by migrants who first began work in the fields.

1950: Ground water supplies more than 50 percent of irrigated acreage in California.

1951: More than 50 percent of California crops are mechanically harvested.

1954: "Operation Wetback" begins. U.S. and Mexican federal governments streamline procedures to deport Mexican immigrants in the United States. Some major cities are targeted but patrols focus on border areas. In the first year, over 1 million immigrants are apprehended and deported. Many deportees are packed onto cargo ships without personal belongings and without being able to contact their families. Most deportees are released in Mexico far from their places of origin, and dozens die. Growers in California and Texas continue to recruit undocumented workers to avoid the conditions of the Bracero Program.

1959: The Agricultural Workers Organizing Committee (AWOC), largely composed of Filipino farmworkers, is chartered by the AFL-CIO and headquartered in Stockton. Led by organizers Larry Itliong and Philip Vera Cruz, the union organizes 158 workplace actions between 1960 and 1962, winning higher wages but no contracts.

1962: Cesar Chavez, with help from Dolores Huerta and Gilbert Padilla, founds the Farm Workers Association. This association later becomes the United Farm Workers (UFW).

1965: AWOC leads a strike of grape harvesters in Coachella, California, which results in wage increases. When the grape harvest shifts to Delano, the growers refuse to pay the higher rate and, on September 8, AWOC members strike again. A week later, the strike is joined by Cesar Chavez and his supporters and turns into a five-year campaign. The UFW's boycott actions attract the attention of the national media and the support of millions of Americans.

1966: Spring—Cesar Chavez leads a 300-mile march from Delano to Sacramento, calling for a boycott of Schenley, a liquor company, and for assistance from Governor Edmund "Pat" Brown. The march arrives in Sacramento on Easter Sunday with 10,000 supporters.

1966: Summer—The National Farm Workers Association (NFWA) merges with the Agricultural Workers Organizing Committee, an affiliate of the American Federation of Labor-Congress of Industrial Organizations (AFL-CIO). Together they establish the United Farm Workers Organizing Committee. That summer, the UFWOC wins the nation's first union election in the field, competing with the Teamsters to represent workers at DiGiorgio, the largest grape grower in the country.

Late 1960s: The Teamsters Union begins to compete with the UFWOC in representing farmworkers.

1968: Chavez goes on a twenty-five-day water-only fast. According to Chavez, he undertook the fast to bring attention to the importance of non-violent acts of resistance, among other reasons. Robert F. Kennedy comes to Delano to break the fast with Chavez and later announces his candidacy for president. The UFWOC campaigns heavily for Kennedy, who wins the California primary but is assassinated on the eve of his victory, just moments after he left a stage with Dolores Huerta and other supporters.

1970: After a five-year strike and national grape boycott, the UFW signs contracts with most of California's table-grape growers. Thousands of lettuce workers in Salinas, sympathetic to the UFW, hold massive strikes after growers sign secret contracts with the Teamsters, granting workers just a half-cent raise per year. Two weeks into the strike, production recovers to only a third of its typical levels. In response, a number of growers cancel their contracts with the Teamsters and sign with the UFW.

1972: United Farm Workers Organizing Committee officially becomes the United Farm Workers of America (UFW).

1973: Grape growers refuse to renegotiate UFW contracts, and instead bring in Teamsters to represent the workers. Chavez receives help from the AFL-CIO to counter the grower-Teamster alliance, and violent conflict breaks out between the competing unions. Chavez completes second water-only fast. This one lasts twenty-four days. Struggles between the Teamsters and the UFW over representation of farmworkers last for years. Media reports suggest Teamsters are colluding with growers to win contracts that are more favorable to the growers than the ones advocated by the UFW.

1975: California enacts the Agricultural Labor Relations Act, granting farmworkers the right to organize into unions and negotiate contracts with employers through collective bargaining.

1975: A nationwide poll finds that 12 percent of the country—17 million adults—is boycotting grapes. Another 14 million refuse to purchase lettuce.

1977: Teamsters and UFW sign a peace pact which grants UFW "the sole right to organize farmworkers and fieldworkers."

Late 1970s: Peso devaluations lead to increased unauthorized Mexican immigration. By the end of the decade, the UFW has about 200 contracts with California farms and about 60,000 members.

Early 1980s: About 25 percent of farmworkers in California are undocumented.

1980s: Farmworker boycott of Bruce Church Inc. Lettuce. The company signs the UFW contract in May 1996.

1988: Chavez completes thirty-six-day water-only fast. By now, the UFW has considerably shrunk in size, having lost many contracts and members. In September, Huerta is beaten in San Francisco by police during a peaceful demonstration.

1993: Cesar Chavez dies on April 23 of natural causes.

1994: Proposition 187, which denies benefits to undocumented immigrants, is voted on and passed. The same year, Cesar Chavez is awarded the Presidential Medal of Freedom after his death to recognize "his nonviolent activism and support of working people."

1997: There are 74,000 farms in the state.

2000s–present: California minimum wage begins to climb. By 2017 it reaches $10.50/hour.

2005: Antonio Villaraigosa becomes the first Latino mayor of Los Angeles elected since 1872 when Cristóbal Aguilar left office.

2011–2015: Statewide focus on water conservation because of major drought. This has an impact on the state's agriculture.

2014: Governor Jerry Brown declares the drought a state of emergency. Orders the first ever state-wide water reductions. California farmers allow about 500,000 acres of farmland to go fallow (5 percent of the state's total farmland). However, overall numbers of farmworkers remains fairly steady at about 420,000 per month during busy months. Generally speaking the drought does not affect availability of farmwork, despite decreased overall farm acreage.

2016: California's population reaches approximately 40 million.

APPENDIX II.
GLOSSARY

Agricultural Labor Relations Act: California state law passed in 1975 that guaranteed the rights of California farmworkers to organize for collective bargaining purposes. Until 1975, California farmworkers had no legal recourse for organizing unions, as farmworkers had been excluded from the federal National Labor Relations Act of 1935.

Agricultural Labor Relations Board: In California, the ALRB is the body that oversees elections to make sure both unions and growers follow the established rules.

border patrol: The U.S. Border Patrol is a federal law enforcement agency. There are over 20,000 U.S. Border Patrol agents charged with detecting and preventing undocumented immigration into the United States as well as preventing other forms of trafficking. The majority of agents are assigned to the U.S.-Mexico border. There are an estimated 400,000 or more border patrol arrests per year of undocumented immigrants as of 2015. This number is down from over 1 million a year a decade earlier.

bracero: *Bracero* means "manual laborer" in Spanish. The United States and Mexico signed a series of agreements in the first half of the twentieth century (most notably the Bracero Program in 1942) to grant temporary work visas to Mexican farm laborers. Guest workers that participated in the program were known as braceros, and today some farmworkers still refer to farmworkers with work visas in the U.S. as braceros.

California Occupational Safety and Health Administration (Cal/OSHA): Cal/OSHA is the state agency responsible for inspecting compliance with state workplace safety regulations. California has 200 OSHA inspectors, a number that makes it difficult to inspect and enforce farmworker safety regulations on California's thousands of farms.

collective bargaining: Legally formalized negotiations between employer and employee representatives to determine contracts and conditions of employment such as wages, working hours, overtime pay, health and safety standards, and procedures for addressing grievances.

contracto: *Contracto* ("contract") farmwork refers to work that is paid based on the weight of produce picked by the individual or by some other quota or benchmark, as opposed to pay based on hours worked. Also known as *piece-rate* contracts.

agricultural cooperative : A form of cooperative in which independent growers pool resources to acquire capital-intensive equipment, share marketing and distribution, and achieve economies of scale to compete with larger corporate farms. Well known agricultural cooperatives in California include Sunkist and Sun-Maid, though there are over 200 agricultural cooperatives in California alone and thousands nationwide.

coyote: A smuggler who helps immigrants pass across the Mexico-U.S. border without documentation. In recent years, *coyotes* may be responsible for contracting with over 1 million undocumented entrants into the United States every year. Revenues may be as high as $7 billion a year.

cuadrilla: A work crew. In California agriculture, *cuadrillas* are generally recruited and operated by *mayordomos*, or supervisors, who are often employed by labor contractors. Cuadrillas can vary in size depending on the work required, but generally range from a few individuals to more than forty. Most farms hire a number of cuadrillas, sometimes through numerous contractors, through the course of a growing and harvesting season.

drought: A cycle of drought began in California in 2011 and has persisted through 2016, marking the driest period in California since record keeping began in 1895. The drought has increased the state's reliance on groundwater to meet water needs. It has caused an estimated loss of billions in agricultural production, with the Central Valley especially hard hit.

Development, Relief, and Education for Alien Minors Act (DREAM Act): A proposed congressional bill that provides eligible minors pursuing education to obtain permanent residency. The act was first proposed in Congress in 2001 and has been reintroduced numerous times for over a decade, though never passed. In 2012, the Obama administration announced that it would stop deporting immigrants that fit the criteria of the DREAM Act. This executive action is known as DACA (Deferred Action for Childhood Arrivals).

farm labor contractor: A farm labor contractor is licensed at the state level to provide workers for seasonal or temporary work to growers for a fee. There are approximately 1,200 farm labor contractors licensed in California, and those contractors provide as much as 60 to 70 percent of the farm labor in California's fields. Using farm labor contractors allows growers more flexibility in hiring practices. For instance, growers can use one or more labor contractors to hire a number of workers that might change from day to day or season to season. Before 2015, labor contractors in California also bore legal responsibility for ensuring worker safety, fair wages, and workers' compensation insurance. The passage of new laws in 2015 made growers equally liable as contractors for ensuring labor law is followed.

green card: In the United States, a green card is also known as a United States lawful permanent resident card. Permanent resident status is granted to non-citizens for periods of either two or ten years, and in many cases green card holders can apply for renewal. After five years of legal residency, green card holders can apply for U.S. citizenship, a process known as *naturalization*. Permanent resident status is granted to immigrants who meet any of a number of conditions, including being the close relative or spouse of a U.S. citizen, meeting certain employment conditions, or having been granted political asylum. Green cards or permanent resident status is different from forms of visa, including travel visas and temporary worker visas (see entry for *H-2A Visa*).

H-2A Visa: A visa that provides temporary legal status for seasonal agricultural work. The provision formally requires sponsorship by agricultural employers that must demonstrate that labor needs cannot be met through the local labor supply, or that a labor shortage is expected. Employers using the H-2A system are expected to provide housing, transportation, and fair wages for those workers who receive the visa.

heat exhaustion: Heat exhaustion is characterized by heavy sweating and a rapid pulse. Heat exhaustion is caused by overheating, especially in humid conditions in conjunction with strenuous activity. Untreated, heat exhaustion can lead to heat stroke, a potentially fatal condition.

heat stroke: Heat stroke is characterized by an internal temperature of 105 degrees or higher, confusion, rapid breathing, dry skin, and loss of consciousness. Heat stroke is the most serious of heat-related injuries and requires emergency treatment. Heat stroke that is not immediately treated can lead to death or permanent impairment.

Immigration and Customs Enforcement (ICE): ICE is a law enforcement agency established under the Homeland Security Act of 2002. The agency replaced the function of Immigration and Naturalization Services. The agency is tasked with enforcing immigration law. Today, ICE is most likely to enforce immigration law among California's farmworkers by auditing the growers that hire those workers, and by relying on the discretion of state and local law enforcement.

Immigration and Naturalization Service (INS): INS was the agency that enforced immigration law up until the establishment of Immigration and Customs Enforcement in 2002.

Immigration Reform and Control Act of 1986: Signed into law by President Reagan, the IRCA transformed immigrant legal status for many undocumented workers in the United States. The act made it illegal to knowingly hire undocumented workers and also granted legal status to formerly undocumented immigrants who had entered the United States before January 1, 1982. The act also provided legal status to immigrants who could prove they worked in agriculture for more than sixty days between 1985 and 1986. Up to 1.3 million farmworkers obtained legal status through the agriculture provision in the bill.

labor camps: In California, labor camps for migrant agricultural workers were first established by the federal government during the Great Depression. These camps generally consisted of tents or single-story plywood structures. During the Bracero Program, additional federal camps were established, and many growers established private labor camps to house workers. Throughout the twentieth century, California's labor camps were notorious for their often unsafe and unsanitary conditions. Reforms including the Migrant and Seasonal Agricultural Workers Protection Act of 1983 set standards for these camps, though many private camps remained uncertified and uninspected. Today, fewer and fewer agricultural workers live in camps—there are fewer than 1,000 camps statewide now, compared with over 5,000 at the height of the Bracero Program. However, many workers continue to live in unsafe and unsanitary private housing, often in cities or unincorporated rural communities rather than land owned by their employers.

mayordomo: The supervisor of a farmworker crew, or *cuadrilla*. In California, the majority of mayordomos are employees of labor contractors, and it is their responsibility to recruit, train, and oversee the work of crews that may range from a few individuals to more than forty.

migra: *La migra* is slang for U.S. Immigration and Customs Enforcement (formerly Immigration and Naturalization Services). Migrants often refer to enforcement agents themselves as *la migra*.

pesticide: Any number of chemicals used to destroy invasive plants, insects, or other life-forms that might eat or damage crops. Numerous pesticides have been linked to adverse health effects in humans such as cancers, nervous system disorders, respiratory disorders, and birth defects.

rancho: In Mexico, *rancho* often refers to a smaller farm or village made up of privately owned farmsteads. In contrast, a *hacienda* is a larger privately owned estate, more like a plantation.

workers' compensation insurance: An agreement whereby employers purchase insurance that provides some wage compensation and medical coverage in the case of workplace accidents. As part of most workers' compensation insurance agreements, workers forfeit the right to sue employers for additional compensation. As many as 25 percent of male workers and 11 percent of female workers in California fields have filed for workers' compensation at least once in their careers.

APPENDIX III.
LEGAL PROTECTIONS FOR CALIFORNIA FARMWORKERS

In terms of both safety regulations and wage regulations, farmwork is subject to a different set of rules than most other occupations. This appendix is intended to provide an overview of some of the protections available to farmworkers in the state of California.

WAGES, HOURS, & WORKING CONDITIONS

Agricultural fieldworkers are often not protected by the laws that safeguard employees in most other occupations. A few California and federal laws do, however, address the workplace rights of farmworkers.

Two federal laws regulate most financial aspects of agricultural employees. The Migrant & Seasonal Agricultural Worker Protection Act of 1983 (AWPA) is the primary federal employment law for farmworkers. The Fair Labor Standards Act (FLSA), first passed in 1938, also regulates some financial aspects of agricultural employment. The U.S. Department of Labor's Wage and Hour Division oversees both laws.

All California workers are protected under the state's labor laws, regardless of documentation or immigration status. California addresses many employment rights of farmworkers through the Department of Industrial Relations and its Labor Enforcement Task Force. The official notice of these rights must be displayed at the worksite. Cal/OSHA, a division of the Department of Industrial Relations, oversees workplace safety.

A significant number of California farmworkers are not employed directly by a grower. Rather, they are hired, organized into work crews, and paid through farm labor contractors, who manage most labor transactions for the grower. This middleman management system has led to widespread abuse, including wage theft. Several laws regulate the responsibilities of farm labor contractors, and as of 2015 growers in California share the burden of legal responsibility for maintaining worker safety and wage standards.

Terms of Employment

At the time of recruitment, employers must inform employees, in writing, exactly what they will be paid, where they will work and what they will do, how long they will be employed, benefits such as transportation and housing and their cost to the employee, and their right to sick leave and workers' compensation in California. These conditions must be written in a language understood by the employee.

If an employer is providing workers with transportation to a jobsite, the vehicle must be in safe working condition and properly insured, and the driver must be licensed.

If an employer offers housing to its employees, the housing must meet federal health and safety standards.

Wages

All agricultural workers in California are to be paid the state's current minimum wage, which as of January 2017 is $10.50 an hour. It will rise to $11 in January 2018, and reach $15 per hour in January 2022. Those farmworkers paid by the piece must be paid at least minimum wage for the hours worked. Despite minimum-wage requirements, full-time, year-round farmworkers earn an average of below $20,000 a year in California. Many earn far less, without full-time, annual employment. Wage theft, including unrecognized overtime, accounts for some of the discrepancy between hourly wages and real annual income.

Overtime pay (time and a half) goes into effect when employees work more than 10 hours per day or 60 hours per week, and for the first 8 hours of the seventh day in a work week; all hours over 8 on the seventh day will be paid double-time. Recent efforts to give farmworkers the overtime pay guaranteed most other workers (after 8 hours/day, 40 hours/week) led to the passage of AB 1066 in September 2016, which will go into effect starting in 2019. The new overtime provision will lower the current 10-hour/day overtime threshold by half an hour every year until it reaches 8 hours/day in 2022.

Currently, employees must be paid at least twice a month on regular designated paydays. The employer must provide a wage stub that shows the employee's name and identification number, pay-period dates, total hours worked and their rate of pay, gross and net wages, and the name and address of the employer.

Workers have the right to inform their employer and/or file a complaint if they believe they are not being paid what they have earned under the law (wage theft). Employers are prevented from retaliating in any way against employees who complain in good faith.

California's Healthy Workplace Healthy Families Act of 2014 mandates sick leave for temporary, part-time, and full-time workers who, since July 1, 2015, have worked 30 or more days within a year. Employees accrue one hour of sick leave for every 30 hours worked and may begin using accrued leave on the ninetieth day of employment. Sick leave is paid at the hourly rate. Accrued sick days must carry over to the following year but may be capped at 48 hours.

Employers must display a poster detailing the sick-leave policy. It must be in a language understood by most workers and in a place where it can be read easily.

Paid time off may be taken under the guidelines that govern sick leave.

Though data on actual wages paid to farmworkers isn't widely available, a 2008 survey of 120,000 indigenous Mexican farmworkers in California found that approximately one third of respondents reported pay below the state's minimum wage. Nationally, the Department of Labor investigates and uncovers thousands of cases of wage violations in agriculture every year. For instance, from the period 2010–2013, over 35,000 agricultural employees nationally were awarded back wages to comply with wage-standard violations and over $15 million in back pay was awarded.

Health and Sanitation

Employers must provide a paid, ten-minute rest break every four hours, and a paid meal break of at least 30 minutes after no more than five hours of work.

With some exceptions, hand weeding, thinning, and hot-capping (covering plants to protect them from extreme weather) is not permitted if these tasks require stooping, kneeling, or squatting. Similarly, employers may not require that workers use short-handled tools for weeding, thinning, or hot-capping when their use requires stooping, kneeling, or squatting.

Employers must provide readily accessible, plentiful, clean, and cool drinking water. This water must be dispensed by fountains or in single-use drinking cups.

For every twenty employees of each sex, employers must provide one easily accessible toilet and hand-washing facility. These facilities must be kept clean and well supplied with toilet paper, soap, and clean water.

Because California's Cal/OSHA enforcement office currently has only 200 inspectors, many violations of health and sanitation standards go unreported. Of California's approximately 80,000 farms, there are around 300 sanitation inspections carried out by Cal/OSHA every year. Based on spot inspections, the organization estimates that as many as one third of farms in California violate some health and sanitation standards.

Farm Labor Contractors

As of 2015, employers whose workers are supplied by labor contractors are held legally responsible, along with the contractors, when workers are paid incorrectly, denied workers' compensation, or other laws protecting workers are violated.

With a few exceptions, farm labor contractors are liable for any wages or penalties withheld from a worker by a previous contractor, and for violations incurred by that predecessor.

Farm labor contractors must maintain written statements of the wages they have received from a grower and the amount they have paid employees. Contractors who fail to provide this statement within twenty-one days of a grower or employee's request must pay $750 to the grower or employee.

Contractors who withhold money from an employee's wages must remit those withholdings to the proper agency, and will not be relicensed until the amount is fully paid.

Collective Bargaining and Unionization

The right to collective bargaining was first guaranteed to most U.S. workers by the National Industrial Recovery Act, which Congress approved in 1933 at the urging of President Franklin D. Roosevelt.

The right was solidified two years later with passage of the National Labor Relations Act. Significantly exempted from those laws were farmworkers.

California changed that in 1975, when the state legislature passed the Agricultural Labor Relations Act, a law formulated with the purpose of bringing "peace to the agricultural fields by guaranteeing justice for all agricultural workers and stability in labor relations." The law was the result of more than a decade of activism by farmworkers and their supporters around the country. Today, California is one of only ten states, and the only major farm state, that gives agricultural workers the right to choose a collective bargaining agent by secret ballot.

Union elections and contracts spiked dramatically in the years immediately following passage of the law. Four decades later, however, fewer than 20,000 of the up to 800,000 farmworkers in California are covered by union contracts—fewer than before passage of the ALRA. This decline has been attributed to weak union leadership, shifts in state politics, the structure of farm employment, and the rise in undocumented immigration, as well as to growers' continual efforts to impede and weaken the law. The law also gives workers the right to file complaints with the Agricultural Labor Relations Board, and exercise all rights guaranteed by the Act without fear of retaliation.

Sexual Harassment

Sexual harassment, including rape, is a common occurrence in the agriculture industry, posing a constant threat to the lives and well being of the more than 560,000 women who work on U.S. farms. According to a report by Human Rights Watch (see Appendix V, page 310–18), nearly all female farmworkers have experienced—or know someone who has experienced—stalking, exhibitionism, obscene language, and rape by men in positions of power in the field. For myriad reasons, among them fear of retaliation, reporting of these crimes is low, prosecution even lower, and conviction nearly non-existent.

The federal Violence Against Women Reauthorization Act of 2013 strengthens protection from predators of all women, including farmworker women and girls.

At the state level, the most recent effort to protect women who do agricultural work from sexual harassment and abuse is Senate Bill 1087, which passed in 2014. The bill primarily includes changes to training and to the licensing of farm labor contractors. Its provisions include the following:

Training

All agricultural employees must be trained in sexual-harassment prevention at the time of hire and at least once every two years. Training must include how to identify, prevent, and report sexual harassment.

Contractor Licensing

A farm labor contractor license may not be granted to a person who has been found guilty of sexual harassment of an employee within the previous three years. Nor may a license be issued to a person who has knowingly hired a supervisory employee who has been found guilty of sexual harassment.

The state labor commissioner is authorized to revoke, suspend, or refuse to renew a farm labor contractor's license if he is guilty of either of the two actions cited above.

Applicants for a farm labor contractor's license must take one hour of training in the prevention of sexual harassment annually, pass a written examination on the laws and regulations governing sexual harassment, and confirm in writing that his supervisorial employees have been trained in sexual-harassment prevention.

Any person who works as a farm labor contractor without a valid license is subject to a fine of at least $10,000 and/or by a prison sentence of 6–12 months.

PESTICIDES

According to an EPA estimate, 20,000 farmworkers nationwide are exposed to dangerous levels of pesticide poisons each year. Immediate consequences of exposure include headaches, nausea, shortness of breath, rashes, blisters, blindness, and seizures. Long-term exposure to pesticides can cause cancer, infertility, neurological disorders, respiratory conditions, and birth defects. California is one of the few states that require blood monitoring for agricultural workers who handle neurotoxic pesticides.

Pesticides are dangerous to people who work directly in the application of pesticides, and to those who live near or work in the fields where pesticides are present. Pesticides can drift from the fields to homes nearby, or can be carried home by workers on their skin and clothes. Once pesticide exposure has caused pesticide illness, farmworkers reach another barrier in the form of medical care. Farmworkers may not have health insurance, and may not be able to afford to take time off work to get medical treatment. It is estimated that only 30 percent of documented farmworkers and 15 percent of undocumented farmworkers carry any form of health insurance. Even if farmworkers are able to seek medical treatment, many healthcare providers have very little training in the identification, diagnosis, and treatment of illnesses related to pesticides.

California growers sprayed, misted, fogged, and injected more than 193 million pounds of pesticides onto and into their fields in 2013. Not surprisingly, California farmworkers report more than twice as many incidents of pesticide-related injury and illness than any other sector of the state's workforce.

The U.S. Environmental Protection Agency and the California Department of Pesticide Regulation (DPR) are foremost among the federal and state agencies that oversee agricultural use of pesticides in California.

The EPA's efforts to reduce the risks of pesticide exposure to farmworkers are formulated under its Worker Protection Standard (WPS). First issued in 1992, the standards were revised in 2015. Most of the new WPS went into effect January 2, 2017; expanded training and some notification requirements will begin two years later, when new materials are available.

California's current rules were most recently amended in 2015, in part to comply with the WPS. While there are many similarities between the federal and state mandates, California's pesticide-protection program operates independently of the EPA's.

Both the EPA and California rules contain specific protections for workers who handle and apply pesticides and for those who work in greenhouses and nurseries rather than in open fields.

Notification, Warnings, and Restricted Entry

All agricultural employers who use pesticides must display general pesticide-safety information in a central location and at sites where decontamination supplies are located. This information must include how to keep pesticides from entering the body as well how to get medical attention if a worker suspects harmful exposure. Among its series of pesticide-safety publications, the California DPR has issued a leaflet that meets this requirement. If the posting is in a language not spoken by the worker, the worker may request that the flyer be read in a language he or she understands.

Whenever pesticides are to be used, employers must display, at a central location and at decontamination sites, details about the specific pesticide, the time and date of application, and relevant hazard and safety data sheets. This information, which must be in a language workers will understand, must be posted before workers enter the area. Postings must be kept for two years and made available to workers, handlers, designated representatives, and medical personnel.

Workers may not enter areas when pesticides are being applied; this area may include an exclusion zone of up to 100 feet around application equipment. Before applying pesticides to a field, employers must warn workers orally or by posting warning signs, or both, depending on the pesticide. In addition to English, warning signs must be in Spanish and/or in the language the largest group of workers understands. All warning signs must meet certain size, design, and language specifications.

Pesticide handlers (those workers who actually apply the pesticides) must make sure no one is in the exclusion zone while applying pesticides, and must immediately suspend work if someone is in the area.

Many agricultural pesticides require a restricted entry interval (REI), which is the length of time after application during which restrictions on who can enter the area are in effect. Employers must post warning signs in both English and Spanish to areas treated with pesticides that have an REI of greater than forty-eight hours. For products with an REI of forty-eight hours or less, either oral warnings or posted signs are allowed.

The REI of a specific pesticide can be found on the label. California has determined the REI for some pesticide/crop combinations; when these times are inconsistent with the label, the longer REI applies.

Early Entry into Treated Areas

Some workers are allowed to work in a treated area during the REI. The minimum age for early entry is eighteen, unless the workplace is owned by the worker's extended family.

Employers must explain the REI exception to workers being asked to enter the area, describe the specific work that is to be done, and identify the required personal protective equipment (PPE). Early-entry workers must be informed of the health hazards posed by the specific pesticide, know how to use the PPE specified on the pesticide label, recognize symptoms of poisoning, know the procedures for getting emergency medical care, and recognize and be able to treat heat-related illness that results from the use of PPE.

Employees may enter a field during the REI only if the employer ensures there will be no contact with anything that has been treated, including soil, water, air, and plant surfaces. Hand work, for example, is prohibited, but operating a tractor from inside a closed cab would meet the "no contact" requirement. Furthermore, inhalation exposure levels listed on the pesticide label must be reached before early entry.

Short-term, limited-contact activities are allowed under certain conditions detailed in the text of the regulations.

Decontamination

Employers must provide decontamination supplies for thirty days after the end of a pesticide application or the end of an REI.

Decontamination supplies must be located no further than ¼ mile from fieldworkers (or within ¼ mile of vehicular access). The decontamination site, which may not be in an area being treated with pesticides or under an REI, must have enough water for emergency eye-flushing and routine washing, and sufficient soap and single-use towels.

Early-entry workers must have access to soap, clean towels, and sufficient water available at the site where they remove personal protective equipment.

Emergency Assistance

Should a worker have reason to believe he or she has been poisoned or injured by pesticides in any way, employers must provide immediate transportation to the appropriate medical facility. In addition to describing the circumstances of exposure, the employer must promptly give medical personnel all relevant information about the pesticide to which the worker might have been exposed.

Training

Fieldworkers and pesticide handlers must receive annual training on how to protect themselves and their families from exposure to pesticides. Employers must maintain records of these trainings and keep them for two years. Employees may request a copy of his or her training record.

Trainings must be held in a setting reasonably free of distraction. Information must be presented orally from written materials or audiovisually, and trainers must remain for the entire session to respond to questions.

Workers who handle or apply pesticides must receive additional, relevant safety training. No person under the age of eighteen is allowed to do either of these tasks.

HEAT-ILLNESS PREVENTION

In 2005, the California Department of Industrial Relations and the state division of Occupational Safety and Health issued regulations regarding growers' responsibility to reduce heat illness and heat-related deaths among their employees.

Ten years, more than two dozen deaths, and countless illnesses later, Cal/OSHA toughened the regulations, which are summarized below. Still, widespread violations—and death in the fields—continue.

Water

Employees are entitled to "fresh, pure, and suitably cool" water, at no cost. Employers must ensure enough potable water to provide one quart per hour per employee for the entire shift.

Drinking water must be located reasonably close to where employees are working so they do not have to go out of their way to stay healthfully hydrated. Individual, single-use drinking cups must be provided.

Shade

Adequate shelter from direct sunlight must be available at all times. Like water, shade must be easy for employees to reach; they should not have to cross traffic or waterways to find relief. When the temperature is above 80 degrees (employers are expected to know if this is the case), natural or constructed shaded areas must be large enough to accommodate all employees on normal, mandated breaks, including meal periods. Employers may stagger breaks to ensure room for all employees to sit comfortably.

Employees are allowed and encouraged to take preventive rests in the shade. He or she must be monitored during the cool-down and asked if symptoms of heat illness—headache, heavy sweating, muscle cramps, fatigue—are present. If heat illness is suspected, emergency medical personnel must be contacted immediately. No one can be ordered back to work, left unattended, or sent home if he or she shows symptoms of heat.

Extreme Heat

The symptoms of heat exhaustion include heavy sweating, pale skin, a fast, weak pulse, nausea, vomiting, and fainting. Signs of heat stroke include a body temperature over 103 degrees, red skin, rapid and strong pulse, and unconsciousness. These forms of heat stress can cause electrolyte imbalance, neurological impairment, multi-organ failure, and death.

When the temperature reaches or tops 95 degrees, high-heat procedures go into effect. (In Fresno during July 2016, only five days were below that threshold; on thirteen days the temperature was 101 or above.) These procedures include continuous monitoring of employees by either direct observation, use of a buddy system, or regular radio or cell phone contact, depending on the number of employees and nature of the worksite.

All employees must be trained to recognize the signs of heat illness and must be allowed to call for emergency help; however, employers must assign that responsibility to specific people on the crew.

High-heat measures also mandate that employers provide one ten-minute preventive cool-down period every two hours for the duration of the shift. These rest periods are not optional—employers must make sure all employees actually take their breaks. These recovery periods are to be compensated as hours worked.

On these extremely hot days, employers must hold brief pre-shift meetings at which employees will be reminded how important it is to stay hydrated and rest every two hours. Employers will let workers know how they are being observed and who on their crew will be in charge of calling for medical help if necessary.

Because people can deteriorate quickly when overheated, employers must take immediate action if an employee shows any signs of heat illness. After contacting emergency medical services and giving precise directions, they must do everything possible to cool and comfort the stricken employee and move him or her to an easily reached place if necessary.

Acclimatization

Employees new to a high-heat area must be closely observed for the first 14 days of work. Employers are encouraged to limit sun exposure and decrease the intensity of work for these employees during this time.

Training

Before beginning work that involves the risk of heat illness, all employees must be trained, in a language they understand, on how to prevent heat-related illness. Employers must ensure their procedures match the information given in the training.

APPENDIX III

Heat Illness Prevention Plan

Employers must develop and put in writing all procedures for complying with the requirements of this standard. This plan, which is to be available at the worksite on request, must be written in both English and in the language understood by the majority of employees.

APPENDIX IV.
FARMWORKER
COMMUNITY
ORGANIZATIONS

The organizations described here represent some of the non-governmental resources available to California's agricultural labor force.

California Rural Legal Assistance, Inc. and California Rural Legal Assistance Foundation

California Rural Legal Assistance, Inc. was founded fifty years ago, and since that time has provided free legal services to the rural poor throughout the state. Its advocacy work focuses on five areas: housing, labor and employment, education, rural health, and leadership development. CRLA also has a special program that addresses the needs of low-income lesbian, gay, bisexual, and transgender people and their families. Its Fund for Rural Equity provides grants and technical assistance to other nonprofits that work with rural communities in the Central Valley. Because CRLA is funded in part by the federal government, it is unable to represent people who do not legally reside in the United States.

That prohibition does not apply, however, to the California Rural Legal Assistance Foundation, which was established fifteen years later. CRLAF receives no federal money, giving it the ability to provide legal aid and services to low-income people regardless of immigration status. As well as focusing on many of the issues addressed by CRLA, the foundation has been involved in the passage of several pieces of legislation crucial to the well-being of all farmworkers.

The two organizations work as partners on several projects, including the Community Equity Initiative and the Agricultural Worker Health Project.

United Farm Workers of America, AFL-CIO

Fifty years ago, grape pickers in California earned an average of $0.90 an hour and paid at least $2.00 a day to live in insect-infested metal shacks with no plumbing. Perhaps no other single organization did more to change that dismal reality than the United Farm Workers of America.

The UFW took shape during the early 1960s, under the leadership of Cesar Chavez and Dolores Huerta, both of whom had been organizing farmworkers for several years before they joined forces. After more than a decade of worker strikes, hunger strikes, grape boycotts, lettuce boycotts, marches, imprisonments, and violent confrontations with the International Brotherhood of Teamsters, the UFW and its supporters finally achieved the seemingly impossible: the right to organize, unionize, and bargain collectively in California.

Since that historic legislation, the UFW has continued to help win significant victories for farmworkers in California and other farmworker states, including improved health and safety regulations in the fields, job security, pension plans, medical benefits, and unemployment insurance.

Although it is currently active in ten states, the UFW's influence is not as great as it was in the late 1970s and early 1980s. Still, the union persists in its long struggle to bring justice to farmworkers, sway lawmakers, and awaken the public to the ongoing plight of the people who feed the country.

Farmworker Justice

From its base in Washington, D.C., Farmworker Justice has worked for thirty-five years on behalf of migrant and seasonal farmworkers throughout the country. Its staff focuses on influencing federal legislation and regulations that affect agricultural workers; representing individuals and organizations in legal challenges to government policies and private employers that deprive farmworkers of their rights; and providing training and technical assistance to unions, community health centers, and advocacy groups that serve immigrants and farmworkers.

Since 1996, Farmworker Justice has been affiliated with the National Council of La Raza, the nation's largest organization that addresses the civil rights of Hispanics. In California, Farmworker Justice has been involved in many farmworker-rights issues, including the successful campaigns for minimum wage and overtime pay for agricultural workers.

National Farm Worker Ministry

For almost a century, NFWM has worked to help improve the lives of agricultural workers. Today, some twenty-eight faith-based organizations comprise the national network, which is based in North Carolina. Guided by core values that include respect, transformation, and resourcefulness, NFWM members throughout the country participate in vigils, pickets, boycotts, and educational efforts in support of farmworker rights. Comprehensive immigration reform is also high on the list of NFWM's priorities.

The organization has been active in California since the early days of farmworker activism in the state. Heeding Cesar Chavez's call for the religious community to take a stand for justice in addition to administering charity, the California Migrant Ministry (the national ministry was formed in 1971) became a critical ally in the United Farm Workers' long struggle for collective-bargaining rights. NFWM continues to galvanize people of faith to support union initiatives and state and federal legislation that promote justice for farmworkers.

Central Coast Alliance United for a Sustainable Economy (CAUSE)

CAUSE came into being in 2012, a merger of two organizations that had focused on living-wage issues in Central California throughout the previous decade. CAUSE is dedicated to bringing about social, economic, and environmental justice to low-wage workers in Ventura, Santa Barbara, San Luis Obispo, Santa Cruz, Monterey, and San Benito counties.

In addition to advocating for meaningful immigration reform, CAUSE supports farmworkers through various housing, education, health, voting-rights, transportation, and environmental initiatives.

During the summer of 2015, CAUSE canvassers went door-to-door in farmworker neighborhoods in Ventura and Santa Barbara counties, asking people questions about the conditions they face in the field, including pesticides, threats to health and safety, wage theft, lack of enforcement of laws and rights, and retaliation by employers. Based on the almost 600 interviews they conducted, as well as on community forums held in Oxnard and Santa Maria counties, CAUSE is now part of an alliance promoting a Farmworker Bill of Rights (a draft of the bill is available on their website). The proposal has widespread support among community organizations, businesses, and politicians.

La Cooperativa Campesina de California

A member of the federal Association of Farmworker Opportunity Programs, La Cooperativa is a state- and federally-funded nonprofit that provides a wide range of services to farmworkers and their families throughout California. Its work is limited to people who are temporarily or permanently authorized to work in the state.

Five member agencies comprise La Cooperativa. Together they offer education programs; job training and placement; housing, healthcare, and childcare assistance; emergency aid; and citizenship and immigration services. La Cooperativa's monthly newsletter, *Voice of the Field,* focuses on such topics as the legal rights of farmworkers, physical and mental health, tax credits and tax preparation, and current legislation relevant to farmworkers.

Center for Farmworker Families

A nonprofit based in Felton, California, the Center for Farmworker Families works on behalf of farmworkers in Central California and their family members who live and labor on subsistence farms in west-central Mexico.

The Center's projects in this country include the Oaxacan Community Shed, which serves as a meeting place for Oaxacan farmworker families and provides them with food, clothing, and other basic necessities; a free, in-home tutoring program for children of farmworkers; and Farmworker Reality Tours, which give participants the opportunity to meet and talk with farmworkers in the workers' own homes.

Its main projects in Mexico are related to sustainable, community-supported agriculture in Guadalajara and Cuquío.

Líderes Campesinas

In 1988, in Southern California's Coachella Valley, a group of farmworker women set up an organization to help better the lives of women like themselves. Now with chapters in seven agricultural regions in the state, Líderes Campesinas is dedicated to educating farmworker women about their human and legal rights, and empowering them to take action.

Through conventional training and theatrical presentations, the organization focuses on issues common to all farmworkers as well as those primarily affecting women: domestic violence, sexual assault, breast and cervical cancer, HIV/AIDS, and teen pregnancy.

APPENDIX V.
"CULTIVATING FEAR"

The following appendix is an excerpt from Human Rights Watch's 2012 report, "Cultivating Fear: The Vulnerability of Immigrant Farmworkers in the U.S. to Sexual Violence and Sexual Harassment." To view the full report, please visit www.hrw.org.

Patricia M. was twenty-one years old when she first came to the United States from Mexico about six years ago. Like most immigrant farmworkers in the United States, Patricia did not have a work visa, but she was able to get work. About four years ago, she got a job harvesting almonds. The foreman would pick workers up and then drop them off at the end of the day at a local gas station. She said he repeatedly offered her food and drink, which "bothered [her] a lot," because she felt he was not offering these things innocently. He insinuated that he could help her, saying, "Listen to me, I'm the foreman, and you'll have a job."

On the third day, he dropped off all the workers at the gas station except her. He told the rest of the workers he was going to pick up the water cooler, but instead, he took Patricia to a remote field.

"From there, he didn't say anything, he just stared at me. I was wearing a hat and a bandanna [that covered my face], and he said, 'What do you have there? An animal?' And I knew he wanted to do something to me."

Patricia described him as "fat, very big." She reported that he got on top of her and tied her hands with her bandanna to the hand grip above the truck door. Then, she said, "He took off my clothes and he raped me... He hurt me badly."

Patricia did not tell anyone. She said, "I felt very sad and very alone." She had no family in the United States, and she did not want to tell her family in Mexico what had happened.

After the rape, Patricia continued to work at the same farm. She could not leave the job because there was no other work available. The abuse continued. "He kept raping me and I let him because I didn't want him to hit me. I didn't want to feel pain." Eventually, Patricia found out she was pregnant. She heard that she could apply for disability benefits and went to a social service agency where the employees asked her whether she had a partner. That question prompted her to tell them everything, and the agency helped her file a police report.

Patricia credits the agency for providing crucial support. She still has not told her family in Mexico what happened. Although she told her mother she was pregnant, she didn't tell her about the rape, "because I don't want her to be sick." Without the counselors at the agency, she knows she would never have filed the police report: "I was afraid they would put me in jail; I was afraid [they'd] send me to Mexico because I was illegal."

Patricia stated that the foreman was not prosecuted and sentenced for the crime. Instead, after arresting him, the police seem to have contacted immigration authorities, as he was soon deported. Unfortunately, this does not mean he is completely out of Patricia's life. She has heard reports from his family that he is planning to come back to the United States and see the child. The rape continues to affect her in other ways as well. Patricia is now married, and her daughter is "so beautiful," despite the painful memories of how she became pregnant. Yet she reports, "Sometimes, I remember and I can't be intimate with my husband." She also worries because, "I don't know what to tell my daughter when she gets older."

Hundreds of thousands of women and girls in the United States today work in fields, packing houses, and other agricultural workplaces where they face a real and significant risk of sexual violence and sexual harassment. While the exact prevalence of workplace sexual violence and harassment among farmworkers is difficult to determine due to the challenges of surveying a seasonal, migrant, and often unauthorized population, the problem is serious.

In researching this report, Human Rights Watch interviewed 160 farmworkers, growers, law enforcement officials, attorneys, service providers, and other agricultural workplace experts in eight states; almost without exception, they identified sexual violence and harassment as an important concern. Victims of sexual violence and harassment are often reluctant to describe these experiences, yet nearly all of the fifty-two workers we interviewed, including many not specifically identified in advance as having been victims of such abuses, said they had experienced sexual violence or harassment or knew other workers who had.

Sexual violence and harassment in the agricultural workplace are fostered by a severe imbalance of power between employers and supervisors and their low-wage, immigrant workers. Victims often then face systemic barriers—exacerbated by their status as farmworkers and often as unauthorized workers—to reporting these abuses and bringing perpetrators to justice. To meet its human rights obligations to these farmworkers suffering sexual violence and harassment, the U.S. government and agricultural employers must take steps to reduce and eliminate these barriers. This report documents the experience of immigrant farmworker women and girls with workplace sexual violence and harassment—with particular attention to unauthorized immigrants—and sets forth detailed recommendations for improving their working conditions and access to services and legal remedies.

Several farmworkers like Patricia M. (whose story is recounted above) reported being survivors of rape and other forms of coercive sexual conduct. Angela G., a single mother in California, told Human Rights Watch that she was raped by a supervisor who threatened her daily afterward. An eighteen-year-old indigenous woman from Oaxaca, Mexico, who spoke no English and practically no Spanish, she reported her rape to a local farmworker women's organization but left the area before the organization was able to help her seek justice. She reportedly told the young woman who tried to help her, "I would like to speak as you speak, but I can't defend myself."

Many more farmworkers reported incidents of humiliating, debilitating harassment in the form of unwanted touching, pressure to engage in sexual relations, and verbal harassment. A woman in New York stated that she had picked potatoes and onions with a supervisor who touched all the women's bodies, and if they tried to resist, he would threaten to call Immigration or fire them. Women packing cauliflower in California described working with a supervisor who exposed himself and made comments like, "[That woman] needs to be fucked!" Knowing that they are likely to be viewed as "sexual objects," women often choose to wear clothes that obscure their faces and their bodies. Susana J., a farmworker who cut broccoli, stated, "Women can't dress normally… You think, 'Oh my goodness, if I wear this, what will happen?' And in that way, the harassers affect you every day."

Such violence and harassment are rarely singular events; many women reported that perpetrators had harassed and abused multiple victims over a period of time. Human Rights Watch's investigation found that, in most cases, perpetrators are foremen, supervisors, farm labor contractors, company owners, and anyone else who has the power to hire and fire workers as well as confer certain benefits, such as better hours or permission to take breaks. Farmworkers frequently depend on employers for housing and transportation, creating more opportunities for those who seek to take advantage of vulnerable workers. Co-workers are also perpetrators, enabled, in part, by an environment that can seem tolerant of abuses. In interviews with Human Rights Watch, farmworkers noted that certain workers are much more powerless and more likely to be victimized than others, including girls and young women, recent immigrants, single women working alone, and indigenous workers.

The impact of such violence and harassment can be devastating. Survivors of sexual violence experience various responses to the trauma, including depression, physical pain, and damaged relationships with their partners and families. Although many of the farmworkers who reported abuse stated they did so after interacting with a rape crisis center or other similar agency providing assistance to victims of sexual assault, few farmworkers have access to such agencies. Even where such agencies are present in rural communities, they are not always able to provide adequate services to limited-English-proficient immigrant victims.

Farmworkers who push back against the abuse, or report incidents to management, say they suffer retaliation, getting fewer hours, more abusive treatment, or, worst of all, losing their jobs altogether. Because many farmworkers work with family members, retaliation can mean the victim is fired along with her family, resulting in loss of income to the entire household. Those who live in employer-provided housing can even find themselves homeless. Some farmworkers who had filed sexual harassment lawsuits reported they were "blackballed" and shut out of jobs at other farms.

In general, survivors of sexual assault and harassment in the United States struggle to report the assault or pursue justice. Nearly one in five women in the United States has been raped at some point in her life. Yet despite the prevalence of sexual violence and decades of legal reform meant to hold perpetrators accountable, in 2008 only

41 percent of victims of rape or sexual assault reported the crimes to the police, and in 2010 less than a quarter of reported forcible rapes resulted in an arrest. Similarly, a 2011 *Washington Post*-ABC News poll found that one in four women and one in ten men have experienced workplace sexual harassment; only 41 percent of women who had experienced harassment said they had reported it to their employers.

Farmworker survivors of workplace sexual violence face the challenges all survivors face, but on top of that, they face particular challenges as farmworkers and as migrants. The agricultural industry has long been treated differently than other industries under U.S. labor law. Agricultural workers are excluded from such basic protections as overtime pay and the right to collective bargaining. The laws that do exist are not adequately enforced, and several studies, including previous Human Rights Watch reports, have found that wage theft, child labor, and pesticide exposure occur with troubling frequency. In such an environment, farmworkers are unlikely to have faith in the ability of authorities to rectify abuses.

The agricultural industry relies heavily on unauthorized immigrants, who make up about 50 percent of the workforce, if not more. Although growers and farmworkers agree that the current situation is unsustainable, the U.S. Congress has failed to pass legislation that would enable farmworkers already here to gain legal status and would reform the existing guest-worker system for agricultural workers. Even many immigrants with work authorization lack English proficiency and education, and those with guest-worker visas are dependent on their employer to remain in legal status, which can discourage workers from reporting workplace abuses.

The lack of any immediate prospect for gaining legal status affects the ability of unauthorized farmworkers to report sexual violence, sexual harassment, and other workplace abuses in myriad ways. Although U.S. law entitles unauthorized workers to workplace protections, and labor enforcement agencies assert that broad application of the law best protects the rights of all workers, the U.S. government's interest in protecting unauthorized workers from abuse conflicts with its interest in deporting them. These competing interests affect unauthorized workers' ability to exercise their rights in several key ways.

Unauthorized workers often struggle to find legal representation, since federally funded legal services organizations are prohibited (with some exceptions) from representing unauthorized immigrants. Moreover, in a 2002 decision, the U.S. Supreme Court in *Hoffman Plastic v. National Labor Relations Board* held that an unauthorized worker fired from his job for organizing does not have the right to receive compensation for lost work under the National Labor Relations Act (NLRA). This decision has raised questions about whether unauthorized workers are entitled to the same remedies for workplace abuse as authorized workers. The U.S. government and worker advocates maintain that the decision is limited strictly to a specific provision of the National Labor Relations Act and does not affect the applicability of other labor laws, but the decision forces lawyers to be cautious in the remedies they seek while also emboldening unscrupulous employers who may feel they have less to lose in mistreating unauthorized workers, including tolerating workplace sexual harassment.

The availability of the U visa—a special non-immigrant visa for victims of certain crimes who cooperate in investigations—provides some relief, but the usefulness of the visa is limited by inconsistent certification of victim cooperation by law enforcement agencies and the unavailability of such visas for most witnesses.

And while police are supposed to vigorously investigate crimes against all victims, regardless of immigration status, the increasing involvement of local police in federal immigration enforcement has fueled immigrants' fear of the police and their desire to avoid contact with the police, even to report crimes. State governments' efforts to get involved in immigration enforcement, through laws like Arizona's SB 1070 or Alabama's HB 56, have further fueled fears of the police and discouraged reporting of crimes in immigrant communities.

Some employers have also failed to meet their obligation to protect their employees from sexual harassment. Few of the farmworkers we spoke with said they received training on sexual harassment or information on how to report harassment. Where farmworkers did report the abuses to employers, many supervisors and employers ignored their complaints or retaliated against them, including with threats of deportation.

Both international human rights law and U.S. law state that all workers, regardless of immigration status, have the right to protection from sexual harassment and other workplace abuses, as well as the right to redress when such abuses occur. The International Covenant on Civil and Political Rights (ICCPR), ratified by the United States in 1992, declares, "Everyone has the right to liberty and security of person." The ICCPR further prohibits discrimination on "any ground such as race, colour, sex, language, religion, political or other opinion, national or social origin, property, birth or other status." U.S. law specifically prohibits workplace sexual harassment as a form of employment discrimination under Title VII of the Civil Rights Act of 1964, and criminal laws prohibiting sexual violence are meant to protect all victims, including unauthorized immigrants. But it is not enough for these laws simply to exist. The ICCPR also requires states parties to "ensure ... an effective remedy" when these rights are violated. The Inter-American Commission on Human Rights has similarly found that the American Declaration of the Rights and Duties of Man requires the United States to take due diligence to prevent, punish, and provide remedies for acts of violence, by private parties as well as state actors.

Sexual violence and harassment in the agricultural workplace is a complex problem which should be addressed in a comprehensive way. The U.S. government and agricultural employers should take steps to ensure that farmworkers, including unauthorized farmworkers, are able to access "an effective remedy" and gain meaningful protection under these laws.

For the full report, please visit hrw.com.

ACKNOWLEDGMENTS

Every book is a collaborative project, but this one was more collaborative than most. That collaboration began, of course, with the seventeen narrators, who are the collective co-authors of this book. Thank you for inviting me into your homes and workplaces and patiently answering my questions, sometimes delivered in garbled Spanish.

A number of people introduced me to those narrators. *Mil gracias* to Lupe Quintero, Lorena Martinez, and Blaz Gutierrez of California Rural Legal Assistance; Armando Elenes of the United Farm Workers; Chris Schneider of Central California Legal Services; and Berry Bedwell of the California Fresh Fruit Association. Thanks as well to Bernice Yeung, Janet Kelly, Sandra Gonzalez, and Raquel Lara.

This book was made possible with generous support from the Burnett Family Fund. Thank you to Verso Books for their care and attention in getting this book out to the world. Finally, a huge thank you to the entire Voice of Witness team—translators, transcribers, and editors—for making this book shine.

—Gabriel Thompson

EDITOR BIOGRAPHY

Gabriel Thompson is an author and independent journalist who has written for the *New York Times*, *Harper's*, *New York*, *Slate*, *Mother Jones*, *Virginia Quarterly Review*, and the *Nation*. His articles about labor and immigration have won a number of prizes, including the Studs Terkel Media Award and the Sidney Award. His most recent book is *America's Social Arsonist: Fred Ross and Grassroots Organizing in the Twentieth Century* (University of California Press).